A volume in the

NIU Southeast Asian Series
Edited by Kenton Clymer

For a list of books in the series, visit our website at cornellpress.cornell.edu.

KHMER NATIONALIST

SƠN NGỌC THÀNH, THE CIA, AND THE TRANSFORMATION OF CAMBODIA

MATTHEW JAGEL

NORTHERN ILLINOIS UNIVERSITY PRESS
AN IMPRINT OF CORNELL UNIVERSITY PRESS
Ithaca and London

First published 2023 by Cornell University Press

Library of Congress Cataloging-in-Publication Data

Names: Jagel, Matthew, 1980– author.
Title: Sơn Ngọc Thành, the CIA, and the
    transformation of Cambodia / Matthew Jagel.
Description: Ithaca [New York] : Northern Illinois
    University Press, an imprint of Cornell University
    Press, 2023. | Series: NIU series in Southeast Asian
    studies | Includes bibliographical references and
    index.
Identifiers: LCCN 2022034302 (print) | LCCN
    2022034303 (ebook) | ISBN 9781501769320
    (hardcover) | ISBN 9781501769337 (paperback) |
    ISBN 9781501769344 (epub) | ISBN
    9781501769351 (pdf)
Subjects: LCSH: Sơn, Ngọc Thành, 1908–1977. |
    Nationalism—Cambodia—History—20th century. |
    Cambodia—Politics and government. | Cambodia—
    History—Autonomy and independence movements. |
    Cambodia—History—1953–1975. | Cambodia—
    Foreign relations—United States. | United States—
    Foreign relations—Cambodia.
Classification: LCC DS554.8 .J34 2023 (print) |
    LCC DS554.8 (ebook) | DDC 959.604—dc23/
    eng/20221101
LC record available at https://lccn.loc.gov/2022034302
LC ebook record available at https://lccn.loc.
    gov/2022034303

To Jes, Mark, and Mirah,
with love

Contents

Acknowledgments

This book would not have been possible without generous research grants from various institutions. The Institute of International Education provided support through a Fulbright Research Fellowship for study at the National Archives in Phnom Penh, Cambodia. Thank you to Debora Pierce of the Division of International Affairs at Northern Illinois University for her help in preparing my application. Thanks as well to the Center for Khmer Studies, which provided a research fellowship for study in Cambodia. A version of this book's first chapter previously appeared as "The First Independence: So'n Ngọc Thành's Controversial Contribution to the Birth of Nationalism in Cambodia" in the flagship journal of the the Center for Khmer Studies, *Siksacakr: The Journal of Cambodia Research*, no. 16 (2021): 87–106. Many thanks to Michel Antelme and the anonymous reviewers there for offering constructive suggestions, making this book stronger.

The US Department of Education, through the Center for Southeast Asian Studies at Northern Illinois University, provided three years of Foreign Language and Area Studies (FLAS) Fellowships, without which I would not have been able to dive into the archives in Phnom Penh. The Southeast Asian Studies Summer Institute provided a FLAS Fellowship for Khmer language study as well. The history department at Northern Illinois University provided two summer grants for archival research at various locations in the United States.

Throughout my travels, several people made my research experience vastly more rewarding than otherwise possible. In Cambodia, thank you to the archival staff at the National Archives of Cambodia for indulging my pursuit of all things Thành. Thank you to Youk Chhang and the staff at the Documentation Center of Cambodia for helping me locate materials on Thành during the Khmer Republic. The archival staff at both the Siem Reap and Phnom Penh Center for Khmer Studies was most helpful. Special thanks to Michael Sullivan for his advice and support. The United States is home to many great collections with dedicated archivists. Thank you to the staff at the National Archives II in College Park, Maryland, and the staff at the Truman and Kennedy Presidential Libraries. Cornell and Harvard were also most welcoming and accommodating on these research trips as well. Special thanks to David Chandler for providing feedback of several draft chapters as I tried to conceptualize Thành's place in Cambodian history. At Saint Xavier University, I would like to thank Matthew Costello for his support and long chats about politics, past and present. Vann Ung provided some fantastic photos from Thành's family and answered many questions. I am very grateful for this contribution.

History, as a discipline, is very much a collaborative endeavor. This work would not have been possible without the generosity and support of many others, especially at the Northern Illinois University Center for Southeast Asian Studies and history department. Both institutions provided welcoming and stimulating environments that allowed me to grow as both a scholar and person. Special thanks to Anne Hanley and Sean Farrell for their advice and encouragement as I inched closer to completing this book.

Northern Illinois University has been my home away from home for nearly two decades, and this book would never have come to fruition without many people's guiding hands. Friends and colleagues at the Center for Southeast Asian Studies have always been of great support, from my time as a graduate student to this very day. Thank you to Kheang Leang for his years of support and aid in the study of Khmer, without which this monograph would not have been produced. Great thanks to the memory of David Kyvig for his advice over the years and long talks on Richard Nixon. Thanks to E. Taylor Atkins for help on all things Japan and for his overall support of this book and of me. Judy Ledgerwood and Trudy Jacobsen offered smart critiques, challenges, and endorsements of this book. They certainly have made it better. Special thanks to Eric Jones not only for the hot tub but also for initially brainwashing me into studying Southeast Asia and for being a constant counselor and friend throughout this journey. I am most grateful to Kenton Clymer, who advised this book from start to finish. He believed in it, even when I had my own doubts. It would not have been possible without his dedication, support, and mentorship.

I am honored to work with some outstanding people at Cornell University Press. Notably, senior acquisitions editor Amy Farranto has been key in guiding this book to publication. Thanks as well to Ellen

Labbate, Karen Hwa, and the entire team at Cornell. I am thrilled that this book will be part of the NIU Southeast Asian Series, itself a historic imprint. Outside readers, including Michael G. Vann, offered great advice on the manuscript and on contextualizing this history. Anne Foster went above and beyond in getting me over the finish line. Her contributions cannot be overstated.

Additionally, thanks to Tyler Jagel for editorial advice and for talking me off the proverbial ledge from time to time. Thanks to Ryan, Maggie, Maran, and Max Jagel for their never-ending love and support. Thank you to my parents, Mark and Monica. They, as always, supported me in this endeavor in more ways than can be counted and are the reason for my initial interest in Southeast Asia. Finally, thank you to my family, Jes, Mark, and Mirah. Your smiles remained the constant in this long, strange trip, and I love you all.

Introduction
A Historical Perspective

Histories of Southeast Asian countries after 1945 have often revolved around one singular, larger-than-life figure. Leaders such as Ho Chi Minh in Vietnam, Ferdinand Marcos in the Philippines, Sukarno and Suharto in Indonesia, or Ngo Dinh Diem in South Vietnam have received outsized attention, crowding out scholarly attention to other significant political figures. Cambodian history also has these dominant, mercurial characters in, first, Norodom Sihanouk, and, subsequently, Lon Nol and Pol Pot. These figures were all significant in the histories of their respective countries; their importance and compelling stories rightly attract scholarly attention. But they did not act in a political vacuum. They came to power in struggles against and alliances with other politicians. Other political leaders challenged them throughout their rule, even if they had little immediate effect in some cases. The political history of Southeast Asian nations should not be seen through the lens of singular political leaders, no matter how compelling they each are. This book offers a corrective to that approach for Cambodia by exploring the political life of one important but understudied political figure, and, in particular, how his political choices shaped and reflected Cambodia's relationship with the United States.

Our story here will focus on So'n Ngọc Thành. As a bête noir to Sihanouk for decades, Thành's story helps provide a richer history of Cambodia, rather than treating the nation as simply an extension of its monarchal ruler. Thành's importance ebbed and flowed; sometimes his voice was dominant in Cambodian politics. Other times it was muted. Without attention to his consistent presence, motivations, decisions, and supporters, however, it is not possible to fully understand Cambodia's march toward independence and its subsequent neutralist-leaning path during the Cold War. Similarly, as the United States struggled to act and react to Sihanouk-centered developments in Cambodia, it also weighed alternative options to Cambodian leadership. Throughout the region, the United States cultivated a range of potential allies, such as the so-called third force in Vietnam or anticommunist elements in Indonesia. During the Cold War, US officials hoped to support political leaders in Southeast Asia who would align themselves with the West and provide an alternative to what they perceived as noncompliant politicians and groups. Thành played a complicated but important role in this American effort not only in Cambodia but also in relation to the broader effects of the war in Vietnam. This book decenters the Cold War and the United States to explore the ways that an apparently peripheral figure in a small nation both navigated in the Cold War geopolitical structures and promoted the politics he thought best for his nation and himself.

To the outside world, Cambodia is well-known for the fabulous wonders of Angkor Wat and the five hundred other Hindu and Buddhist structures built from the ninth to the fourteenth century. In modern times, while Angkor became a major tourist attraction, the country drew attention during the war in neighboring Vietnam, where it was subject to an infamous, intense bombing campaign and was ultimately drawn into the war in 1970, when the longtime ruler, Sihanouk, was overthrown. Five years later, the notorious Khmer Rouge took over the country, and Cambodia became known for its "killing fields," as the Khmer Rouge slayed as many as a quarter of the country's seven million inhabitants. The Khmer Rouge period has been among the most scrutinized eras in studies of modern Southeast Asian history.[1]

But, although often ignored, modern Cambodia existed before the Vietnam War, and before the Khmer Rouge. It was a colony of France, a part of French Indochina. And, like Vietnam and Laos, it struggled to gain its independence. The young king, Sihanouk, who ultimately persuaded the French to leave and later caused the Americans much heartburn, has also deservedly received considerable popular and scholarly

attention.[2] At times, however, other nationalist leaders were as important as Sihanouk himself. Foremost among them was Sơn Ngọc Thành,
about whom little has been written. My hope in this book is to bring
attention to Thành's importance as a nationalist leader who influenced
both the internal political development and the regional and international pressures that impacted Cambodia from the 1930s to the 1970s.

In addition to Thành's significance in developments within Cambodia, he became an important, if covert, ally of the United States in its
anticommunist efforts in the region. Throughout the 1950s and 1960s,
Thành and his group, the Khmer Serei (Free Khmer), had connections
to both the American Special Forces and the Central Intelligence Agency
(CIA) in South Vietnam. The Khmer Serei exacerbated tensions between
Cambodia and its Thai and South Vietnamese neighbors. Thành was
involved with the coup to unseat Sihanouk in 1970, which the Nixon
administration, at the very least, applauded. He returned to the new
Khmer Republic government later that year, where he remained until
his retirement to South Vietnam in 1972.

This book will address the following issues : How did Thành influence the creation of an independent Cambodian state? How did he
influence Cambodia's relationships with both its neighbors and the
superpowers during the Cold War? What was his precise relationship
with United States and its intelligence agencies? What was his role in
overthrowing Sihanouk in 1970? What was his role in Cambodia after
Sihanouk's ouster, leading up to the Khmer Rouge takeover in 1975?
Thành's addition as a key figure in these developments complicates our
view of the Cambodian trajectory from colonialization to the Khmer
Rouge, especially who our key actors are. The gravitational pull of Sihanouk, who traditionally dominates histories of Cambodia of this period, often does not allow for a more nuanced, rich, textured view. My
attempts here are not to ignore Sihanouk's outsized role, but, rather,
to broaden our understanding of developments in modern Cambodian
history.

Previous accounts of Thành's role in Cambodian history have been
mostly limited and cursory. He is, at best, mentioned in passing, and,
at worst, ignored all together.[3] Given Thành's importance in the rise
of Cambodian nationalism, the fight for independence from France,
the brief period of Japanese dominance, and Cambodia's postwar
relationship with the United States, Thailand, and Vietnam, this lack
of attention is conspicuous. Additionally, Thành's role in the ouster
of Sihanouk and his subsequent service in the dysfunctional Khmer

Republic bolsters his importance in recent Cambodian history. This book will thus challenge and revise the existing accounts by demonstrating the centrality of Thành in these developments. By focusing on Thành's role, we can better understand how he influenced both the internal political development and the regional and international pressures that impacted Cambodia throughout this period.

Though many different factions of resistance to France sprouted up throughout the country even before World War II, Thành was an unquestioned leader of Khmer resistance to France at the dawn of the war. From the perspective of the United States, he was a rumored communist sympathizer and a troublemaker. From the perspective of many in Cambodia, he was that nation's first independent ruler. The period of 1945 to 1975 saw dramatic changes both inside of Cambodia and in the United States's responses to political developments. These transformations can be directly connected to Thành's various political incarnations, where he morphed from agitator to leader to dissident. During that period, he went from being Cambodia's prime minister to political outcast, while Sihanouk transformed himself from a royal figurehead to a political authoritarian. The United States gradually moved from an advisory and supporting role for France, as the last remnants of its colonial empire disintegrated, to the main geopolitical player in Southeast Asia as it attempted to thwart the spread of communism in Southeast Asia. By that time, Thành had turned from an American adversary to an American ally. For the United States, a country it might have preferred to ignore became impossible to overlook. In this respect, the case of Cambodia is similar to that of Indonesia. While the latter was geographically bigger and a larger trading partner, it too attempted a neutralist path during the Cold War under Sukarno that, by the mid-1960s, was deemed no longer tenable by American officials.

Because he was very much a man of mystery during his life, locating source material on Thành is a problematic undertaking. There are periods in which little information is available on Thành's specific whereabouts or motivations. His own voice is similarly absent from much of the available sources of this era. Tying his story together is a task akin to a complicated jigsaw puzzle with missing pieces. But there is enough to allow meaningful conclusions about his influence and importance. Most of the existing source material, including those sources found in Cambodia, are in the French language. While there are Khmer sources incorporated into the narrative, this research relies on French- and English-language sources for much of its historical information. Many other potential sources were lost during the tragic civil war between 1970 and 1975, and many more were intentionally destroyed during the subsequent brutal Khmer Rouge regime from 1975 to 1979. While far from ideal, this does not obstruct the overall analysis of Thành's significance to both modern Cambodian history and to US relations with Cambodia during the Cold War.

Chapter 1 briefly discusses the history of nationalist resistance to occupying French forces in Cambodia. These instances were sporadic and generally insignificant in reaching the broader collective thought of Cambodians to spur them on to nationalistic confrontation. It was not until Thành came of age during the interwar years in France that he developed his earliest political motivations that would carry him on to great highs and lows for the remainder of his life. By the late 1930s, Thành began to affect the national conscious through the political newspaper *Nagaravatta*. During World War II, the conquering Japanese sheltered Thành after a number of his followers were arrested during a protest he organized. He was hidden in Japan for two years, after which he returned to Cambodia to enter the government and was soon appointed prime minister. Following Japan's defeat in the war, France regained control of its territory, and Thành was sacked. His influence, however, was instrumental in creating the political base to begin to challenge French hegemony.

Chapter 2 focuses on the period in which Thành was imprisoned in France. During that time, Norodom Sihanouk began to press France for political concessions and autonomy. This move was largely due to the influence of Thành's followers, the Democrats. Thành returned to a hero's welcome in late 1951, but he soon joined the anti-French dissidents, the Khmer Issaraks, in the *maquis*. Despite his absence from the capital, Thành was still a highly influential political figure who pressed Sihanouk to take a hard-line stance with France that, ultimately, resulted in Cambodian independence.

Chapter 3 follows Sihanouk's push to marginalize his political opponents and Thành loyalists in Phnom Penh. Thành saw his support dwindle as he lived in self-imposed exile on the Thai border. By the end of the 1950s, he had founded the Khmer Serei to begin armed dissent against Sihanouk's regime. The governments in Thailand and South Vietnam assisted him, which brought him closer to the Americans, who had grown weary of Sihanouk's grandstanding and neutralist Cold War foreign policy.

As the 1960s began, a rapprochement of sorts seemed possible between the United States and Cambodia. However, as will be discussed in chapter 4, severe tensions between Cambodia and its Thai and South Vietnamese neighbors remained. Thành was a major factor in these developments. Sihanouk began to feel boxed in not only by his so-called Free World neighbors but by the United States as well. He in turn shifted toward an accommodating position with China, further exacerbating his tensions with the Americans.

By the late 1960s, as the war in Vietnam heated up, Thành and the Khmer Serei cemented their ties with certain segments of the American intelligence apparatus and worked closely with the US Special Forces. Chapter 5 discusses the events that led up to the Lon Nol and Sirik Matak-led coup that unseated Sihanouk in 1970. Although much of the picture during this period remains foggy, it is clear is that the Khmer Serei was a highly respected and utilized force under the direction of American Special Forces in the Vietnam War. Thành was crucial to recruiting the Khmer Serei, both in aid of the Americans and to battle Sihanouk's forces. Thành was also a key figure—along with American officials—in this coup. This chapter examines the exact nature of these relationships in depth.

Chapter 6 follows the floundering Khmer Republic government in the aftermath of Sihanouk's ouster. During this time, Thành reentered the government and hoped to play a large role in creating and maintaining the new republic. But, despite his role in the coup that led to the formation of the Khmer Republic, the new rulers of Cambodia mostly sidelined him. Thành would continue to recruit Khmer Krom (ethnic Cambodians who lived in Vietnam) into the Cambodian army, while Lon Nol attempted to placate him by appointing him as an advisor to the government. Due to his continued popularity among some segments of society, Thành would later briefly find himself appointed as prime minister. Politically marginalized by Lon Nol, he had little influence by this point and was finally ushered away to retirement in South Vietnam.

To many historians, Thành was a peripheral player during these years. While often relegated to the margins simply in terms of proximity to the capital, Thành was, instead, fundamental to the dramatic changes that Cambodia faced in the fight for independence and during the Cold War. Thành was essential in the dissemination of nationalist thought, the brief gain and loss of independence during World War II, the battle that ultimately resulted in a free Cambodia, and the establishment of ties with the Americans that kept Sihanouk on edge until his downfall in 1970. Although naïve and power-hungry, this overlooked person was one of the most important figures in modern Cambodian history.

CHAPTER 1

The First Independence, 1908–1945

Nationalistic resistance movements in Indochina were as diverse as the people, cultures, and religions. While regional differences impacted how each individual movement progressed and how Western powers perceived them, the one constant was the desire of the indigenous population to throw off the shackles of French colonialism. As the leader of resistance to the French in Vietnam, Ho Chi Minh struggled for forty years against French, Japanese, and US forces before Vietnam was unified. While Ho was undoubtedly the most famous Indochinese nationalist, a very different kind of resistance movement was born in Cambodia.

Although sporadic incidents of resistance to the French protectorate arose occasionally in the years following the French takeover of Cambodia in 1863, during the early 1940s, nationalist resistance to France emerged to a degree not previously seen. Though many different factions of resistance sprouted up throughout the country at various times during French occupation, Sơn Ngọc Thành was the unquestioned leader of Khmer resistance to France at the dawn of World War II. This chapter will focus on Thành's early years, his entry into political resistance to French rule and his years abroad in Japan during World War II. The idea of both contested and fluid national boundaries, a prominent theme throughout this book, is introduced here as well. The chapter will conclude with an analysis of Thành's return to Cambodia in 1945, rise to power as prime minister, and eventual imprisonment by returning French forces.

US foreign policy toward French Indochina also changed dramatically during this period. American reactions to French and Japanese policy in the protectorate of Cambodia, as well as the response to the bourgeoning nationalist sentiment, will also be discussed. Although peripheral to other major issues of US foreign policy at the time, this is a period when the internal political factions in Cambodia that would, years later, come to haunt the United States are established.

Perhaps indicative of the lack of regional expertise among American officials, oftentimes during this period when they discussed events in Vietnam, Laos, or Cambodia, the three are lumped together as Indochina or French Indochina. Generally speaking, when referring to US policy toward French Indochina, that included Vietnam (Tonkin, Annam, and Cochinchina), Cambodia, and Laos. Vietnam, which received more attention from the United States than Cambodia or Laos, is also at times referred to as Indochina in documents. Cambodia is sometimes referred to by name (as is the French-language version, Cambodge) but is far from a priority for the United States during this period and, like Laos, is generally seen as a backwater. Thành was, at this time, similarly not on the radar of American diplomats.

Thành was, however, a key figure who helped lay the groundwork for an independent Cambodia. Not only was he at the forefront of the Cambodian nationalist movement for independence from France centered on a modern Buddhist-Khmer identity, but he was also a key player in Japan's relationship with Cambodia, its temporary wartime possession. Through Thành, we can see the many external forces that applied pressure on Cambodia: France's interest in retaining its beloved colonial outpost and Japan's desire for a buffer against Allied invasion. The United States had interests in the region as well. Begrudging acquiescence of a French return to the region became, by war's end, the official American position, and it aided its regional allies, the British and French, to ensure that outcome. Cambodia as the increasingly troubling "sideshow" to developments in Vietnam, which would be a dominant theme for the following thirty years, begins here.

Thành, like many other future Cambodian political figures, was born into the Khmer Krom population of southern Vietnam. He was born to an ethnically Khmer father, a landowner, and a Sino-Vietnamese mother on 9 December 1908 in the Keylar Commune, Korki district of Travinh (or Preah Trapeang, as it was known to ethnic Khmer), Cochinchina. There he began his primary school education before moving to Phnom Penh. Like many of his political peers, Thành was educated in France, a rare privilege for a small minority of ethnic Khmer living in Vietnam at the time. His affluent family sent him to study in Montpellier and Paris for secondary school and university. In 1933, he completed a law degree. Overall, he spent six years in the metropole. As with other bright young men from the colonies, Thành's nationalism was likely developed and was nurtured in the exciting intellectual milieu that existed in interwar France. By the time he returned to Indochina in 1933 the seeds that would grow into a determination to eradicate colonialism in Cambodia had been planted.[1]

While the concepts of independence and nationalism began to flourish during the late 1930s with Thành as a central figure, anti-French resistance was, in fact, not entirely new to Cambodia. Buddhist monks led the "First Great Uprising" in 1864, where they protested new taxes and the growing presence of French missionaries and their influence on the royal court. That Buddhist monks were to later play a major role in the push for independence stems from this initial protest.[2]

Around this time the first Americans visited Cambodia. Big game hunters, scientists, and adventurers lured by the mystique of the temples of Angkor would be followed in the coming decades by tourists and missionaries. The first glimpse of Cambodia for many Americans was through Frank Vincent Jr.'s travelogue *The Land of the White Elephant*, published in 1872, but the kingdom remained peripheral to both the general public and American diplomats alike. While the envoy extraordinary and minister plenipotentiary for Thailand Hamilton King, for example, dutifully reported back to Washington on evolving border negotiations between Siam and France (which ultimately restored previously lost Cambodian territory to the kingdom, including Angkor, in 1907), Cambodia was generally no more than an afterthought until after World War II.[3] Siam, for its part, would settle into a temporary position as a buffer between dueling world powers in the British and the French, but its territorial ambitions to reclaim what it felt was unjustly lost during this period will return as a theme later in our story.

While the great powers shifted pieces on their global boardgame, spasmodic bursts of resistance continued in Cambodia. The "Second Great Uprising" of 1885 to 1887 occurred in response to the reduction of the king's powers and that of the mandarins that the French had imposed on King Norodom. Although Cambodian rebels were able to fight the French to a standstill, according to the historian John Tully, "the effects of the war were disastrous. When it was over, large swathes of the countryside were ruined, famine stalked the land, and the population was in decline." While the rebellion was felt across the entire country, there was no nationalistic impetus to revolution at this time. The rebellion ended, in fact, when King Norodom called for peace.[4] As the historian V. M. Reddi recounted, "The rebels were united by sentiment and xenophobia, . . . but there was no definite and compact organization, nor a constructive approach."[5] General unrest and lack of unifying purpose would also prove to be hallmarks of the later Issarak movement of the 1940s to the 1950s.

Although sporadic incidents of resistance to the French protectorate such as these arose occasionally in the years following the French takeover of Cambodia in 1863, it was not until the turn of the century that religious-inspired tensions in Cambodia mounted to push for reforms from the French government. In the 1910s and 1920s, Chuon Nath and Huot That, both ordained in the Mahanikay sect, were instrumental in modernizing Cambodian Buddhism. By publishing religious texts in the Khmer language, they made a claim for a nationalist, Cambodian form of Buddhism, and by making the Buddhist *dhamma* accessible to novice monks and laypeople, they expanded their reach. This was an inherently political shift, and in many ways, they were religious reformers, embracing modern science and rejecting the more superstitious strains of the Mahanikay, the largest sect of Theravada Buddhism in Cambodia. By the late 1920s, there was a pushback from certain sections of the laity that wanted to retain Buddhism's supernatural elements.[6] Within this context, the Indigenous Institute for the Study of Buddhism of the Little Vehicle, or Buddhist Institute, was established.

Inaugurated in May 1930, the professed mandate of the institute was for the study of Theravada Buddhism among the Khmer, Laotian, and Kampuchea Krom populations.[7] Being stationed at the Royal Library in Phnom Penh, however, insured a Cambodian focus, as did the appointment of Suzanne Karpelès as the secretary of the institute. Karpelès was a French expert on Cambodian Buddhism and language who, according to the historian Penny Edwards, "devoted sixteen years in Cambodge to the establishment and management of several key cultural institutions and journals, all keenly oriented towards the purification and salvation of Khmer Buddhism from degeneration and 'foreign' contamination." Not surprisingly, Sơn Ngọc Thành and others would find the Buddhist

Institute the perfect place to exchange ideas on modernity, reform, religion, and colonialism. It would prove to be the perfect staging ground for the dissemination of nationalistic thought.[8]

After returning to Indochina, Thành began work as a civil servant, first as a secretary in Cochinchina from 1933 to 1934. By 1935, he had moved back to Phnom Penh, where he took a job as a clerk in the Royal Library, working on translation. He also worked as a judge in a Cambodian court, a professor, and a member of the council of prosecutors.[9] Throughout this time he continued to nurture his nationalist ideas carefully and quietly. He soon moved on to work on the Mores and Customs Commission at the Buddhist Institute and later became its secretary general. Through this institution, Thành was able to recruit Buddhist monks, the one source of institutionalized nationalism that had not been stamped out by French colonial rule, to educate soldiers throughout the country on Cambodian nationalism. Thành chose only those monks who were strongly nationalistic and good public speakers. These monks then contacted Thành with the names of those who seemed especially interested in the movement, whom Thành would then attempt to recruit. According to the historian Henri Locard, one such monk, Achar Hem Chieu, "was a natural choice as he was skilled in explaining and convincing the solders, using Buddhist teachings, to love their country, and to prepare for what they called 'the struggle.'" The Buddhist Institute became, in the words of Elizabeth Becker, "the first home of anticolonialism in Phnom Penh."[10]

Thành also founded, along with the nationalist Pach Chhoeun, the Khmer language newspaper *Nagaravatta (Angkor Wat)* in 1936, Cambodia's first unabashedly political newspaper. Weekly circulation grew quickly to over five thousand by 1940. The paper was widely read by mainly young intellectuals and modern-minded Buddhist monks.[11] Thành and his associates promoted a Buddhist doctrine seeped in modernism and supportive of nationalist inspirations. This promotion of modernism linked Thành's agenda with the Tommakay faction of the Mahanikay.[12] By encouraging a Buddhist education among the Cambodian population, especially among lay workers, *Nagaravatta* and the Buddhist Institute promoted the idea of a joint Khmer, Buddhist nation. The hope was that these contacts would be a unifying force as Thành looked toward the future.[13]

Over time, *Nagaravatta* moved further in a political direction, and Thành was the essential figure here. The Khmer Issaraks' history of Cambodia's nationalist struggle, published two decades later, dates its inception to 1935, when Thành and the Cambodian elite began their push for independence and commenced with open antagonism toward the French. One of the ways they did was through *Nagaravatta*. Another was the establishment of the Association of Friends and Alumni of the Lycée Sisowath (AFALS), which Thành worked on in late 1934 and early 1935. French police described organizers as "pretty active, evolved Cambodians, with a rebellious temperament." According to Penny Edwards, groups such as this "stretched the parameters of the newly emerging public cultural sphere in ways that translated the sense of imagined collectivity and imagined community." The idea of a Cambodian "nation" was beginning to take hold. But what would this "nation" look like?[14] Again, according to Edwards, "Son Ngoc Thanh and Pach Cheoun's promulgation of an ethnically homogeneous but territorially elastic vision of the Khmer nation allowed for the incorporation of the Khmer Krom in Cochinchina as well as ethnic Khmers in Siam into their visions for the nation."[15] The territories of the Kampuchea Krom and Khmer Surin (ethnic Khmer living in Thailand), both part of the long-lost Angkor Empire, will be major factors in later chapters as they become co-bases for an exiled Sơn Ngọc Thành.

In a bid to weaken Thành's organizational skills and popularity, in 1937, French officials transferred him from the Buddhist Institute to Pursat, where he served as a prosecutor. Thành remained unperturbed, and shortly thereafter, a new branch of the AFALS was opened in Pursat. During this hectic and tense period, he found time to return to his home. Beginning on 9 November 1938, Thành began an eleven-day respite in Tay Ninh, Vietnam, during which he married a Vietnamese woman, Nguyen Thi Tri.[16] He would go on to father seven children, one son and two daughters from his first marriage, and two sons and two daughters from his second.[17]

Thành's search for personal stability contrasted with the onset of world war. Cambodia would not be spared. With France's fall to Nazi Germany in June 1940, French Indochina became the first area in Southeast Asia with Japanese boots on the ground. According to the historian Mark Peattie, initial designs for a Japanese Southeast Asian empire can be dated back to the Meiji period, although the actual execution was undertaken in an opportunistic fashion when Western powers floundered during the World War I. This phase of Japanese imperialism "was the consequence of a complex interplay of circumstances and motivation, of ideology and hard interest; but it took place within a context of the formal authority of Western colonialism."[18]

Prior to World War I, the Japanese presence in Southeast Asia was limited to small-scale economic enterprises, but the acquisition of Micronesia made southern expansion possible. When European capital slowed during the war, new markets were opened to Japan. At this point, Southeast Asia was not viewed in terms of security or military strategy. Japan's interest was strictly an economic policy of expansion that was quite successful due to low labor costs and proximity. When Japan's success eroded the distribution systems of the colonial powers, the West reacted with "hostility and alarm" and put restrictions on Japanese trade, which resulted in a restructuring of established trade patterns, a heightened anti-Western and anticolonial sentiment among the Japanese, and merged Japan's economic and strategic goals in the region.[19]

According to Peattie, the East Asian Co-Prosperity Sphere was, for the Japanese, "an amalgam of rock-hard self-interest and vaporous idealism" that was more concerned with economic self-sufficiency than with colonial liberation, although some intelligence operations in the region did attempt to stir up colonial opposition. Although the Dutch East Indies was the primary target, Japan worked with Southeast Asian nationalists throughout the region to subvert the colonial powers. Cambodia was no different. The main goals of Japanese plans for Southeast Asia were to secure resources (which was the most prominent motivation) and to galvanize support among the local population, with the caveat that the "welfare of indigenous populations was to be sacrificed to Japanese military requirements." In actual practice during the years of 1942 to 1945, Japanese imperialism became a rougher version of the Western variety, and despite the idealism emphasized in Pan-Asianism rhetoric, no ideology existed that would allow for Japanese and Southeast Asians to live harmoniously together. According to Peattie, the major failures on the part of Japan were a lack of knowledge about the region and a failure to plan, which led to its downfall at the hands of the Allies.[20]

As for Indochina specifically, according to an Office of Strategic Services (OSS) report, after Japan faced major problems with installing military administration in Malaya and Java, utilizing the French for day-to-day administrative issues seemed to make the most tactical sense. Because Japanese forces lacked the experience and training to handle the "racial and linguistic complexity of Indochina," the existing French administration could be most helpful in navigating the exploitation of the region for raw materials and foodstuffs.[21] Through agreements with France in Vichy and Hanoi, Japan was thus free to concentrate on further Southeast Asian expansion while France retained day-to-day control over Indochina. The OSS also reported that Japan intended to strengthen its position in Indochina by making "an intensive effort to promote a rift between French and native resistance elements, and to enlist native support with promises of 'independence' as soon as conditions permit."[22] Although there was little appetite on the part of the United States to get involved, developments were monitored with a close eye.

American officials saw an example of this in Japanese entreaties for Thai support, with territorial acquisition of western Cambodia an easy selling point. By the fall of 1940, Thai prime minister Plaek Phibunsongkhram was, according to the US minister to Thailand Hugh Grant, "out in the open with the program . . . that Thailand will not take one step backward and is bound to secure her [territorial] objective[s.]" Grant reported that the Thai government was "dominated by a powerful military clique which is linked with the Japanese and encouraged by the Germans," that an especially provocative speech from the prime minister was "belligerent and smells strongly of Tokyo." According to Grant, the prime minister "resort[ed] to the most dangerous sort of demagoguery which seems to be thoroughly in line with the Japanese programs of Asia for the Asiatic, in referring to the French as white, eating bread and meat and living in towns, while the Thai brethren are yellow, live in the jungle and eat rice and curry."[23] The subsequent Franco-Thai War lasted until the following January 1941, when Thailand's latest territorial ambitions were realized.

On 11 July 1942, a treaty between Thailand and French Indochina was finalized and signed, settling disagreements over national boundaries. It was the result of the peace treaty signed the year prior by the two nations that provided for a special commission to settle any disagreements over borders within one year. Japan, fully engaged in the Indochinese peninsula, mediated the talks.[24] Japan's dual goals of shoring up Thai support while France maintained day-to-day operations in Indochina were thus realized, allowing for continued focus on the broader war effort.

As Japan moved into the region during World War II, *Nagaravatta* turned increasingly harsh in its anti-French rhetoric as this demonstration of Asian power emboldened the editors. Japanese officials in the region partially supported these nationalist sentiments, although anti-French Cambodians likely overestimated their backing. As the French were still in nominal control of the day-to-day activities in Cambodia, they attempted to restrict Cambodians' anticolonial activity, and many Cambodian activists were jailed. French authorities censored several editorials following defeats in Europe in 1940 and Thailand in 1941, the latter of which resulted in the loss of western Cambodian territories. Thành himself became outwardly politically active and was forced into hiding in Phnom Penh after a number of arrests were made at a demonstration of bonzes (monks) against French rule and the arrest of two Buddhist monks in July 1942 that he had helped organize. The tipping point that led to the demonstration was the arrest of the respected monk Achar Hem Chieu two days earlier. The *Nagaravatta* editor Pach Chhoeun was also arrested and eventually taken to Poulo Condore, the French penal island off the coast of Cochinchina and home of the infamous Con Dao prison. This event would come to be known as "the revolution of the umbrellas," or the "Umbrella War." With the aid of Japanese officials, Thành fled to the Thai-controlled province of Battambang and, later, to Bangkok.[25]

The Umbrella War of the summer of 1942 was the culmination of years of burgeoning nationalist, anti-French sentiment. Thành had been at the forefront of this political movement, where Buddhist monks were used to recruit Khmer soldiers serving in the French army. Thành's success in recruiting monks to support his nationalist goals is clearly demonstrated at the Umbrella War, where out of over one thousand demonstrators, around half were monks, many of which represented the modernist Thommakay faction.[26] As recounted by Bunchan Mul, a key figure in the events that led up to "the revolution of the umbrellas," Thành made his initial contacts with Japanese officials as far back as spring 1941 "to ask for military intervention in case the French uncovered the plans for the revolution." Contacts between Thành and the Japanese army continued for the next year. When Achar Hem Chieu was defrocked and arrested for allegedly conspiring against colonial authorities on 17 July 1942, Thành ordered a mass demonstration in front of the *Résident Supérieur* to call for his release. Thành directed planning from Japanese police headquarters to avoid arrest by French authorities. With the help of a Japanese army captain, Thành instructed that the protests must remain peaceful, or Japanese officials could not intervene on the monks' behalf. The hope was that, with Japanese intervention, a path toward independence could be paved. When the demonstration turned violent, French officials crushed the revolt. According to Bunchan Mul, "at the point when the demonstration was in chaos, the Japanese army sent two truckloads of soldiers who stopped nearby.

But how could they possibly make any intervention with the French government? The plan was carried out wrongly, different from how they had been told, so they stayed still."[27]

As Thành later recounted, his decision to get involved with politics during this period was done "in order to protect the interests and independence of Cambodians while the French were defeated in World War II."[28] Despite the setback of the Umbrella War, he still saw this as a prime opportunity to expel the French once and for all. While in Bangkok, Thành wrote often to Tokyo, where he indicated his desire for a "reorganization of Cambodia in accordance with the New Order instituted by the Empire of the Rising Sun." Thành fashioned himself the "representative of the Khmer Nationalist Party," and, while in many ways unrelated to the actual wishes of the people concerned, he claimed its members consisted of:

> the entire peasant population of Cambodia[,] all Cambodians who were not functionaries, the entire population of the territories ceded (to Thailand in 1941), as well as of the Khmer portions of Thailand, the entire Cambodian population of Cochinchina, and all the Cambodians living in Bangkok. In Cambodia itself, only the King, his close associates, the royal family and those functionaries loyal to France are ineligible to participate in our movement.[29]

He later wrote to Saigon and informed a Japanese official that "all of us, monks and lay people, are quite attached to Japan in the cause of Cambodia's independence, knowing that we can form with all the other states of yellow Asia a compact bloc around Japan, the Liberator and Defender of the Yellow World."[30] Japanese officials reacted cautiously to Thành's overtures. It is not clear how much of Thành's smooth rhetoric was a naïve attempt to swap one belligerent, dominant power in Cambodia for another that he hoped had more sympathy for his country's plight, or whether he hoped to exploit Japanese regional power to get what he wanted. Either way, it is quite obvious that he attentively studied Japanese wartime propaganda and weaponized that rhetoric for his own goals for Cambodia.

On 28 November 1942, at Vichy, the Japanese ambassador to France Takanobu Mitani discussed a possible reorientation of the Japanese role in Indochina. He suggested to officials in Tokyo that:

> although we will nominally respect their sovereignty, actually we hold the real power, and it can be said that Indo-China should cooperate completely with us as a political and economic member

of the East Asia Co-Prosperity Sphere. It is to the interest of both parties to settle all possible questions concerning French Indo-China with the local authorities, and I believe it will be best to increase their independence from France proper and make them more and more dependent on us.[31]

A similar sentiment was expressed in a Japanese message to Tokyo from Madrid, dated 30 November. That note stated that Indochina was now a "danger zone because of the secret plots of England and America, who are passing things through to Chungking. . . . Therefore it is a matter of course that we should have nothing to do with Vichy, but should pursue a policy of disposing of all matters only with the officials on the spot. Furthermore, we think it absolutely vital for us to take over at once at least the police power of the country." The Greater East Asia minister also noted that a closer relationship with the French governor general in Indochina was desired.[32]

A Japanese broadcast from Tokyo on 7 January 1943 announced that Indochina had advanced from the status of a French colony to "the Indo-China of Greater East Asia." It stated that Indochinese authorities had decided to follow Japanese directives on political and military policies without Vichy approval. According to the broadcast, the economic relationship with the metropole had also been severed, and Indochina would now contribute to the economic prosperity of the East Asia Co-Prosperity Sphere and the greater war effort. Although matters had been heading in this direction for some time, Ambassador Mitani protested the report in communications with Tokyo, stating "articles like this may infuriate not only France but Germany. Furthermore, such articles serve our enemy well as propaganda."[33]

By early 1943, American intelligence had picked up on a series of Japanese communications that discussed a "Cambodian independence leader" who went by the name of Son Niyotuku Tan, the Japanese rendering of Sơn Ngọc Thành's name. Thành had taken refuge in the Japanese embassy in Bangkok until 23 January 1943. He then boarded a Japanese army plane and traveled to Tokyo for what Japanese officials referred to as "safe-keeping." Days earlier, the Greater East Asia Ministry ordered its representatives in Formosa and Thailand to take extraordinary precautions with Thành's flight. It added, "Under the present circumstances of course we must keep absolutely secret the fact that Japan is patronizing him and especially the fact that he has come to Japan, so please be specially careful about the newspapers."[34]

Thành's travel to Japan during the war was not an aberration for Southeast Asians during the era of the Japanese empire. The historian Ken'ichi Goto examines the case of Indonesian students moving to Japan, for example. Spurred on by nationalist intent, anti-Dutch sentiment, and new Japanese overtures to the south, many Indonesian students studied in Japan in the prewar period. There some joined Japan's advocacy of Pan-Asianism and even aided in the formation of Japan's southern strategy. These students were the creators of the Sarekat Indonesia student organization, which promoted relations between the two countries, as well as Indonesian nationalism. As Japan moved to a wartime setting, foreign student programs were seen as an essential part of implementing its overseas policies. The plan was to foster the education of would-be future leaders who would then lead their respective countries in establishing the Greater East Asia Co-Prosperity Sphere. For Indonesians, in this instance, traveling and studying in Japan was a desirable prospect. During their stay in Japan a national consciousness was strengthened, which was an essential ingredient in the postwar push for liberation from the Dutch.[35] Thành demonstrated a similar hardening of his already established beliefs during his time in Japan.

In hopes of playing on the inspirations of Asian nationalists, Tokyo granted independence to the Philippines and Burma in 1943. It also hosted the Greater East Asia Conference from 5 to 6 November 1943, where representatives of states liberated from Western colonialism (Manchukuo, Burma, the Philippines, Thailand, and the Reform Government of China) joined Japan in solidarity, at least on the surface. Pan-Asianism was stressed, and according to the historian James L. McClain, Ba Maw, the representative from Burma, thanked the Japanese for helping Asians "recapture a sense of common brotherhood and destiny." A communiqué issued at the conference declared that the only path to "universal understanding, peace, and stability" was through a Japanese-centered so-called co-prosperity.[36]

Overall, the Japanese military administration supported nationalist inspirations among local Southeast Asian populations insofar as it was useful in garnering local support for the empire against the West.[37] Like those from other Southeast Asian countries who went to Japan, Thành was a willing participant, and would spend the next two years under an assumed Burmese identity, where his political views further hardened; he also attained the rank of captain in the Japanese army. Through letters home, Thành urged his supporters to wait for Japanese victory and to collaborate with them at all times against France and the incursions of Thailand.[38] Japan, however, had broader concerns.

In February 1943 the Greater East Asia minister Kazuo Aoki expressed concerns that certain elements of the French military in Indochina were less than sympathetic to Vichy French administration and Japanese occupation. They were followers of the former governor general Georges Catroux and opposed his Vichy replacement Jean Decoux. According to the Japanese, local French military officers and men met secretly on a weekly basis to discuss potential resistance measures. A Japanese message from Saigon to Tokyo stated that "the growing strength of the resistance against a policy of cooperation with Japan on the part of the upper strata of society in French Indo-China is a reflection of the vain hopes which they have regarding the stalemate in the war situation in Europe and in the Southwest Pacific, and also with regard to the landing operations on the mainland of Europe which they are expecting."[39] For the time being, however, French administrators in Indochina remained compliant with Japanese wishes.

In a 5 March 1943 message Aoki relayed that since France was following an agreeable policy toward China, Japan intended to cooperate with French authorities in Indochina. He disingenuously claimed that Japan was also "strictly refraining from all scheming with respect to the so-called independence movement" among the Vietnamese and other groups, as he made no mention of the "Cambodian independence leader" to whom Japan had already granted asylum.[40]

In Phnom Penh, the local power of the Buddhist Institute was not lost on the Vichy French, and in an effort to reduce its impact, Suzanne Karpelès, its founder, was forced into an early retirement in late 1941. Her forced retirement left members of the institute vulnerable. As recounted in a letter from Thành to Karpelès in 1947, without her, "on the grounds of simple suspicion, mass arrests were made among your staff, without the slightest explanation. . . . All personnel were threatened with arrest from one moment to the next. . . . It was this extraordinary police brutality which led me to abandon my family and my children, to leave my country, for Japan." He went on to say, "it was these events of 1942, concocted by the police, that threw me squarely into politics, in spite of myself. I took this road out of the duty that I must fulfill towards my Khmer country, [which was] in danger."[41]

Like his royalist adversaries, Thành utilized Angkor's symbolic value as a political tool. In July 1943, in a letter from Tokyo to a contact in Battambang, Thành wrote, "Khmers, show yourself worthy of your race, worthy children of the builders of Angkor." The politicization of Angkor and other such themes began under the French and would continue later under Sihanouk, Lon Nol, and Pol Pot.[42] For Thành, Angkor, and the strength and ingenuity that it symbolized, was the perfect encapsulation of his version of nationalism based on a Buddhist-Khmer identity.

The Allied liberation of France in 1944 left issues confused in Cambodia. According to the historian Justin Corfield, "it was expected that the French in Indochina, including Cambodia, might have decided to arrest the Japanese there, and try to aid the British, US and Australian forces fighting Japan." With its overall war effort going poorly, Japan had to take the initiative.[43] As it became clear that the Allies were not going to make landfall in Indochina, the Japanese diplomatic initiatives to grant some semblance of independence to Indochina, which would, in theory, undermine French authority, took precedence over the military insistence of stability.[44] There was also concern that with the imminent collapse of Hitler's Third Reich in Germany that the pro-Vichy garrisons could switch sides.[45]

A memorandum for President Franklin Delano Roosevelt on 13 January 1945 stated that "there is substantial sentiment for independence or self-government among the Indochinese," and while France had plans for future "increased native opportunity in business and participation in the government," it "oppose[d] Indochinese self-government." At this late stage in the war, there was concern that "the United States may have little practical influence on the future of Indochina if French and British forces are in possession of the country at the conclusion of the war unless advance agreement is reached with the French and British." There was a sense that if the prewar status quo returned to the Indochinese peninsula after the war, "American influence among Asiatic peoples will suffer." As the local population would undoubtedly be looking toward the United States to set the tone in the region following the war, "our policies toward Indochina should be consistent with our policies toward the other countries in Southeast Asia."[46] In these instances, mentions of Indochina refer most specifically to Vietnam. Before the war, the only US consular representation was in Vietnam, speaking to the prominence it had for both French and American officials. Roosevelt likely would have viewed Cambodia and Laos as nothing more than remote outposts of the French empire.[47]

During the war, Roosevelt developed a skeptical approach to the European colonial powers as they sought a resumption of the prewar status quo. He often saved his toughest rhetoric for French Indochina, proclaiming at one point, "France has had the country—thirty million inhabitants—for nearly one hundred years, . . . and the people are worse off than they were at the beginning." He proposed a trusteeship for French Indochina that would result in independence, but the angry response of the European powers threatened the close alliance between the imperial powers. If they were alienated in the Pacific, they could not be reliable partners in rebuilding Europe. By early 1945, according to the historian Robert Dallek, Roosevelt had backed away from international trusteeship planning, changing "the scope but not the substance of his plans." Roosevelt still desired, however, according to the historian Robert J. McMahon, "a liberalization of colonial rule."[48] By early February 1945, Japan's policy with respect to Indochina had also begun to shift. The French embassy in Chungking reported that Japanese forces displayed "a more arrogant attitude toward the French" and that French forces could be disarmed in the near future.[49]

French governance in Indochina ended abruptly on 9 March 1945. Air raid sirens echoed throughout Phnom Penh, and French citizens were summarily disarmed and interned by the Japanese. There was scattered resistance, but overall, the *coup de force* went off with little trouble. Even pro-Japanese Cambodians were taken by surprise.[50] Japan quickly declared a state of martial law. It took over "all industries, barracks, airfields, Government residences, police stations, railroad stations, and utilities."[51]

Following the internment of French soldiers and officials, Japan allowed the Cambodian king Norodom Sihanouk to declare Cambodia's independence, which he did on 12 March, and a week later, he appointed a new government. These new ministers were to act under the advice of the Japanese.[52] Ung Hy was appointed to the position of *akkamohasena*, a title with precedence over other ministers.[53] Japan, in turn, filled the void as Cambodia's regional protector left by France. The Japanese news agency Domei announced on 12 March the Cambodian declaration of independence and noted Cambodia's promise to utilize resources in conjunction with the Japanese for the "realization of their common objectives."[54] Symbolically, the enforced romanization of the Khmer script and use of Gregorian calendar were gone in an instant, and Sihanouk "proclaimed [Cambodia's] place in the Greater East Asian Co-Prosperity Sphere."[55] According to the Japanese colonel Hidezumi Hayashi, Japanese policy in Cambodia was centered on "non-interference in internal politics" and "close collaboration in all domains." Economically, Japan saw Cambodia as a source of cotton, fish, rice, beef, and labor.[56] The OSS reported that Japan intended to strengthen its position in Indochina by making "an intensive effort to promote a rift between French and native resistance elements, and to enlist native support with promises of 'independence' as soon as conditions permit."[57]

On 13 March 1945, the US ambassador to France Jefferson Caffery met with Charles de Gaulle to discuss the current military situation and postwar outlook for France. De Gaulle was perplexed by American refusals to allow Britain to transport French reinforcements to Indochina, stating "we do not understand your policy. What are you driving at? Do you want us to become, for example, one of the federated states under the Russian aegis? . . . When Germany falls they will be upon us. If the public here comes to realize that you are against us in Indochina there will be terrific disappointment and nobody knows to what that will lead. We do not want to become Communist; we do not want to fall into the Russian orbit, but I hope that you do not push us into it."[58] In response, a proposed statement on Japanese actions in Indochina was quickly drafted: "In accordance with its constant desire to aid all those who are willing to take up arms atainst [sic] our common enemies, this Government will do all it can to be of assistance."[59] Roosevelt had in fact ordered US air forces to assist the French in Indochina as long as it did not impede the broader war effort against Japan in the Pacific.[60]

While tensions remained between the United States and France, Cambodia and Japan strengthened their ties. After 9 March, a special bureau was created to handle relations between the Cambodian government and the Japanese army. The minister of interior initially handled this, but the post of minister of foreign affairs was soon created. Even before his return to Cambodia, it was decided that Thành should head this post due to his experience in Japan. Sihanouk made the decision in consultation with Kanichiro Kubota, a former diplomat who was named supreme advisor to Cambodia shortly after the 9 March coup and who later worked as a counselor to the king. Kubota was responsible for all questions that arose between the Japanese and Cambodian governments and represented a new era of close collaboration that would remain in place for the duration of the war.[61] American intelligence theorized that "the hard-pressed Japanese probably cannot at present afford the manpower to undertake radical changes in the local governments and therefore are trying to enlist the support of the present officials as an emergency procedure."[62]

In April, Sihanouk requested that Kubota intervene with the Japanese army to aid in repatriating Cambodian citizens who were residing outside of the country. This was not a specific request for Thành's return, as it applied to all Cambodians, but Thành was seen as an important part of a new Cambodian government in collaboration with the Japanese. Sihanouk specifically noted the desire for the return of students currently in Saigon and Hanoi.[63] Soon after, the Japanese brought Pach Chhoeun back from Poulo Condore, and in early May 1945, three years after it was suspended, he began publication again of *Nagaravatta*.[64]

Over the years, anti-French sentiment had grown in Cambodia. The fact that an Asian power could displace a European one gave hope to nationalist aspirations throughout Asia. Renowned for his nationalist credentials, Thành had become a political folk hero of sorts in Cambodia. While Sihanouk claims to have begged the Japanese for Thành's return, it was more likely to have been a Japanese decision, as Thành had never been close to the king, and his ardent opposition to French control did not ingratiate him to many in the royal family.[65]

Thành arrived in Saigon on 21 May 1945, where he stayed for just over a week. He arrived in Phnom Penh on 30 May by car, escorted by several Japanese officers, including Colonel Sadaharu Kodo, who had temporarily replaced Hayashi as "l'Etat-major de l'armée."[66] A group of Japanese advisors was present at the first meeting between Sihanouk and Thành. Two days later, Thành was named the minister of foreign affairs, the post created especially for him "to ensure liaison between Jap [*sic*] army and Cambodian [government], and in particular to centralize all requests presented by Kubota for labor and supplies."[67] Here, we see the dichotomy of Thành's political maturation. On the one hand, he was a reformist, nationalist, and independence leader. On the other, he was not only reliant on but also a collaborator with the occupying Japanese forces.

The position of minister of foreign affairs included the duties of "form[ing] and maintain[ing] good relations with foreign nations," the creation of treaties and other actions related to international commerce, creation and organization of representation in foreign nations, and to submit nominees for positions of ambassador to the king and his advisory council. Thành's other responsibilities included: receiving and presenting foreign representatives to the king; monitoring treaties, conventions, and diplomatic documentation; protecting Cambodian nationals of foreign soil; and monitoring and regulating immigrants into Cambodia.[68] At the same time, Thành helped local Japanese officials organize and recruit five hundred "Cambodian Voluntary Troops" to assist the continuing war effort.[69]

Upon his return to Phnom Penh in May 1945, Thành found that "Annamite influence, supported by the Japanese," was strong. According to Thành, those who worked for the Japanese were favored over ethnic Khmer, and some displayed an "openly anti-Cambodian" prejudice. There were noticeable tensions between Khmer and "annamite."[70] Such tensions had deep historical roots and would remain a constant in Khmer-Vietnamese relations for the foreseeable future. But Thành saw a closer relationship with the Vietnamese as a means of thwarting a French return.

In June 1945, a policy paper prepared by the Department of State expressed concern by both French and US officials that the independence granted by Japan to Cambodia could complicate the return of colonial France.[71] To ensure a French return to the region, which the United States now supported, a return to the parameters of the French colonial regime was essential. In Phnom Penh, however, the nationalist sentiment that had been building would soon find itself in the seat of power.

On 9 August, seven young Cambodians led a coup d'etat, where, except for Thành and Prince Sisowath Monireth, all ministers in the government were arrested. Their hope was to force Sihanouk to abdicate and install an independent government before the French returned.[72] The next morning, eleven militiamen broke into the palace and demanded that the king dissolve Ung Hy's cabinet. Members detained the previous night were released after Sihanouk yielded to the intruders' demands.[73] According to later accusations made against Thành during his trial, the Japanese authorized the coup. According to the French, the objectives of the Japanese were to "increase the influence of" Thành, to reinforce the pro-Japanese position of cabinet, and lessen the "prestige of king" Sihanouk.[74] The result of the coup attempt on 9 August was that the king elevated Thành to become the prime minister of Cambodia. Thành summarily had the seven suspects arrested. Statements from the trial record imply that the Japanese may have pressured Sihanouk to install Thành as minister, although Thành denied any knowledge of this, as he was out of the country at the time.[75] Whatever the case, Thành was now in the position of power that he had craved for over a decade.

According to Kubota, the Japanese had no knowledge of the coup and had "no interest in changing [government]." Kubota also claimed that Thành was unaware of any coup plot, but that he was the "idol of the group . . . because he represented pure nationalism."[76] Whatever the discrepancy, according to later accusations made at Thành's trial, as prime minister, he attempted to cement a close, collaborative relationship between Cambodia and Japan, and according to the French, Conseiller Kubota and Colonel Hayashi closely advised him.[77]

Indicative of Thành's close relationship with the Japanese, on 13 August, in one of his first actions as prime minister, Thành wrote to the Consul General of Japan requesting the urgent intervention of the Japanese army to occupy waterworks and electricity plants in Phnom Penh and additional major provincial locations in hopes of avoiding any disruptions to essential facilities in the capital.[78] Despite the grave situation Japan found itself in, Thành still needed its help. That same day, Takeshi Tsukamoto, a minister in Saigon, informed Tokyo of the mindset of the local population in the twilight of the Japanese empire. "The local inhabitants are petitioning the Japanese to prevent the return of the French at all costs. If the French can be kept out they would prefer independence but, failing that, they would be content to come under some sort of international trusteeship. This appears to be the earnest desire of all three peoples of Indo-China [Vietnamese, Laotians, and Cambodians]."[79] Though two atomic bombs had been detonated over Japan shortly before this, it is unclear whether Thành was aware of this fact, or how it influenced his approach toward Japan. It seems he remained dedicated to a close relationship with Japan, even with its defeat imminent.

A new cabinet was proclaimed on 14 August and installed the next day. Many of the new ministers were actually holdovers from the previous cabinet. Pach Chhoeun and Khim Tit, both collaborators with Thành, were also included as new members. In addition to being elevated to prime minister, Thành retained the position of minister of foreign affairs.[80]

On 15 August, the day of Japan's surrender to the Allies, Thành was officially named Cambodia's prime minister. A corps of Cambodian volunteers known as the "green-shirts," a one thousand–man group formed by Japan a month prior, supported him. By the end of September it had nearly doubled in size. In addition, Thành maintained a "personal secret police" force, as he undoubtedly was concerned with the long-term prospects of his political survival.[81]

In his speech at the cabinet's installation, Thành spoke not only on his plans for the future, but he also connected them to his vision of a Khmer-Buddhist nationalist Cambodia. Thành pledged to "'nourish

FIGURE 1.1. Sơn Ngọc Thành, undated photo. Courtesy of Vann Ung.

and defend' Buddhism, the king, and the royal family, to consolidate the Cambodian people, to defend the state, to strengthen independence, and to improve education." A strong alliance with Japan was again emphasized, and he stressed the importance to expanding Cambodia's alliances with other Asian nations, including Vietnam.[82] Soon after, Thành expressed his desire to "work for the development of his country by cooperating completely with Japan, in time of peace just as in time of war." He added that if the French returned, he would "resign and take refuge in Japan," perhaps signaling that he acknowledged his and Cambodia's impermanent independent status.[83]

With the end of the war near, US officials were less concerned with postwar reconstruction in Southeast Asia than they were with delivering a final blow to Japan. As recounted by the historian Robert McMahon, at the Potsdam Conference in July and August, with the specter of a land invasion of Japan on the horizon, "Truman agreed to transfer the responsibility for the liberation of . . . the Southern half of Indochina, along with Thailand, to the Southeast Asia Command of British Admiral Lord Louis Mountbatten." This decision effectively dampened the US presence, at least in the short term, in reshaping postwar Southeast Asia.[84] But it was also more than this. Roosevelt had a strong anticolonial sentiment and carried an anti-French prejudice, but with his death, support for these ideas diminished. As the historian Lloyd Gardner puts it nicely, "In a sudden gust at Roosevelt's death, the pieces all flew apart."[85]

The French position in postwar Indochina, however, was still of great concern to American officials. In late August, a series of talking points for President Harry S. Truman to discuss with General de Gaulle was drafted that laid out the American position with respect to Indochina. The United States considered a strong France as essential "to stability in European and world affairs" in a postwar world and sought to maintain a close relationship with it. While the United States would not "aid her in restoring control" over Indochina, it had no "intention of opposing restoration of French control." That being said, stability in East Asia was of great concern to American officials, and there was "deep concern with the policies which France may pursue in regard to Indochina as such policies may affect such peace and stability."[86] The United States also agreed "with the French government in not recognizing the validity of the transfer of territories acquired by Thailand from Indochina in May 1941."[87] American officials "believe[d] that it is of great importance to the peace and stability of Southeast Asia that a border be designated which will actually remove sources of discontent and potential conflict."[88]

Because the United States played the essential role in the defeat of the Japanese empire, it demanded a major say in the postwar political situation. The greatest fear was that "the peoples of Southeast Asia may embrace ideologies contrary to our own or develop a Pan-Asiatic movement against all Western Powers." The best way, strategically, to thwart such tendencies in Indochina was for it to "be run for and increasingly by the Indochinese themselves so that within a reasonable period of time Indochina may be fully self-governing and autonomous." American officials felt that any use of French forces to suppress the "political sentiment at the conclusion of a war fought to establish democratic principles and the right of peoples to choose their own form of government" would leave the American public "severely shocked." Although mostly in reference to the overt "Annamite" desires for independence, "French prestige and the influence of all Western Powers in Asia would be enhanced" if all Indochinese people were on the path to self-governance.[89]

If France began to exhibit signs of "an intransigeant [sic] attitude" and relations with the local population deteriorated "into another Syria-Lebanon affair," American policy might have to change. It was also snidely noted that France had, in fact, failed in its role as protectorate over Annam, Tonkin, Laos, and Cambodia when it surrendered to Japan.[90]

On 20 August a meeting of the Cambodian Permanent Commission of the Council of Ministers was held. This group included Sisowath Monireth, the counselor of the government, Pach Chhoeun, the minister of the national economy, Khim Tit, the minister of national defense, and Penn Nouth, the finance minister. Prime Minister Thành presided over the meeting, where a variety of topics were discussed, most notably the "delicate situation in which Cambodia finds itself," namely its tenuous hold on independence. Thành expressed a desire for the people of Cambodia to come together and to work with the government to prove to the world that "we are capable of self-government." Thành stated that "of course, it is not a question . . . of a resistance leaning on violence, but purely and simply a moral resistance." The Council of Ministers approved his point unanimously.[91]

Thành's, and Cambodia's, perilous position was reinforced two days later when leaflets were dropped just west of Phnom Penh from an Allied plane announcing the return of French forces. The following week, eight French officers parachuted into Cambodia.[92] On 25 August a Japanese advisor to the Kingdom of Cambodia sent a message to Tokyo stating that "It is universally felt among all classes of the population that, if the Japanese are to evacuate, the Cambodians would like to have the British and Americans come in rather than get the French back. This is quite understandable. If the French were to return at once the situation would immediately revert to the old state of affairs and all sorts of political and economic upheavals would ensue."[93]

While this was the general sentiment among many in Phnom Penh, it was not universal. Many in the traditional circles of power, whether administrative, monarchal, or the courts, were open to the return of the French. Thành's abrupt rise to power and his methods of gaining it left many resentful. Fears that long held privileged positions could be jeopardized, combined with suspicions of Thành's connections to Vietnam led to the creation of an opposition group.[94] Khim Tit spearheaded the pro-French faction within the cabinet. He later expressed concern that Thành had "rushed to maintain himself in power and disorder would result upon return of French," although Kubota felt that this was exaggerated. Kubota, in fact, later stated that Thành "expressed . . . most clearly desire to resign if his presence in [government] was not" supported by the allies. Kubota recalled that Sihanouk expressed similar support, and that "Son Ngoc Thanh's presence at head of [government] appeared desirable until [the] arrival of [the] allies."[95]

During his short stint as prime minister, Thành revealed little about his political leanings or positions. One of the few policies he enacted was replacing French with Khmer as the language of instruction in primary schools, once again centering his vision for the country as a predominantly Khmer one. Additionally, many intellectuals in the capital pushed for Vietnamese to be introduced as the replacement for French as the primary foreign language, reorienting Cambodia toward a regional identity as opposed to one beholden to a colonial past. Many of Thành's French-schooled peers took positions as teachers, where they began instructing students about Cambodian nationalism. These students would later provide considerable support for Thành's next political reincarnation in the years to follow.[96]

To legitimize his actions as prime minister, Thành held a plebiscite on 3 September, with lists of questions being sent to various governors of the Cambodian provinces. This was the first time that a "democratic" vote took place in Cambodia, although the vote was itself a sham, with most provincial governors simply returning questionnaires having marked their approval of Thành's proposals. Over 540,000 ballots were returned, only two of which were not votes of support for Thành.[97] This would later become the blueprint for the many "votes of confidence" Sihanouk would hold during his long tenure.

Soon after, on 13 September South East Asia Command (SEAC) dispatched Major General Douglas Gracey to remove Japanese forces from the peninsula. General Jacques Philippe LeClerc was sent as commander of the French forces.[98] By mid-September Gracey had led his British and Indian forces into the heart of Saigon. They quickly began the process of releasing French prisoners and disarming the Japanese, but met immediate resistance from the Vietminh, who viewed Vietnam as an independent state. Ho Chi Minh had, in fact, previously declared Vietnam's independence on 2 September.[99] Although retaking Saigon proved more difficult than expected, it was a signal that the days of an independent Cambodia were few in number.

On 6 October, Thành sent Pann Yun as a "special delegate" to Thailand to discuss a potential collaboration between the two anticolonial governments. According to some later reports, Thành authorized Yun to offer Pridi Phanomyong, regent in Thailand, continued control over Battambang and Siem Reap in exchange for military support. This would have been a shocking concession, given how the loss of this territory had been a rallying cry for nationalists. While no formal agreements were finalized, this is another example of Thành valuing independence

from France over past regional tensions. It also foreshadowed his future close relationships with neighboring Thailand and South Vietnam.
At this point, Thành also reached out to the Vietminh with the hope
of collaborating in resistance to the returning French. He even visited
Vietnam himself. It seems his aspirations at this point were to simply
solidify regional support for his government before the inevitable return of French forces to Cambodia. Thành sent a delegation to meet
with Vietminh military leaders, but talks broke down after the delegation insisted on Cambodian territorial rights to the Mekong Delta.[100]

Cochinchina, and specifically Saigon, had been the most important
jewel in the French Indochinese empire. As France returned, it found
Saigon in chaos. French civilians were being killed, and the Vietminh
surrounded the city, cutting it off from outside supplies. Cambodia
had traditionally supplied much of the food stocks for Saigon under
the French. To secure a return to power in Saigon, Cambodia needed to
be brought under French control.[101]

On 7 October 1945, the Cambodian Council of Ministers met to discuss the current political and military situation. As he later recounted,
Khim Tit, the president of the council, posed the question of whether it
was necessary to resist a return of French forces to the area. Thành responded that it was. He had already recruited a force of about one hundred men to oppose units of the French military. Khim Tit expressed
concern that the minimally armed, small units recruited to oppose a
French return were no match for the heavy machine guns and canons
of the French military. Years later, he recounted the absurdity, in his
view, of Thành's proposal. "Here is how our 'national hero' conceived
the resistance of French forces!" he quipped.[102]

At the same meeting, according to Khim Tit, Thành proposed an
evacuation of Phnom Penh in the event of a disembarkation of French
forces, whereby Kompong Cham was to be the site for a relocated government. All objects belonging to the state and the crown were to be
removed from the capital and relocated, along with the government.
In case the French followed them to Kompong Cham, Thành proposed
Tay Ninh in Vietnam as a second location, to which Khim Tit replied,
"We no longer revere . . . [the] precious heritage of our ancestors."[103]
If true, this certainly implies that Thành had lost the confidence of at
least some in his cabinet.

The story is a fanciful one, to be sure, and is, on its face, hard to believe, especially considering its source Khim Tit would in later years be
close to Norodom Sihanouk and work in his government. That being

said, it does have value in framing how Cambodians, and Thành in particular, viewed the lower Mekong Delta region of Vietnam. Whether Thành was about actually implementing such a plan is certainly in doubt, but that Thành would choose Tay Ninh as a potential (albeit temporary) location for the Cambodian head of state says much about his views on both the Vietnamese and lower Cambodia. Thành viewed that area as an historical part of Cambodia and the people who lived there to be Cambodian, as would future leaders of the country. The importance of lower Cambodia was highlighted in discussions between Japanese authority and the Bao Dai government the previous summer over the transfer of Cochinchina back to the nominally independent Annamese government. Cambodia expressed its displeasure, which Bao Dai dismissed. The idea of instead awarding a section of Laos to Cambodia as compensation was floated, although the idea did not progress past this stage. In any event, Thành and Sihanouk both would have undoubtedly not been receptive to such a compromise.[104]

On 8 October, Lieutenant Colonel E. D. Murray arrived in Phnom Penh. Two of his most pressing concerns were to ensure "that the Japanese troops there really complied with the surrender terms," and to guarantee calm in the country, as Cambodia was the major supplier of fresh food for Saigon, which was "not obtainable in Cochinchina owing to the Annamite food blockade." Thành was seen as a detriment to completion of both pressing tasks.[105] Three days later Murray flew to Saigon with the request that General Gracey, his commander, authorize Thành's arrest by French forces. Generals Leclerc and Gracey agreed.[106]

It is possible that at this point both Thành and Sihanouk saw the writing on the wall. There were reports on 11 October 1945 that Sihanouk had reached out for support from the French government. Thành reportedly declared Cambodia's willingness to return to the prewar status quo as a protectorate as long as reforms were made, indicating that his own status was of foremost importance to him at this stage.[107]

According to records from Thành's subsequent trial, Vietnamese and Cambodians alike, spurred on by rumors and false news reports propagated by the Japanese, were set to "massacre" the French population that was imprisoned in Phnom Penh's French quarter. The danger was reportedly so real that an unnamed Cambodian minister (actually Khim Tit) dashed off to Saigon to discuss the situation with Allied authorities.[108] When he returned to Phnom Penh, Khim Tit reported that he had been negotiating with the French, when in actuality he was collaborating with the allies in Thành's overthrow.[109] On 14 October

Sihanouk and his parents conveniently left Phnom Penh to visit a Buddhist wat, perhaps with the foreknowledge of what was about to occur in the capital.[110] A later report claimed that the "neatly planned and executed manoeuvre" that was to follow was intended to be "carried out without compromising the position of the King," whose neutrality could only be guaranteed by choosing a day to act when he was on a pilgrimage.[111] Whether Sihanouk was involved or not, time was running short for Sơn Ngọc Thành.

The *Times* of London reported on the situation in Cambodia, and in doing so prophesized Thành's demise. According to the *Times*:

> The Japanese have been openly assisting the Annamites in this area and, as in most inland places, have been selling them arms. There are about 1,500 armed Annamites surrounding Pnom [sic] Penh and at least 300 armed men inside. This British party has made contact with a leading member of the Cambodian government [again, referring to Khim Tit]. Additional French troops are flying into the town, and others are following to defend it from the attack which is expected when the Prime Minister, a half-breed Annamite, is arrested.[112]

On the morning of 15 October 1945, Thành received a letter from the allied "état-major" in Phnom Penh that requested his presence at the Résidence Superieur for a 10 a.m. meeting. After arriving, he was kept waiting for an hour and passed the time talking with the "sous chef d'état major and a French officer" until the French commander General Leclerc arrived, who promptly ignored him. The "sous-chef d'état major" briefly spoke with an officer, who then instructed Thành to "follow us." Placed in a car beside Major Gallois, he was taken to the airport, and then loaded on a plane bound for Saigon.[113] Murray recalled the scene in an interview in 1982: "Poor little Prime Minister thought Leclerc was welcoming him and got up sort of to say, 'How lovely!' He was taken by the scruff of the neck by this gunman [Leclerc's bodyguard] bundled into a car and off."[114] Interrogation began the following day and lasted until 20 October.

The *Times* of London reported that "the allies have ousted the Prime Minister . . . because his activities threatened the security of the allied forces in Indo-China."[115] The *New York Times* added, "he was working against Cambodian interests."[116] Concerns about supplying Saigon were alleviated almost immediately, as food convoys carrying rice, pigs, and cattle traveled from Phnom Penh to Saigon within days, although they were met with sporadic resistance along the riverbanks.[117]

On 18 October, a new Cambodian ministry was sworn in. Sihanouk reluctantly acquiesced to French demands and, according to Chandler, five days later "officially welcomed the reimposition of the French protectorate, reading aloud from a message composed for the purpose by the reinstated *résident superieur*."[118]

Reports from his trial recount that during his two-month reign, Thành, who was being secretly advised by Colonel Hiroo Saito, "persisted in . . . hostile attitude toward allies," both domestically and internationally. These included orders to provincial governors to organize manufacturing, coordinating "propaganda tours," and fomenting "patriotic sentiment against [the] return of French." The "organization and execution of plebiscite" vote was also noted. In terms of foreign policy, Thành's "rather obscure negotiation" with the Vietminh and his calls for aid to China and Siam were both mentioned.[119]

For his part, Thành maintained that he "always acted for country," that he "collaborated with Japanese by patriotism and necessity," and was "never anti-French." He stated that he did not agree to create, with the Japanese, a Cambodian army to fight against France, and that his intentions were only to protect Cambodia against foreign aggression (one could certainly argue that fighting against France fit into this criteria).[120] Thành maintained that he never received marching orders from Kubota or Hayashi and that his collaboration with the Japanese was done on his own "free will because of [his] desire to save [the] country in danger." Any collaboration was not conducted against allied forces. Japanese policy, to Thành, "seemed to want to keep Cambodia peaceful," but that "Cambodia could not live without a protector."[121]

Following interrogation and trial, Thành was sentenced to life in prison and exiled to France. His sentence was later reduced to twenty years imprisonment, then commuted to "administrative surveillance" in Poitiers, France. While interned there he completed a law degree.

Although Japan's impact on Cambodia was short-lived, it had a lasting impact on the role of nationalism within the country. According to a US National Intelligence Survey from 1955, this period "gave the Cambodian nationalists a brief taste of freedom from French control and laid the basis for the anti-French movements that characterized Cambodian politics during the first decade after World War II."[122] This movement would be led by, among others, So'n Ngọc Thành.

While ostensibly a failure, Cambodia's first period of independence, from March to October 1945, gave most Khmers their first taste of participation in the political process. Many also dove head-on into the anti-French and anticolonial spirit that had been brewing for years but was finally unleashed with the claim of independence. People learned of historical anti-French movements, joined militias trained by the Japanese, or marched in parades. As David Chandler notes, "the catalyst for much of this activity was Son Ngoc Thanh." Although Chandler characterizes the writings and speeches of Thành as "a *mélange* of garbled history, race pride, and half-digested Japanese ideas," he notes that, "at the same time, we should not discount the *appeal* of such ideas, or of such a leader, to Cambodians accustomed to being treated like *bons enfants.*"[123]

Anti-French sentiment in Cambodia was far from widespread at this point, but looking back to the status quo at the dawn of the French protectorate, much remained the same. As the assistant chief of the Division of Southeast Asian Affairs Kenneth P. Landon put it to the secretary of state James F. Byrnes in a 30 January 1946 telegram, Cambodia was still "a small country of 3,000,000 squeezed between two hostile nations, namely Annamite and Siamese."[124] This was not only an animating factor in Sihanouk's acceptance of the return of French power, but also a subject that will be present for the remainder of this book.

Chapter 2

Return to Exile, 1946–1955

The next phase of the fight for Cambodian independence from French authority would mostly be fought with Sơn Ngọc Thành on the other side of the world. Following his capture by French forces in the aftermath of World War II, Thành was shipped to Saigon for trial and then to France where he was to serve a twenty-year sentence. In his absence, the Khmer Issarak, an all-encompassing term for all divergent political groups fighting for independence, would grow in stature and prove to be a constant thorn in the side of both the French and Norodom Sihanouk. Many Issaraks were former supporters of Thành. One of their leaders was Pach Chhoeun, who had founded *Nagaravatta* with Thành. As one of the group's leaders, Chhoeun was instrumental in forming a Khmer Issarak committee and a makeshift government in exile. Although Chhoeun surrendered in April 1946, the Issaraks would survive for the next eight years.[1]

Thành would return to Phnom Penh in 1951 to great fanfare and almost immediately flee to join the resistance in the jungles on the Thai border. From here he attempted, with some successes, to consolidate the various Issarak factions and press Sihanouk to take a strong stance against French intransience. By 1953, due in large part to the propaganda success of Thành, the political mood of the country was ripe for change, and Sihanouk adroitly shifted his tactics vis-à-vis the

French. The result was independence by November 1953. Thành's self-proclaimed goal was realized with him relegated to the background.

The United States walked a bit of a tightrope during this period. In this chapter we see that there is a general desire to not get heavily involved in internal developments in Cambodia, and also an ignorance on the part of American officials of the intricacies of Cambodian politics in the waning years of French domination. Sympathies toward a French presence in the country, however, dwindled over the years, and as the Cold War became a reality, of paramount concern for the United States was potential communist infiltration in Cambodia. Sihanouk, perhaps once seen as a stable presence, was beginning to be seen as less so by the middle of the 1950s.

It was with some trepidation that the United States, under the guidance of President Harry Truman, decided to invest in the future of French colonial aspirations in Indochina following Japan's defeat in the Pacific. A "Policy and Information Statement on French Indochina" laid out US policy in the aftermath of the war. Although policy planners were conscious of the importance and need for "the resurgence of France as a strong, friendly world power," they were also "keenly aware of the need . . . to recognize the natural political aspirations of the colonial peoples of Southeast Asia." This was of utmost importance in Indochina, where nationalist sentiments, which predated the war, were only growing stronger. "Accordingly, although we recognize French sovereignty of French Indochina, we have adopted the policy of not aiding the French in the reestablishment by force of their control over that area." That meant no arms, munitions, or military equipment, nor were "American flag vessels" permitted to carry troops or equipment to the area.[2] The month prior, however, Truman approved the transfer of eight hundred Lend-Lease trucks from the British to the French in Indochina.[3] While Vietnam was a hotbed for resistance for returning French authority, Cambodia, although granted autonomy within the French Union on 6 January 1946, was host to its fair share of independence-minded fighters as well.

With France back in power following the war, Thành's supporters fled to the jungle near Siem Reap and the Thai border, where they formed the Khmer Issarak movement. Sympathizers were found in the Democratic Party, which benefited from French attempts to stem the growing nationalist sentiments in the protectorate. France granted political concessions, including liberalized male suffrage, (theoretical) freedom of speech and assembly, and perhaps most importantly, allowed for the establishment of political parties. In the election for the National Assembly of 1947, Democrats won 73 percent of the total vote. This was due in large part to the party's connection to Thành and its commitment to independence.[4] Thành was respected throughout the country as a true patriot, "particularly among students, intellectual groups, and younger army officers who see in him the embodiment of Cambodian independence aspirations." An early supporter of Thành was none other than Saloth Sar, who would later be known infamously as Pol Pot.[5] That Thành gained an immense following while he was on the other side of the globe worried the throne.

US officials, however, continued to view developments through the prism of how they would impact the French presence in the region, and for the time being were far more concerned with developments in Vietnam. The American consul at Saigon Charles S. Reed was dismissive of the potential of the Issaraks. In a confidential communication to the secretary of state George Marshall, Reed commented that Cambodia would continue to accept French leadership, and that "the Issarak movements could largely be dismissed as attempts to make dynastic changes rather than revolts against the French position."[6] Despite such sentiment, French officials maintained a watchful eye on groups like the Issaraks.

While the French administration made gradual concessions that allowed for additional political freedoms in Cambodia, it continued to keep tabs on the burgeoning independence movement that continued to grow in Thành's absence. One piece of propaganda collected by the Sûreté, the department tasked with criminal investigations within the French government, was a political cartoon. Its headline asks, "Do all Patriots know Son Ngoc Thanh?" In a series of panels, the cartoon depicts a sarcastic history of Thành's role during the Japanese occupation period. In the first, a diminutive Thành, wearing suit, tie, and glasses, stands next to a towering Suzanne Karpelès, insinuating the subordinate role he played to her at the Buddhist Institute. The caption, in Khmer, states that Thành "is protected under the skirt of Karpelès." The cartoon goes on to lampoon Thành for his past connections to the Japanese and minimize his contributions to the nationalist movement.[7]

In the immediate postwar years, Bangkok became a center for the various nationalist movements in Indochina. Thai officials, still wistful for a return of lost provinces on the western edge of Cambodia, saw the Issaraks as a useful tool in destabilizing Cambodia. Perhaps a politically marginalized Sihanouk would open the door to a return of the sacred

FIGURE 2.1. Political cartoon depicting Sơn Ngọc Thành and Suzanne Karpelès in caricature. Courtesy of the National Archives of Cambodia.

temples of Angkor to Thai control. Khmer Issaraks initially organized in Battambang, the western province of Cambodia situated on the Thai border, with various groups aided by either Siam or the Vietminh, the latter of which also hoped to utilize the rebels for their own political gain. By the end of 1946, Battambang was a war zone, and the Angkorian temples were no longer safe for visitors. Issaraks went to Bangkok to reorganize, although they never united. Each Issarak chief continued to operate independently, in which they ruled a set piece of territory and maintained a private militia.[8]

On 6 August 1946, five hundred Khmer Issarak moved on Siem Reap under the cover of night and attacked French positions. French reinforcements came north from Phnom Penh and drove the Issaraks from the city, whereupon they withdrew and took shelter at the temples of Angkor. On 12 August, six aircraft strafed the rebels at Angkor Thom, while one hundred paratroopers and a detachment of the French Foreign Legion assaulted Issarak positions. Sihanouk made a request to the French high commissioner in Indochina to lodge a formal protest with the Thai government, which supported the Issaraks, against the "profanation of the monuments of Angkor."[9]

On 14 January 1947, Prince Norodom Chantaraingsey, representing the "Free Cambodian Committee," penned a letter to the former US senator and representative to the recently established United Nations Warren R. Austin that detailed "the determination of all Cambodians desirous to attain their Self-Government." Peppered with idealized Cambodian history, a damning critique of the French, and quotations from Presidents Franklin Roosevelt and Harry S. Truman that supported the concepts of humanitarianism and self-governance, Chantaraingsey appealed to the secretary general "for the cause of our independence." In a closing plea to Austin, Chantaraingsey wrote, "for the sake of our country, we shall be most grateful, if your Excellency will be so kind as to assist us in the attainment of our independence by submitting our appeal to your Excellency's Government."[10] Austin forwarded the letter to the secretary of state, and by mid-February responded to Chantaraingsey, stating, "In accordance with your request that your letter be placed before the United States Government, I have forwarded it to the United States Department of State."[11]

American officials, however, were not sympathetic to the Issaraks and believed that the upstart Issarak movement would have collapsed long before if not for outside aid. Additionally, it was thought that "the promulgation of [a] liberal constitution . . . and [its] implementation by free elections; turn-over of administrative and legislative functions to the people, . . . these have given Cambodia . . . about all the democracy that [it] can handle." The Issaraks were dismissed as "a motley gang of Cambodian non-entities" who "issue manifestoes, hold cabinet meetings, plot with various Siamese political factions and do a lot of empty boasting about a non-existent revolution that they purport to lead." They were no more than "a pack of conceited prima-donnas whose sole objective is the seizure of power for their own personal benefit."[12]

Also dismissive of the Issarak's anti-French sentiment was the *Far Eastern Economic Review*, which editorialized that "French influence, especially cultural, is increasing in . . . Cambodia and the development of [Cambodia] can be viewed with confidence as there exists no friction between the French and the native population." It went on to say, regarding the Vietnamese population in Cambodia, that they "are not politically opposed to the native population and good domestic relations between all peoples exist."[13] Such utopian fantasies belied the realities on the ground. Cambodia's king was well attuned to the growing dissent to French rule in the country. In late November 1948, with the French high commissioner among the thousands of captivated

Khmer, Sihanouk stated, "I [speak] of independence because I am fully convinced that this word and everything it implied constitutes the key to our problem."[14]

Although derided by some American officials, opposition forces of varying political incarnations were a growing concern. According to the British author Norman Lewis, who traveled extensively throughout Indochina at the time, in addition to the Vietminh, the French were up against "five bands of Issarak nationalists, all well armed with fetus amulets and automatic weapons."[15] Dap Chhuon had been heading up a sixth, but he rallied to Sihanouk in 1949 and was awarded with the governorship of Siem Reap province.[16] By the late 1940s, the Issaraks had become restless, and support from refugees in Siam continued to increase. American officials believed that Sihanouk would continue to preserve the relationship with France, if for no other reason than to maintain the protection it offered from potential Vietnamese and Siamese expansion.[17]

This may have been true to a degree, but Sihanouk did push French officials for some internal autonomy. In September 1949 he demanded several assurances from the high commissioner of France, including internal sovereignty for Cambodia, the replacement of French military forces with Khmer soldiers, pardons for Issaraks, and "a favorable attitude on the part of France looking to liberation and complete amnesty for prisoners or Khmer political exiles—first of all for Son Ngoc Thanh."[18] Léon Pignon, the French high commissioner, agreed to the requested terms.

On 29 January 1950, the French Assembly ratified a bill that in effect established Vietnam, Laos, and Cambodia as putatively independent states within the French Union. State Department officials recommended continued support of French efforts in Indochina "or face the extension of Communism over the remainder of the continental area of Southeast Asia and, possibly, farther westward." This support would include military aid, but not US troops. Shortly thereafter, Secretary of State Dean Acheson suggested that the United States recognize the newly created states, which President Truman approved. Acheson next advised Truman to write a letter to Sihanouk expressing that the president "looks forward to early exchange of diplomatic representatives between the two countries."[19] This was the first step toward open US support for Sihanouk in Cambodia.

Acheson felt recognition of the Laotian, Vietnamese, and Cambodian states "appears desirable and in accordance with United States foreign policy" of "encouragement to national aspirations under non-Communist leadership for peoples of colonial areas in Southeast Asia; the establishment of stable non-Communist governments in areas adjacent to Communist China . . . and as a demonstration of displeasure with Communist tactics which are obviously aimed at eventual domination of Asia, working under the guise of indigenous nationalism."[20] On 4 February 1950, Truman sent a letter of congratulations to Sihanouk to mark Cambodia's newfound status as independent state within the French Union, which was ratified two days prior.[21]

For years, the Cambodian Democrats and Sisowath Monireth had been urging Sihanouk to pressure the French for Thành's return. The king likely hoped Thành could be used to exploit a political rift among the Democrats, and his popularity could be used to extract concessions from France. Sihanouk, for his part, owed Thành a debt of gratitude for the latter's intervention during the Japanese occupation when Japan wanted to replace him as king. Sihanouk reportedly paid for Thành's return himself. France was seemingly unconcerned, feeling Thành's political capital had been spent. After six years in exile in France, Thành was released and immediately made the journey back to Cambodia. Upon his return on 29 October 1951, Thành was greeted by over one hundred thousand supporters carrying banners reading "So'n Ngọc Thành, National Hero," and "So'n Ngọc Thành Our Hope." Sihanouk, anxious over the potential loss of power, did not share in the camaraderie, nor did the French authorities.[22] Buoyed by the strong show of support he received upon his return, Thành returned to his strident nationalist rhetoric. Thành's nationalist, anti-French rhetoric marked a clear distinction from Sihanouk's relatively compliant, gradualist policy with respect to the French.

Thành's time in the sun was short lived, however, as he quickly ran afoul of French officials. Under an agreement with French authorities, Thành agreed to abstain from political activities, but by December 1951 Thành publicly stated that true Cambodian independence could only be secured with the departure of French forces. In January 1952, he began publication of *Khmer Krauk!* (Khmers Awake!), an anti-French newspaper designed to rouse such feelings that were spreading throughout the capital. Not surprisingly, the French deemed this a violation of Thành's repatriation agreement.[23] French authorities briefly and unsuccessfully attempted to portray Thành as a communist, but quickly decided to arrest and exile him once again.[24] Thành was tipped off, however, and soon found himself on the run, fleeing to the jungle along with

Ea Sichau on 9 March 1952, the seventh anniversary of the Japanese *coup de force* when he announced that he was leading an anti-French resistance movement and that Sihanouk was an impediment to true political revolution in Cambodia. According to Thành, he left Phnom Penh to "struggle to fight back against imperialist France in order to gain Cambodian independence."[25] Thành went directly to the Dangrek mountain range near the Siem Reap and Oddar Meanchey provinces.[26] Among those who followed Thành into the jungles was Lek Sam Oeun, who later served as colonel in Lon Nol's army.[27] The transformation to Issarak dissident and continued denouncements by Sihanouk pushed Thành to consider the possibilities of Cambodia shifting from a constitutional monarchy to a republic.[28]

By the time Thành fled the capital, the overall strength of the divergent Issarak forces was estimated to be around three thousand men strong, with around half armed. Thành's goal was to consolidate these groups under one umbrella organization, which proved difficult. French officials charged that Thành had merged his forces with the Vietminh, which both sides denied.[29] French officials urged Sihanouk to declare Thành a fugitive dissident, but the king was wary of issuing such a declaration due to Thành's popularity in the country. Sihanouk confided to Donald R. Heath, the US chief of mission for Vietnam, Laos, and Cambodia, that he felt that Thành and the Issarak "could do less damage as guerillas than conspiring in Phnom Penh."[30]

Thành explained that he fled "to join real patriots to win back Cambodian independence taken away by France." Although there was a fear that he might join forces with the Vietminh-supported communist forces in Cambodia, former associates of Thành asserted he was an anticommunist nationalist. Thành used appeals over the radio to call on Cambodian public officials and army recruits to join him. Thành was resolute in his stance that Cambodia's treaty with France did not constitute the genuine independence he felt he had secured under the Japanese.[31] Thành's real hope was to consolidate the various bands of Issarak guerillas, which had split into pro- and anticommunist camps.[32]

As of 1952, according to Chana Samudavanija, who served as deputy police chief in the Surin province in Thailand, the Thai government did not explicitly aid the Khmer Issarak groups positioned on its border, although some Thai ministers sympathized with their efforts. Samudavanija kept tabs on the Issaraks, but did not approach them or arrest any individuals. The Khmer Issarak leader at the time, Kao

Tak, lived across the Thai border in Surin. Following World War II, the Thai government had a policy of providing Thai citizenship to Cambodians from Battambang, Siem Reap, and other areas returned to the French. This policy simplified movement between borders for Issarak soldiers.[33]

According to Samudavanija, Thành "had some followers, and at the same time, there were some hundreds of Khmer Issarak at the Cambodian border, close to Surin," near O Samat. Members of the Issaraks soon approached Samudavanija and requested to transfer rice and medicine to others in the group. They arranged for a meeting with Thành and other Issarak officials near the Thai border. Subsequent meetings were held at Issarak headquarters. Samudavanija expressed sympathy with Thành's efforts against the French and agreed to turn his head to any activity between borders. On one occasion he accompanied an Issarak transport of rice and medicine from the market in Surin to the border to allow for easy crossing.[34]

According to Samudavanija, the Issaraks were financially supported by local Cambodians and Khmer Surin.[35] Thais also sympathized "because they were fighting for their independence and their freedom . . . and we [Thailand] also had conflict with French in past history," notably the annexation of Siem Reap and Battambang provinces in 1941.[36]

It was around this time that Thành, in the eyes of some US officials, became associated with the Vietminh, Ho Chi Minh's nationalist-communist front organization that sought both Vietnamese and Cambodian independence. CIA intelligence noted that on 10 March 1952 that Thành and Ea Sichau disappeared while on a tour of eastern Cambodia. At this point, US intelligence was unsure of Thành's intentions, speculating that he might have been kidnapped by Khmer Issarak rebels or the Vietminh, but they were fearful of a potential Issarak-Vietminh coalition.[37]

Later that month, the Issarak leader Phra Phiset Phanit met with Robert Anderson, the assistant attaché in the US embassy in Bangkok. Now that Thành had joined the Issaraks, he claimed, there was a change "to begin forming a government which would save Cambodia from the Viet-Minh and from French domination." He boasted that with American weapons and equipment that the Issaraks "could defeat the Viet-Minh in Cambodia within three months," that Khmer communists would defect "if they knew that French domination would be overthrown," and that France "would voluntarily relinquish . . . control in Cambodia" once it "saw the 'might of his forces.'"

Anderson certainly saw such outlandish claims for what they were and was noncommittal, but in another example of a lack of understanding of Cambodian politics, he asked Phra Phiset if Thành was related to Hanoi-supported communist leader So'n Ngọc Minh. He stated that Minh "had been given his name by the Viet-Minh" to gain support among the Cambodian population. Anderson seemed unconvinced, and the rumor that the two guerillas were related would persist for years.[38]

Feeling the pressure of Thành's continued popularity, Sihanouk began to push for French recognition of full Cambodian independence.[39] For a true coalition to work, however, Thành was needed within the government. Cambodia was splintered, and a peaceful transfer of power could not be realized without Thành's acquiescence. In a vast understatement, Tillman Durdin of the *New York Times* reported that "Cambodia's political stability would be greatly enhanced if he [Thành] should rally to the government," a sentiment that was echoed by many in the US, French, and Cambodian governments.[40]

Even at this stage, some American officials felt that the writing was on the wall for French rule in Indochina. On 31 March 1952, the counselor of the embassy in France, Philip W. Bonsal, wrote to the director of the Office of Philippine and Southeast Asian Affairs, William S. B. Lacy. Bonsal laid out a variety of scenarios, but came to the conclusion that "the French are finished in Indochina," and "that all is not well is shown by . . . the desertion of Thanh in Cambodia. The French have not convinced enough Indochinese that the real enemies are Ho Chi-Minh and the Chinese communists."[41] In Cambodia, however, French authorities continued to see Thành as a major threat.

There were reports that some in the Cambodian government were supportive of Thành's activities. The French cabinet minister responsible for the Associated States Jean Letourneau informed Sihanouk that "France's contract to defend the country would be 'reconsidered'" if any support continued. Letourneau was wary of the Democratic Party, which remained supportive of Thành, and he criticized the fact that it was the dominant political faction in Cambodia. Letourneau felt that, in order to remedy the situation, Sihanouk could dissolve the National Assembly and create a new constitution "more in accordance with political realities."[42]

Although the Khmer Issarak movement was slowly gaining popularity, the many different resistance factions and splinter groups prevented a unified alternative to Sihanouk's government. There was no consensus, even among members of the Issarak faction, that Thành was really with them. Krot Theam, a member of the Khmer Issarak movement, for example, insisted that Thành was "on the other side."[43] Thành, however, maintained that he was not a communist, and, curiously, that he was a great admirer of American and British colonial rule. He simply wanted France out of Cambodia.[44]

Despite some internal struggles, the Khmer Issarak movement was deemed worrisome enough to warrant an official response from Sihanouk. A combined French-Cambodian force soon routed the nationalist group from its base west of Siem Reap and chased it toward the Thai border.[45] It was later reported by French headquarters that 40 per cent of the now one thousand–strong forces behind Thành had been killed during the raids that Sihanouk personally orchestrated.[46]

Although the number of people that actually followed Thành into the jungle was relatively small, he maintained a great deal of support throughout the country, especially among students in Phnom Penh.[47] Because of his popularity, the United States was concerned with the reaction of the populace to the joint French-Cambodian move. These concerns would prove justified when student demonstrations erupted in May 1952 in Phnom Penh, Kompong Cham, and Battambang in protest of alleged French brutality in their efforts to suppress Thành's influence.[48] Despite the military success of the operation, Thành remained a significant political force in Cambodia, and the Issaraks were a constant thorn in the side of the French.

Issarak guerilla Nguon Hong wrote a scathing, propagandist piece against French rule titled, "Who is the Thief?" In it he complained that "the French have robbed us for eighty years" through high taxes, stolen resources, arresting the innocent, and driving the country into poverty. He claimed that French teachers, on a daily basis, urged students to hate the true Cambodian "patriots . . . for example, Son Ngoc Thanh," but that only drove them to love and respect Thành more.

Corruption was another theme, with the French coffers being stocked to feed their "useless" functionaries. The Ministry of Defense failed to adequately protect Cambodia. Speaking of the French, Hong states, "they put a stick in the wheel of the cart" in order to prevent Cambodia from living in harmony. "Cambodian blood flows and soaks the earth" because of the French, which is why "Son Ngoc Thanh seeks all means to get rid of the French." He resists and struggles from the jungle, "so we should support him by giving food, money, and help hide his soldiers." He called for all Cambodians to help implement Thành's goals to achieve independence. The Committee of Khmer Issarak, Building the Nation issued this pamphlet on 20 August 1952. At the top it includes a political cartoon in which a French man slits the throat of a traditionally dressed Cambodian man, his blood collecting in a pan below. To their left a French woman drinks Cambodian blood from a glass, while her child begs at her feet for a taste.[49]

Such calls to arms did not go unnoticed by Sihanouk. To retain his rule unchallenged, the prince dissolved a Democratic Party assembly in early June 1952, and Huy Kanthoul was removed from his position as its leader. According to Thomas J. Corcoran, the US chargé d'affaires at Phnom Penh, on 17 June 1952 Sihanouk explained that the dismissal of Huy Kanthoul (by which Sihanouk became premier of Cambodia) was due to the Democrats' failure to take a stand against Thành, which therefore made them unable to solve the insecurity problem.[50] Thus with the aid of the French, Sihanouk subsequently took over as prime minister and appointed a non-Democratic cabinet.[51] In addition, the former premier Yem Sambaur was arrested "on charges of plotting against the internal security of the state." According to the CIA, such developments "underscore[d] the growing political unrest in Cambodia."[52]

In his proclamation, Sihanouk promised to win victory and independence for Cambodia within three years. After that time, he would submit to the judgment of the people in a national referendum.[53] Sihanouk also spelled out the differences between himself and the Issaraks. "The Issaraks claim to be fighting for Cambodia, and so do the Army and the police. As Son Ngoc Thanh has said, all Cambodians must join together on one side. Only, one has to agree on what side." He continued, stating "that the so-called heroes have never done anything constructive, that they have only brought disorder, disunity, and ruin while shouting that France has not given real independence. They speak of public servants sucking the blood of the people, but they help themselves to the wealth of the country without any vote or control. If the Issaraks win, there will be unbridled arbitrariness."[54]

The chargé at Saigon Edmund Gullion wrote to the Department of State on 30 June 1952 detailing a verbal attack by Thành against what he felt was French influence over Sihanouk. Sihanouk minimized Thành's importance as a dissenter and curiously referred to him as a good man and a friend. US officials agreed, as they did not believe that Thành, the Issaraks, or the Vietminh would fundamentally prove to be a great threat in the immediate future.[55] That did not mean, however, that there was no need for concern on the part of the United States with respect to the internal stability of the country. A CIA report from 23 August conceded that "political unrest will probably continue in Cambodia."[56]

These concerns were affirmed on 29 August 1952 by a National Intelligence Estimate that reported that because of Thành's defection and mounting student protests, Sihanouk felt forced to dismiss Premier Huy Kanthoul. This allowed the king to rule by royal prerogative.[57] The United States supported these measures, as concern with the communist sympathizers in the Democratic Party took precedence over democracy, and a near absolute monarchy began in Cambodia.

Still, Sihanouk claimed that he wanted Thành to return to the government. Supposedly Thành and the Democrats had become too close, and the king used the Democrats as a scapegoat. Sihanouk argued that the Democrats had led Thành astray from the true fight for Cambodian independence, which only the king could provide. Sihanouk was also quick to point out that Democratic Party actions had forced him to instill a more authoritarian form of government. American intelligence pegged getting rid of the French as Thành's primary goal, leaving Thai and Vietnamese border disputes as secondary concerns. Sihanouk felt this course of action an impossibility because he believed that the French were needed to maintain a "free" Cambodia.[58] Eerily similar prognostications had been made by the Cambodian elite nearly a century earlier that allowed for the creation of the French protectorate.

On 1 October 1952, Dean Acheson sent a memo to various diplomatic and consular offices throughout South and Southeast Asia detailing various aspects of recent developments with respect to Cambodia, Laos, and Vietnam. He reported that the government (likely a reference to the Democrats) was sympathetic to Thành, and described him as an "anti-French agitator and former collaborator of Japanese" who was steadily fomenting rebellion and anti-French feeling in Cambodia. "French let matters proceed with no action other than mild remonstrance to King. French fear was that if situation became too unstable in Cambodia, it would favor the infiltration of Viet Minh Communist forces. They thus stepped up their remonstrances but only to point of warning King they could no longer be militarily responsible for defense and internal security of kingdom unless corrective action was taken." This is when Sihanouk decided to dissolve the government.[59]

When the National Assembly reconvened in January 1953, Democratic leadership decided to confront the king. Having been successful in previous elections, the Democrats felt they should be leading the country. When Sihanouk addressed the assembly on 11 January, he asked it to grant him special powers on the grounds that the kingdom was in danger. Sihanouk cited strikes at high schools and the assassination of a provincial governor, both of which he blamed on Thành and the Democrats. The Vietminh had been the actual perpetrators of the assassination, but Sihanouk was determined to expand his powers. Cambodian troops soon surrounded the assembly, dissolved it, and suspended many civil rights.[60]

Heath suggested that Sihanouk's strong stance against the Democrats might have been partially a result of his fragile state of mind following the death of his daughter the previous week.[61] While it is impossible to know the exact mindset of the king at this time, what is clear is that Sihanouk had made a successful power play for himself, leaving a democratic Cambodia in the dust. Thành was again the scapegoat for the king, who blamed the dissident for ordering the Democratic Party to obstruct the government.[62] French officials were doubtlessly pleased with these developments.

Despite Sihanouk's political success, a strong sentimentality for Thành remained among the young population of Phnom Penh and in intellectual circles. Joseph J. Montllor, the US chargé in Phnom Penh, would later state that Thành was able to capture people's imaginations "because he stands for something, anything. This is more than [the] weak leadership of the constantly changing royal government has given them."[63] This, along with a French government that seemed more than reluctant to give up its Indochinese empire, kept Thành at the forefront of both the Khmer nationalist movement and the minds of American officials, even though he remained hidden to all on the Thai border.

American intelligence attempted to keep tabs on the reclusive Thành. A CIA Information Report on 31 December 1952 about Thành's whereabouts specified the number of troops and arms that were at the dissident's disposal just across the border from Ban Dan, Thailand. According to the report, "200 armed and trained guerillas" comprised of the main force, with two units being recently dispatched to Kompong Speu and Kompong Chhnang. An advanced guard camp of twenty-five men was located two kilometers from the main camp. Much of Thành's arms were old Japanese weapons, including rifles, ammunition, and grenades. Two radio stations, from which he broadcasted his announcements to the nation, were located on nearby mountaintops. Thành also had support from Thailand, which supplied him with additional arms and equipment. The Cambodian population in Bangkok and Surin, Thailand, were great supporters of Thành and agreed to contribute twenty-five baht per head to Thành's group of rebels. The rearmament from Thailand was being done in preparation for a supposed planned attack on Siem Reap the following month.[64] Although many of these specifics are impossible to corroborate, and while a major battle never ensued, that Thành was able to gain such support from both the Thai government and the Cambodian population within Thailand showed the dissatisfaction with France's continued presence in Cambodia.

While many people took Sihanouk's word when he claimed that Cambodia was independent, his subjects were increasingly suspicious of French motives. Heath felt that Thành had diluted Sihanouk's message as the rebels gained prominence throughout the country. To counter people's apprehensions, and to ostensibly pull support away from Thành, Sihanouk offered a harsh analysis of the situation in Cambodia, to which he surmised that additional French concessions were necessary. This would not only further expand his power, but would also gain him popular support, and it was deemed the only remedy.[65]

On 5 March 1953 Sihanouk sent a lengthy letter to the French president where he laid out the reasons why Cambodia should be allowed its independence:

> The Issarak propaganda speaks of me as the principal obstacle to complete independence . . . they say that I and my government are too Francophile to make our country really sovereign. Now, I ask you, Mr. President, what am I to reply to this propaganda when I am denied the means to fight effectively to defend my people . . . ? What am I to reply when the Issarak propaganda points out to the people . . . that Cambodia is not really independent since its king . . . has no power over the Frenchmen, Vietnamese, and Chinese living in the country?[66]

Thành's support among the Cambodian elite was growing, Sihanouk claimed, by depicting the king as "more French than the French themselves."[67]

Sihanouk was evidently aware of the potential political draw for the Issaraks, as he attested to in his letter to the French president. "Native sons, peasants and even townspeople . . . [Issarak] patriotic proclamations find a favorable response among the population and also among the clergy whose influence is enormous throughout the kingdom and they are assured of faithful followers among the masses as well as amongst the elite of our nation."[68] This is a similar diagnosis to one given by the former prime minister Yem Sambaur, who in an interview with Norman Lewis a few years prior stated that "we can take care of the Issarak, without French help. . . . If the country were really independent there would be no Issarak. There would be no reason for them."[69]

In the spring of 1953 Sihanouk traveled to Paris where he pushed harder for full independence. When that failed, he moved on to the United States, where he met with Vice President Richard Nixon and Secretary of State John Foster Dulles. Sihanouk claimed that unless independence were granted, Cambodia could very likely succumb to the communists, which he tied closely to Thành, "within a few months."[70] As Martin Herz states, "There is irony in the fact that [Sihanouk] used the danger of Son Ngoc Thanh and the Issaraks as his most effective argument, while continuing to excoriate Thanh himself and even lumping him with the Communists," which he did when he wrote to the president of France that his country's policy "risks throwing the Cambodians into the arms of Son Ngoc Thanh, *i.e.* of the Communists."[71] This would not be the only time that Sihanouk used Thành as both a domestic and international political wedge and as a means of boosting his popularity at home. Sihanouk left the meeting disappointed, as neither Nixon nor Dulles offered support for his demands. The two instead reminded the king that maintaining a unified Franco-Indochinese front against communist aggression in Cambodia was of paramount importance.[72]

In a 28 April 1953 memo to secretary of state Dulles, Heath related Thành's history of resistance since his return from France, and "his almost immediate taking to the brush and rebellion again. Thanh's propaganda has been increasingly effective and has diminished the national support, almost veneration enjoyed by the King." According to Dulles, that was likely the principal cause of Sihanouk's anti-French outburst given in an interview to the *New York Times* on 19 April 1953, where the king warned that unless it was granted further independence, Cambodia would be swallowed up by the Vietminh movement.[73]

Sihanouk's displeasure with French rule was further evident when on 14 June 1953 he went into a self-imposed exile in Thailand while touring Siem Reap. He accused the French of not wanting to grant Cambodian independence, and said he would not return until the French agreed to full and complete Cambodian independence. The king was now moving, once again, closer to Thành's policies, and in the view of Montllor, Sihanouk was likely inspired to action by Thành.[74] He also began forming plans for an armed rebellion of his own against the French. These efforts later became known as the "Royal Crusade for Independence."[75]

Just before taking voluntary exile in Bangkok, Sihanouk had gone on what Montllor described as a "rebel tour" of the northwestern provinces. Sihanouk attempted to secure Issarak support, along with other resistance factions, and made contact with Thành, which was one of the motivations for Sihanouk's drastic change in tactics.[76] This was done in hopes of consolidating disparate anti-French factions under his leadership, including communist forces. It was Lon Nol who was dispatched to discuss with Thành the king's plan for a united, anticolonial force. Thành categorically refused, saying in response, "We will each work on our own side."[77]

A background paper, "Cambodian Crisis," detailed Cambodia's ambassador to the United States Nong Kimny's dismay over recent developments. These included Sihanouk's visit to Thailand for the sole purpose of broadcasting his dissatisfaction with the Franco-Cambodian relationship and his return to Cambodia but outright refusal to step foot in Phnom Penh. Following these events, French and African troops reinforced the capital, ostensibly to protect French citizens. Perceiving the influx of troops to be a threat, Sihanouk responded on 29 June by ordering the National Army to occupy key governmental buildings.[78]

US officials lamented Sihanouk's actions and apparent dismissal of American advice offered during his state visit the previous April. At the time, Washington advised the king to "continue negotiations with the French toward a peaceful solution." Not only was this ignored, but it also gave "rise to the King's suspicions that [the United States] backed the French." American officials perceived that Sihanouk's subsequent actions increased tensions and not those of French authorities. That being said, for the most part US officials wanted to maintain a distance in the diplomatic wrangling.[79]

Meanwhile, the US government continued to be most concerned about communist influence in Cambodia, although some uncertainty on how to proceed with respect to communist infiltration in Cambodia remained. In September 1953 Montllor relayed to the Department of State Sihanouk's proposed concept of offering some sort of amnesty to dissidents in hopes that Issarak rebels would choose to join the government instead of continuing a fight against it, the idea for which was formed while in exile.[80] Heath had declared days earlier that the "Cambodian situation has taken serious turn for the worse" and decried Cambodia's Cold War neutrality and Sihanouk's offer to the Issarak and communist forces to join the government.[81] The prospect for reconciliation with France now seemed impossible.

Frustration mounted for France as 1953 came to a close. The French general Pierre de Langlade, who had initially come to Cambodia a good friend of Sihanouk, was demoralized, saying "he despised this country and its people." Anarchy seemed close at hand due to the political forces Sihanouk had unleashed in his country. To French leadership, there seemed no other recourse than to abandon Cambodia.[82] That French officials absurdly feared a united right-wing, Siam-backed Thành and communist, Vietnam-backed Minh front made the decision to capitulate to Sihanouk all the easier.[83] With public opinion in Cambodia clearly shifting behind Sihanouk by midsummer, and with France so ensconced in a never-ending war with the Vietminh, the metropole was apparently willing to do anything to keep hostilities from spreading further. France quickly capitulated. Thành himself was apparently so moved by the king's efforts that he felt compelled to call him "a true patriot."[84]

Sihanouk made his triumphant return to Phnom Penh on 8 November 1953. French colonial troops left the next day, and Sihanouk considered his country independent. Issarak leaders, however, including Thành, did not. Over time, some dissident groups joined the government. Ea Sichau, Thành's so-called right-hand man, even made the three hundred–mile journey from Thành's jungle headquarters to Phnom Penh on foot to discuss terms for the acquiescence of the rebel leader.[85] Despite overtures such as this, Thành remained isolated and defiant, and in April 1954 rebels laid siege to the western city of Pailin.[86] The CIA reported on 9 June that "there are also in Cambodia several hundred armed non-Communist dissidents, who are followers of the nationalist leader, Son Ngoc Thanh."[87] Despite setbacks such as these, there was still hope that Thành would leave the insurgency as the Geneva Conference approached.

On 23 April 1954, the the commissioner general for French Indochina Maurice Dejean notified the American embassy in Saigon in an alarmist fashion of his deep concerns for the situation in Cambodia. The French felt that a coup d'etat was imminent, and that, paradoxically, the Vietminh and Thành would be left in control. French authorities in Phnom Penh were less alarmed than their counterparts in Saigon, however. The day prior, the acting high commissioner in Cambodia stated that situations had improved of late. Thành, for his part, while the most important noncommunist insurgent figure in Cambodia, was believed to have fewer than one thousand armed followers.[88]

It was in Geneva that France, Vietnam, the United States, and other major powers negotiated an end to the First Indochinese War. Although the main task for negotiators was finding an end to the bloodshed in Vietnam, Cambodia's future was discussed as well. France did not want the Associated States, of which Cambodia was one, to participate at Geneva. As the date for the conference opening drew near, the United States pressured France to allow the Associated States to participate, which France finally agreed to a short time later. While the Vietminh resistance movement in Vietnam could not be denied participation due to the fact that it controlled significant portions of that country, the same offer was not extended to resistance movements in Cambodia and Laos. This was true for both communist and noncommunist groups. Son Ngoc Minh, the leader of the Hanoi-supported communist "Liberation Committee," and Thành both attempted to be recognized as representatives of Cambodia, but were eventually rebuffed. The pervasive thought was that Cambodian resistance movements were negligible, as they had not even been recognized by the Soviet Union. Despite that fact, following the conference the Khmer Issarak movement, to speak of it in broad terms, seemed fully satisfied that independence had been achieved.[89] One declaration from the Geneva Conference would be put to the test in short order. "The Conference takes note of the declarations made by the governments of Cambodia and of Laos of their intention to adopt measures permitting all citizens to take their place in the national community, in particular by participating in the next general elections, which, in conformity with the constitution of each of these countries, shall take place in the course of the year 1955, by secret ballot and in conditions of respect for fundamental freedoms."[90]

The British prime minister Anthony Eden viewed the Geneva Conference as the international community proclaiming in unison that peace was preferable to war. It was, however, controversial at the time and would remain so for years to come. James Waite has argued that "The Geneva Conference . . . contributed to the uneasy global *détente* of the 1950s but set the conditions for future turmoil and conflict in Indochina."[91] That would certainly become the case for Cambodia. The most notable result of the conference aside from the end of war and colonialism on the peninsula was the temporary division of Vietnam at the seventeenth parallel. This was to be only temporary until nationwide elections could be held in 1956 to unify the country. Those elections, of course, never took place, and Indochina once again succumbed to war.

In the months following the Geneva Conference in July 1954, Sihanouk was more determined to consolidate his power and keep nationalist insurgents like Thành out of the Cambodian government.[92] Returning to Phnom Penh following the Geneva accords under amnesty, Thành briefly left his jungle hideaway and sought an audience with the king. He instead received a cold rebuff, with Sihanouk telling him:

> You would not serve His Majesty The King at the critical hour when he was accomplishing his royal mission. You have broken promises, you have openly attacked the King and his government, saying that they have done nothing but play a comedy to lull the people to sleep so that the French could oppress the Cambodians. . . . If the Monarch had not obtained the independence of Cambodia, the people would have condemned him and his entourage to death, for you and your men have denounced them as traitors.[93]

Sihanouk feared that Thành might win the scheduled elections and establish a republic. Sihanouk decreed that no one could vote without proving that they had resided in the same location for three years, which would dramatically reduce the chances of a Thành victory because his followers had been guerillas for years, living throughout northwestern and western Cambodia.[94]

At this point, the United States's fears of resistance movements in Cambodia had largely dissipated. According to a National Intelligence Estimate, "Post-Geneva Outlook in Indochina," written on 3 August 1954, "Non-communist dissidence appears to have abated and the principal dissident leader, Son Ngoc Thanh, no longer poses any real threat to the government. The King retains widespread popular support."[95] Thành's influence had finally been marginalized, although tabs were still kept on his movements.[96] In October, he and his followers accepted amnesty, although the crown continued to view them with great suspicion.[97]

Soon after, Thành relented and attempted to join the government. A National Intelligence Estimate from 23 November 1954 stated that "Son Ngoc Thanh, the last and most important of the non-Communist dissident leaders, rallied to the King," but that "his loyalty to the King is questionable."[98] Still fearful of Thành's potential for political success, Sihanouk refused to see him. The two never met again. Thành retired to the Thai border, and following Sihanouk's refusal to join the Southeast Asia Treaty Organization (SEATO) in late 1954, Thành became a willing partner with Thailand, South Vietnam, and the United States.[99] In a possible last gasp attempt at some sort of reconciliation, Thành requested an audience with the king in February 1955 after pledging his loyalty but was again refused.[100]

Suggestions that Thành deserved at least a small degree of credit for that great achievement that was independence would gnaw at Sihanouk for the rest of his life. For Sihanouk, this was a prize he could not share. "It is entirely wrong to pretend, as some have done," the prince stated on one occasion, "that the Conference of Geneva in July, 1954, or the 'flight' of Son Ngoc Thanh played a role in the acquisition of independence."[101] Thành was, in fact, a major player in the push for Cambodian independence, and should be remembered as such.

Now that Thành's role as a nationalistic insurgent had ended, he began a new phase of resistance. With his goal of seeing French forces leave Cambodian soil complete, he shifted his angst fully toward the monarchy, yet he remained an outsider. As Sihanouk worked to solidify his stranglehold on Cambodian politics, he continued to complicate American anticommunist initiatives in the region. By the end of the decade, American goals would align with Thành's.

CHAPTER 3

Lost in the Wilderness, 1955–1959

Following the Geneva Conference and Cambodian independence, Norodom Sihanouk was more popular than ever. Buoyed by his success in ousting the French, he set on marginalizing political opponents, especially those close to Sơn Ngọc Thành. This was a period when Thành found himself, both figuratively and literally, lost in the wilderness. It began with Sihanouk's abdication of the throne and the formation of the Sangkum political party, which allowed him to enter the political field more directly and capitalize on his burgeoning popularity in the aftermath of a successful campaign for independence. It also marginalized the Democrats and Thành. The throngs of people that greeted Thành upon his return from exile were a distant memory, as he grew more secluded and isolated on the Thai border, his popular support nearly sapped. He needed a rebirth or sorts. By the end of the decade, Sihanouk had completely co-opted the political sphere. A different means of fomenting dissent was needed. This led Thành to form the Khmer Serei. This group of dissidents, working in the shadows alongside some Thai and South Vietnamese officials, would be the constant antagonist to the prince throughout the next decade. It would also lead him to the Americans.

It is also during this period when a pattern begins to emerge that would repeat itself for more than a decade. In the mid-1950s Cambodia remained on the periphery for most American officials. Focus remained on Vietnam and the potential regional growth of communism. As the decade moved on and Thành solidified his relationships with Thailand and South Vietnam, American diplomats in the region by and large saw South Vietnamese and Thai support for Thành and the Khmer Serei as detrimental to not only the United States, but to Saigon and Bangkok as well. Other officials, generally those emanating out of the State Department in Washington or American intelligence, worked more closely with the friendly governments in Bangkok and Saigon. Despite urgings from some American diplomats to end support for the dissidents, Saigon and Bangkok for the most part maintained it, with encouragement from American intelligence. This incongruous policy toward Cambodia helped to bolster Thành's aspirations and would work to isolate Cambodia from both its neighbors and the United States. This culminated in the historically overlooked coup attempt in 1959 that resulted in both further strained relations between the United States and Cambodia and a hardened, empowered, and defiant Sihanouk.

The year 1955 was to be a year of change in Cambodia. Democrats maintained strong political support and expected, despite some push-back from the throne, to solidify their control in elections scheduled for that summer. Yet early in the year, Sihanouk moved up the date for national elections from June to 17 April. According to American intelligence, the decision to do so "reflect[ed] the king's determination to head off the budding political campaign of the ex-rebel leader Son Ngoc Thanh," which had been given a recent lift when Indian officials expressed sympathy and support for Thành. As early as the previous October, an Indian official with the International Control Commission (ICC) stated that both he and his colleagues thought of Thành as an "ideal national leader, under whom the country could experience the kind of democracy" that India favored. US intelligence reported that a recent letter from Thành to Sihanouk was actually drafted by Indian officials. Sihanouk attached a great deal of importance to Cambodia's ties with India, which, according to American intelligence sources, "restrained [him] from taking direct repressive measures against Thanh."[1] Far removed from his days as the French-appointed boy king, Sihanouk had matured into both a resourceful and skilled diplomat, but one that was both ruthless and politically calculating. This led to the development of underground resistance movements against him, some communist inspired, some not.

Beginning on 7 February Cambodians flooded the polls to vote in a referendum in which the respective political strengths of Sihanouk and Thành were to be put to the test, at least in theory. Sihanouk hoped it would reduce Thành's influence and base of support in the country and discourage continued Indian encouragement for him. The question at hand, "Have I kept my promise to give you total independence?" was a reference to the pledge Sihanouk made three years prior on 15 June 1952 to liberate Cambodia from France. Those voting in support cast white ballots, and those against him used black ones. Although the outcome was all but preordained, government forces took measures to ensure as few dissenting ballots as possible were cast. Thành's newspaper, *Khmer Thmey* (Modern Cambodian) was shuttered, and twenty of his key supporters were arrested. Sihanouk counted on the support of traditional Thành loyalists when he granted suffrage to both monks and members of the military. Voting lasted two days, and voters cast their ballots in the open, in front of election officials and their neighbors as opposed to in secret. One government official in Phnom Penh said that of the tens of thousands of ballots cast there, "there were five or six black ballots [cast] by mistake. The voters, after learning their mistake, wanted to retract them, but it was too late."[2] The final vote in the crooked election was recorded as 925,667 in support of Sihanouk and 1,834 opposed.[3] The CIA reported the results a "smashing victory."[4]

Although rebuked at the polls, Thành pressed on. By February 1955 he had amassed two thousand supporters based on the Thai-Cambodian border operating with Thai support. An American official from Bangkok visited the camp and was summarily rebuffed by Ambassador John Peurifoy for reporting on its existence. Thai officials viewed Sihanouk in much the same way that Thành did: untrustworthy, leftist, and corrupt. Thai grievances were not only geopolitical, but historical, as Cambodia and Thailand had long been enemies. While many in American circles were sympathetic to the views of Thành and Thailand, in the eyes of US officials Sihanouk was both too powerful and too unpredictable to move against.[5]

Sihanouk knew he had to smash the political wing of the Thànhists. In the lead up to the election, Sihanouk considered banning the Democratic Party "on the ground that it has recently fallen under the control of crypto-Communists and followers of the Republican leader, Son Ngoc Thanh." The possibility of a postponed election also became more of a reality at this time. The ICC, which consisted of noncommunist Canada, communist Poland, and nonaligned India, was created to oversee the implementation of the Geneva Accords and was wary of such moves. Sihanouk ran the risk "of alienating the Indian and Polish members of the International Control Commission, who favor holding elections in conformity with the Cambodian government's pledge at Geneva."[6] This response from the international community had at least some impact on Sihanouk's next move—his abdication from the throne.[7]

Sihanouk announced his decision to the country in a radio broadcast. He stated, in part,

> My people are not unaware of the work accomplished by their King in the past three years, nor of the importance of the constitutional reforms which I envisaged to avoid a return to chaos. Certain political parties, among them the Democratic party of Son Ngoc Thanh, have intervened with the [ICC] to prevent me from carrying out my work. That is why, today, I announce publicly my intention to abandon power and to step down from the throne in order to live among my people a life that will hereafter be humble like that of my subjects. I will retire to the country and I will refuse to take with me anything from the palace.[8]

In fact, Sihanouk's abdication was a response to the political difficulty he faced in rewriting Cambodia's constitution. In turning the throne over to his father, Sihanouk would be free to form a new political movement, the Sangkum Reastr Niyum, or People's Socialist Community. To join, one had to renounce membership in any other political group or party. It is clear that the intention was to starve other political parties, especially the Thànhist Democrats, of members.[9]

Any lingering doubts as to the extent of Sihanouk's patriotism were severely dampened following his abdication. The main calling cards for rebels of varying political stripes (that Sihanouk was a French puppet, that he was a tool of the communists, or that he was a self-serving egomaniac) was, on the surface at least, stripped away in an instant. In a show of deference and respect, many returned from their rural encampments to join the Royal Cambodian Army. Thành himself was reported to have stated in a radio broadcast, "I was mistaken about the King in thinking him a tool of the French. He is a patriot."[10]

The thrust behind Sihanouk's proposals to secure and insulate the position of the king and expand his powers was thus successful. Sihanouk's proposal called for the indirect election of members of the National Assembly. Candidates would need to have been residents for three years. Such a rule would impede many of Thành's followers from candidacy. The ICC reportedly stated that the proposed rules would fail to satisfy the requirements laid out at Geneva for a true democratic election.[11]

With the consolidation of his political power seemingly complete, compromise was not on Sihanouk's mind. The Indian delegation to the ICC sought in vain to bridge the gap between Sihanouk and Thành, even attempting to bring them together in a show of reconciliation. Some of Thành's followers reached out to the United States for intervention, but American diplomats stood firm that the United States would not get involved.[12] This is possibly due to the mystery that continued to surround Thành. Confusion about Thành's political allegiances remained. American newspapers at the time referred to him as a "former Prime Minister and pro-Communist rebel."[13]

American officials were, in fact, concerned that if "the present trend continues and elections are held April 17th, the Democratic Party now under radical control will likely return a majority to Parliament and possibly give government leadership to Son Ngoc Thanh." If that were to happen, the fear was that Thành would expedite the shift toward neutralism (possibly due to the influence of his contacts with Indian prime minister Jawaharlal Nehru), which could ultimately result in "a rejection of western influence."[14] Elections were, in fact, delayed, allowing Sihanouk time to shore up his political base and thoroughly smash his political opponents. As his Sangkum party would win a decisive, yet controversial, victory, international onlookers considered what Cambodia's future would hold.[15]

Sihanouk's political maneuvering left leaders worldwide considering the ramifications and the United States in search of a response. Among those global voices was Arnold Smith, the chief of the Canadian delegation for the ICC, who inquired as to American interest in further Indian involvement in Cambodia. He was especially interested in an Indian training mission for the Cambodian army. Smith "made it clear that Canada favored any scheme which would further this development," and "thought an Indian training mission for the Cambodian army would be particularly useful." The United States was not ready to make such a move. While the potentially beneficial influence of India in the region was welcomed, issues such as India's neutral seat on the ICC, French reaction to the mission, and Cambodia's reluctance to accept such an initiative were all impediments to such a development. In addition, "The Indians have for sometime antagonized the Cambodian government by criticizing the government's actions and by unnecessarily friendly contacts with the dissident leader, Son Ngoc Thanh."[16] Dulles also noted that Indian "lobbying in favor [of the] Crown's arch enemy Son Ngoc Thanh will make it difficult to respond to Indian guidance or offers [of] assistance."[17] But presumably the US reluctance about an Indian training mission was that the United States wanted to take over training operations from the French. And of course, Indian neutralism made its advice problematic from an American perspective.

The prince, too, was keenly aware of the importance India played. Two weeks after his abdication, Sihanouk traveled there for an eight-day visit, where he met with the nation's first prime minister, Jawaharlal Nehru. Nehru noted his approval of Sihanouk's decision to take a more overt political role. He also urged Sihanouk to take a neutralist path forward in Cambodia foreign affairs, to which Sihanouk was receptive. Thành's overture to Nehru, secretly made earlier during the latter's trip to the temples of Angkor with his daughter, Indira, was also relayed to Sihanouk at this time. As Sihanouk recounted in his memoirs, Nehru "advised Son Ngoc Thanh to forget his differences with me and cooperate in the interest of national unity. Thanh replied with a diatribe against me. Among the reproaches was that I was 'anti-American' which did not impress Nehru." That being said, there was concern on the part of the Americans that Nehru and the Indian government were too close to Thành and could potentially marginalize progress in the region.[18]

The Cambodian relationship with India not only clouded the international picture, but it also contributed to domestic turmoil inside Cambodia. Cambodia's internal political situation was of enough concern that it was raised by Robert Amory, a member of the National Security Council Planning Board and recently promoted to the deputy director of the CIA with a background in intelligence gathering as opposed to covert operations. During a speech before the Army War College in Carlisle Barracks, Pennsylvania, on 29 March 1955, Amory touched on a variety of topics with respect to the current world situation and the United States's role in it. Although not a major feature of his speech, the situation in Cambodia was highlighted. After discussing the political situation in Vietnam, Amory opened his discussion of Cambodia by noting that it was "in worse shape." He recounted being alongside Ambassador to Cambodia Robert McClintock in Manila when they received the message that Sihanouk had abdicated the throne. In a comment revealing his patronizing attitude, McClintock, a career Foreign Service officer, commented, "That dirty rat, my King has run out on me." Amory then discussed the internal political situation in Cambodia, which was in trouble due to Sihanouk's alienation of the middle class. Amory admitted that Sihanouk had "a certain degree of mass support," but that "everybody who can speak French [implying the educated class] . . . think that he is just a reactionary." These were the same people that supported Thành and felt that the only future for the country lay with him, and that "Son Ngoc Thanh is one of the estimable group of people who think that he is the only one who has found out how to deal with Communists."[19] But could the United States continue to count on Thành's supposed anticommunism?

That summer, the Thai general Phao Sriyanon met with the American ambassador to Thailand John Peurifoy. Peurifoy's anticommunist credentials were well established, notably as the ambassador to Greece, where he supported the new anticommunist government following the Greek civil war, and as the ambassador to Guatemala, where he was instrumental in the overthrow of the left-wing Jacobo Arbenz government and installation of a right-wing authoritarian government more friendly to the United States and American commercial interests. The latter of these two events is an example of how President Dwight D. Eisenhower's "New Look" foreign policy stressed covert action as a tool in foreign policy, where left-leaning or communist governments were targeted for disruption or worse. Other examples famously include intervention in Iran in 1953 and, as we will see later in this chapter, in Cambodia. According to the historian Walter LaFeber, Eisenhower believed that "the overriding threat to world stability was communism, not starvation, inequality, or other wants that led the have-nots to rebel against the haves."[20]

The two discussed what the Thai and American approach to Cambodia should be in light of Sihanouk's shift. Peurifoy suggested support of both Sihanouk and Thành, and that if the latter were to win election it was desirable "to be in a position to influence him to support the West." He emphasized that while Thành was not communist, if the West ignored him, he could easily convert to the communist bloc.[21] For Peurifoy, this potentiality was of greatest concern. Victory would not be in Thành's immediate future, however, as Sihanouk's Sangkum Party swept the 11 September elections, marginalizing the Thànhists in the Democratic Party. Thành remained on the sidelines through the elections because, while receiving amnesty from the crown, he feared assassination at the hands of Sihanouk.[22]

Sihanouk's power grab marked a dividing line in Thành's political life. He was essentially marginalized, both politically and militarily. A US National Intelligence Survey in October 1955 referred to the Khmer Issarak movement as "of no present importance . . . whose armed dissidence degenerated . . . into disorganized armed banditry and petty warlordism."[23]

Perhaps as a display of genuine reconciliation, an acknowledgement of his approval of Sihanouk's shift toward neutralism, or realization that Thành was no longer a feasible substitution, Nehru later commented on Sihanouk's abdication following their meeting, calling it "a rather unique and possibly unparalleled thing. I do not know if there is a similar example anywhere else. Many kings have disappeared as kings and people have chosen their leaders in a different way. I do not know any example of a king giving up his kingship and joining with the people and functioning as the national leader of the people. That is remarkable."[24] The Indian prime minister, however, still did not fully trust Sihanouk, and he hinted as much to the South Vietnamese secretary of state Nguyen Huu Chau during the latter's trip to New Delhi.[25] Cambodia's political future remained very much in flux, in large part due to Thành and the Issaraks.

Also contributing to Cambodia's uncertain political future was that the political infrastructure still existed for communism to emerge as the dominant force, despite the fact that the Vietminh had removed the majority of its ground forces following the Geneva conference the previous year. US Army intelligence was concerned that the few remaining Issarak rebels were susceptible to communist influence due to their "venal nature." Thành was again singled out as a potential problem. If he were to join with the communists, it "could create a situation whose suppression could be difficult for the Cambodian army, at its present state of morale and training."[26] It was this fear, along with Sihanouk's overtures to the political left in his country, which caused a shift in US policy toward Thành.

In many ways this shift made sense, at least on the surface. Sihanouk's neutralism brought suspicion to both Thailand and South Vietnam as Cambodia's neighbors grew paranoid in the face of what they perceived to be communist aggression. Zhou Enlai's personal approach at Bandung in April 1955 planted the seeds in Sihanouk's political shift. When Sihanouk turned down a Philippine effort to secure Cambodian entry into the Southeast Asia Treaty Organization (SEATO) the following February and accepted $22.4 million in Chinese aid soon after, his neighbors took notice.[27]

Those who felt the brunt of Sihanouk's oppressive wrath during the election season of 1955, predominantly Democrats and their supporters, saw little future for themselves in Cambodian politics, and many fled to the former Issarak stronghold in the northwest and joined Thành. This new breed of dissidents brought with them, and perhaps understandably so, a decidedly antimonarchal attitude, something that was only a moderate feature of the previous Issarak incarnation. But this motley crew was far from the relative powerhouse of the Issaraks of years prior. They were in need of external support for their crusade against the prince. Luckily a receptive partner was a stone's throw across the border that would attempt to destabilize Cambodia in the most subversive fashion: through a coup.[28]

American officials were aware of the potential for a coup to arise in Cambodia, as Alfred Jenkins, the deputy director of the Office of Southeast Asian Affairs, noted in a memo to the assistant secretary of state for Far Eastern Affairs Walter Robertson on 21 August 1958. If one were to occur, Thành was seen as a possible candidate to lead an overthrow of Sihanouk.[29] Thành had become a sought-after asset, and the United States was not the only nation aware of his potential.

The end of the decade culminated in a series of plots, supposed or otherwise, against Sihanouk. Generally referred to as the Sam Sary-led "Bangkok Plot" and the Dap Chhuon Affair, they marked a turning point in how Sihanouk viewed his neutral position in the Cold War, as he now found himself surrounded by Western-aligned enemies. The end of the fifties also signified a shift in how the South Vietnamese and Thai governments viewed Cambodian neutrality (or in their minds, left-leaning neutrality). Communist subversion, according to Saigon and Bangkok, could not effectively be fought with Sihanouk in power. He had to be replaced with a like-minded "cold warrior." Thành was to play an integral part in these developments. It was also this period that saw the United States become associated with subversive activities plotted against Sihanouk. In doing so, the Americans became linked with Thành, among others. This link would last until the fall of the Khmer Republic in 1975.

While several histories do cover the Dap Chhuon Affair in great detail, the most important recent contribution with a strong focus on US involvement is William J. Rust's *Eisenhower & Cambodia: Diplomacy, Covert Action, and the Origins of the Second Indochina War*. In it, he provides great documentary support for US complicity in the plot to overthrow Sihanouk. My goal here is not to contradict any of his conclusions but instead to augment his findings, especially with respect to the role of Son Ngoc Thành.[30]

Sary was a longtime advisor to Sihanouk. He was intimately involved with previous negotiations with France and was a member of Cambodia's delegation to the Geneva Conference. Never drawn to leftist circles, he was an important and trusted Sihanouk associate, and was named ambassador to London in late 1957. By that time, however, he had embraced pro-Western views, which, in the words of David Chandler, "cooled his intimacy with the prince." While in London, a scandal erupted in which Sary was charged with beating an ex-mistress, which led to him being recalled.[31] Ostracized from Cambodian politics, Sary looked for revenge, and found willing accomplices both in Cambodia's neighbors and its one-time prime minister.

According to Sihanouk, a secret meeting was held in Bangkok in December 1958, presided over by Field Marshal Sarit Thanarat. Others in attendance included Thành, Ngo Trong Hieu, and several CIA officials from Peurifoy's staff. At this meeting the secret bilateral committee made the decision to overthrow the prince. These representatives from Western-aligned groups and countries would theoretically, if successful, steer Cambodia in a more US-friendly political direction. Thành would establish a base on the Thai-Cambodian border, Ngo Trong Hieu would recruit Khmer Krom on the Cambodian border with South Vietnam, and Chhuon and Sary would organize an uprising within Cambodia itself. The CIA agent Victor Matsui would coordinate all contacts.[32] Much of Sihanouk's account has proven to be accurate.

Bitter toward the prince for recalling him, Sary began attacking Sihanouk in his political newspaper *Reastrthipodei* (Democratic People) and began making contacts in search of support from foreign sources discontented with Sihanouk's neutralist Cold War posture. In January 1959 Sihanouk alluded to a "Bangkok Plot" against him, supposedly spearheaded by Sary and the new Thai premier marshal Sarit Thanarat. Sary had, in fact, fled to Thailand where he received support from Major Channa Samudavanija, Thành's former contact in the Thai government.[33] A small group of Khmer Krom from Vientiane reportedly joined him.[34] In a speech, Sihanouk detailed the plot as "drawn up by a marshal, head of the government of a neighboring kingdom, by the envoys of a neighboring state, and by Thành. Like nocturnal birds of prey blinded by the hunter's torch, dark schemes hatched in secret will come to nothing once they are dragged out into the light."[35] Sihanouk's assessment was strikingly close to reality.

The plotting culminated in the mysterious case of Chhuon's coup attempt. Chhuon had a long history as an ardent anticommunist and as a resistance fighter, working against the both the Japanese and Vietminh. He was a committed Issarak until rallying to the king in 1949, and he was of aid to Sihanouk during the fight for independence. Due to this support, he was seen as a loyal ally to the prince and served as the minister of the interior and security.[36] The cabinet, however, was dissolved in 1957. Chhuon's ouster was highlighted by American officials, who labeled him as "the mysterious tough anti-Communist Army officer whom Sihanouk and other Cambodians suspect of being overly ambitious."[37] Chhuon was then appointed governor of Siem Reap province, as well as its military commander. While the armed forces that served under him were officially part of the national army, in essence Chhuon had his own private militia and ruled over his own personnel. His was notorious for his ruthless and brutal governance.[38] The quasi-official publication *Réalitiés Cambodgiennes* (Cambodian Realities) would later refer to Chhuon as a "brutal," "relentless," and "greedy" tyrant who ruled by terror.[39]

Chhuon had long maintained contacts within Thailand, and by the mid-1950s Diem began to consider him a potential ally, as Diem had been growing further estranged from Sihanouk from 1957 to 1958 due to the prince's requested aid from communist China in settling border disputes with the South Vietnamese. This eventually led Sihanouk to kick nationalist Chinese representation out of Cambodia. Chhuon was also quite leery of this dramatic shift to the left. He expressed his frustrations in a letter to the US ambassador McClintock, and also asserted that he was waiting for the opportunity to "frustrate" the prince's policies and declare a "diplomatic rupture" with communist nations.[40] He also approached the queen to intervene, and while she was sympathetic to his anticommunism, she failed to sway Sihanouk. Chhuon also complained to the British embassy in Phnom Penh that Sihanouk was "leaning towards the Communists," although nothing came of this. It was at this point that Chhuon turned toward Saigon, which was eager to help.[41]

While there remains much to uncover with respect to the Dap Chhuon plot of 1959, the basics of how events eventually unfolded are generally agreed upon. After being tipped off by various sources, including the French and the communists, Sihanouk's troops, led by Lon Nol, moved in on Chhuon's stronghold of Siem Reap on 21 February and easily squashed the coup attempt before it had a chance to get off the ground. Chhuon was killed while allegedly attempting to escape, and in addition to a cache of arms, money, and gold, a CIA radio was found. *Réalités Cambodgiennes* would later report that messages between Saigon, Siem Reap, Bangkok, and a representative of the CIA in the American embassy in Phnom Penh were also found at the scene.[42] Such evidence, alongside the failure of the United States to make him aware of the existence of the plot, was enough for Sihanouk to implicate the Americans in the attempt to overthrow his government, and relations between the two nations subsequently went into a tailspin. The Dap Chhuon plot, however, turns out to be far more complex.

On 25 June 1958, the outgoing Cambodian prime minister Sim Var criticized a recent South Vietnamese penetration of Cambodia at Stung Treng. He stated that the Vietnamese troops still remained in Cambodia and "were actively organizing themselves with a view to an attack in depth" on Cambodia. He appealed to the United States to intervene, but warned that if aid were not forthcoming, Cambodia would be forced to turn to "other friendly powers."[43] Two weeks later Sihanouk affirmed this when he stated, "For our tranquility we ought to choose a great ally who is not too far from us and who is ready to aid us." The Stung Treng crisis continued to frustrate Cambodians for some time to come and provides an ominous foreshadowing of where relations were headed.

By midsummer the ambassador Carl W. Strom saw Cambodia as clearly at a crossroads. He felt that Sihanouk saw "Cambodia's true friends . . . in the West," but that he felt abandoned by them. It was possibly the last chance to forge a dénouement to hostilities between Cambodia and South Vietnam, and Strom urged the State Department to intervene and push Diem to soften his stance of antagonism toward Sihanouk.[44] The South Vietnamese ambassador Elbridge Durbrow and the embassy in Saigon saw things differently. "From here Cambodia does not appear to be at crossroads but rather somewhat past that point along the road to the left. Sihanouk has already recognized USSR and accepted Soviet aid and for most practical purposes has also recognized Communist China." Durbrow went on to add, "I translate Sihanouk's talk about 'pure' neutrality and 'active' neutrality as nothing more than 'pure' opportunism or smokescreen."[45] Evidence for the ambassador's concerns presented itself ten days later, when Sihanouk recognized the People's Republic of China, but the countering narratives about Sihanouk continued.[46]

Strom felt that it was Diem's intransigence that pushed Sihanouk to move toward communist China.[47] Diem felt that Sihanouk's territorial ambitions with respect to Cochinchina were the main stumbling block for progress between the two sides. He believed that Sihanouk was fearful of Chinese power and was convinced that China would soon dominate Southeast Asia, and he hoped that China would aid in recapturing the lost territories in South Vietnam.[48] While the reclamation of lost territories was, and would continue to be, a constant theme in Sihanouk's rhetoric (as it would for his successors Lon Nol and Pol Pot), Diem's concerns are nonetheless overstated.

Diem also expressed his conviction that opposition to Sihanouk was growing within Cambodia, and that within the next year opposition would be so strong that the prince would be forced to flee the country. Diem referred to Thành as a "Cambodian national hero who fought [the] French and is now in Thailand as [a] potential leader of opposition." Durbrow disagreed, telling Diem that Sihanouk remained, in fact, quite popular and that any effort to overthrow him would play right into the hands of the communists. After their meeting, Durbrow commented that Diem's "insistence on growing opposition may indicate he [is] actively trying operate in this field."[49] Dulles was concerned that "if coup should be attempted by Vietnamese and/or Thai and as appears highly likely should fail, US and SEATO would receive [the] brunt [of] adverse repercussions in Cambodia and elsewhere."[50] British officials felt similarly, and they expressed concern that the potential coup would push Sihanouk "even further to the opposite side."[51]

Although reluctant to support a coup attempt at this point, Dulles and Durbrow were clearly skeptical of Sihanouk's motives. Strom was more sympathetic to Sihanouk's position and dubious of Diem's objectives. He felt the results of a coup would be catastrophic. While there was disagreement among American officials on several of these key points, it was agreed that while Sihanouk might have been drifting to the left, the alternatives to his leadership (or the road to them) could prove disastrous.

Potentially dampening any US support for a coup, Trinh Hoang, a member of the Cambodian National Assembly, informed Edmund H. Kellogg, counselor of the embassy, on 30 September 1958 that Thành had lost much of his appeal among the population. He also stated that the Democrats were basically inactive, with no organization on the provincial level.[52] External support was a necessity if Thành were to become a viable replacement for Sihanouk, and linking up with

Chhuon was certainly a viable option for him at this point. Although Sihanouk had managed to isolate and diminish the Khmer Serei's political stature to a certain extent, the group was still a prominent feature of Surin Province in Thailand at this point, which bordered Chhuon's Siem Reap.

After Sihanouk officially recognized communist China, Chhuon sent word through his brother that he wanted a meeting with Ambassador Strom, held on 2 October in Siem Reap. Chhuon stressed the importance of improved relations between Cambodia and its neighbors. When asked what he thought of Sihanouk's policy of neutrality, he responded adamantly with one word, "Impossible!" At the meeting, Chhuon informed the ambassador that he had three battalions of hardened, seasoned men at the ready. He reminded Strom of his previous service as the minister of the interior and security the year prior, where he controlled the police forces throughout the nation, the implication being that he retained their loyalty. Members of the Royal Guard in Phnom Penh were also "his men," he insisted. Chhuon maintained that he was loyal to his country, but could not follow if "the King did wrong."[53]

Chhuon did not persuade Strom to support him or a coup. On 20 October the ambassador wrote to Robertson, concerned "by evidence that the Vietnamese delude themselves that it may be possible and useful to work for the overthrow of Sihanouk." At the same time evidence of such plotting was "almost conclusive." The Saigon government had, in fact, "considered a coup to overthrow Sihanouk at the height of the Stung Treng crisis," but, unsure of American support, had canceled it.[54]

Possibly in response to the developing situation on the ground, the next month, Strom characterized it as quite feasible for South Vietnam to find a diverse group of dissatisfied players in Cambodia. The problem was uniting them, and according to Strom, "Son Ngoc Thanh can hardly be considered a likely leader [of] these disorganized groups. He is widely respected for his fight for Cambodian independence, but . . . he is considered increasingly disgruntled man who has abandoned principles and only seeks return to power by any means. He has no organized following."[55]

On 7 February Chhuon himself greeted an Air Vietnam plane loaded with several cases of wireless equipment, along with two operators, in Siem Reap. Two hundred seventy kilograms of gold was also furnished for Chhuon to pay his troops. Additional material was flown in from Thailand.[56] It was also around this time that, according to the historian

Milton Osborne, Matsui visited Chhuon in Siem Reap and delivered a radio transmitter and receiver.[57]

On 16 February 1959, Strom wrote to Robertson about his continued concerns over Saigon's interference in Cambodia. He lamented that, unless "some modus vivendi among Thailand, Cambodia, [and] Vietnam" could be reached, that the American goal of denying communism a foothold on the Indochinese peninsula could not be achieved. The recent Sam Sary and Chhuon plots with the support of South Vietnam would only lead to trouble. "The countries supporting Western cause in SEA have been in position of football team with two quarterbacks calling opposite signals." Strom was on his way out as Ambassador and was anxious to have such issues cleaned up as much as possible. He was once again adamant that the United States "insist in the most categorical manner that GVN break off all relations with Dap Chhuon conspiracy . . . and that GVN . . . take positive steps for settlement of its principle [sic] differences with Cambodia," yet he made no effort to inform Sihanouk of the plotting.[58] Here we again see the clear frustration of the American diplomat, impotent, nearly, to effect change that would benefit, in his eyes, both the United States and its regional allies. At the same time, he never informed the Cambodian prince. This would, after events unfolded, only increase Sihanouk's suspicions.

Saigon did not listen, and days later, on 21 February, Sihanouk's forces moved in on Chhuon and broke up the plot. The 24 February issue of the Cambodian newspaper *La Dépêche du Cambodge* (Cambodian Dispatch) triumphantly announced in a front-page headline, "Another Traitor Unmasked: Chhuon Mchulpich." The paper also blamed the international "powers sponsoring the implementation of the Bangkok Plan against Cambodia."[59]

It was an exasperating time for the ambassador, who in another telegram bemoaned the " 'free man's burden' that we have assumed as a nation that we are many times held responsible for actions of governments we do not control."[60] But is that statement an accurate one? Was the US government or its agencies closer to Chhuon, Sary, and Thành than Strom was able or willing to admit? And were all government agencies on the same page with respect to diplomatic relations with Cambodia?

William Colby, later the CIA director but at the time deputy chief of station in Saigon, claimed that the agency, while aware of the plot beforehand, attempted to dissuade Bangkok and Saigon officials from encouraging a coup attempt against Sihanouk. When it became clear that no such advice was taken to heart, the CIA recruited Matsui, who was reportedly close to Chhuon, and gave him a radio to keep the CIA up to date. According to John Prados, it was Richard Bissell, the deputy director for plans, who ordered that a mole be placed among coup plotters so as to ascertain how such operations worked and to keep tabs on events as they unfolded. When Cambodian troops moved in on Chhuon and captured him, Matsui was captured as well, along with a CIA radio, American weapons, South Vietnamese coconspirators, and a large sum of cash.[61] The Saigon government had furnished a mobile broadcast station, as well as a "box of gold bars," for the express purpose of supporting a coup attempt against Sihanouk. American officials were well aware of these facts ahead of time, as were they of Thành's efforts at the time to quadruple his forces in Thailand to two thousand men with the help of Cambodia's neighbors.[62]

This is confirmed in a letter from Strom to his successor, William C. Trimble, in September 1959. In it, he states that following an emphatic denunciation to the Thais to end all plotting, they acquiesced. Yet the same instructions were not relayed to South Vietnam, and on 7 February "Diem sent his radio equipment, gold, technicians, etc. to Siemreap." Strom went on to state that "it was recognized from the start that the mainspring of the plot was in Saigon." This is clear evidence that the United States was, at a minimum, aware of the coup attempt, and the failure to intervene with Diem undoubtedly led to the participation of American intelligence officials, including Matsui.[63]

There is some evidence that supports a deeper American involvement than officially acknowledged, though much of it could be seen as circumstantial. The US ambassador to Thailand at the time, Peurifoy, was, according to Prados, "the same man who was instrumental during the Eisenhower administration in mounting a CIA operation to overthrow the Guatemalan government in 1954." One could surmise that, if a coup were so desired, he would be the man to design and implement one. Sihanouk proposes the same theory for the same reason in his memoirs.[64] Another component is that of Edward Lansdale. While Lansdale agrees with Colby that the matter in question was a joint South Vietnamese–Thai plot that the CIA discouraged, he claims he was, at a minimum, vaguely connected to the planning.[65] In his memoirs, Lansdale refers to Chhuon as "a Khmer patriot," and laments never having met or working with him, "although I wish I had, since he was beloved by the people of Cambodia," a laughable statement, as Chhuon's people in Siem Reap considered him a brutal tyrant. Here Lansdale plays the victim, as he states that "the weird assassination canard set me up as a straw man for Sihanouk to attack in his frequent tirades."[66] This is certainly in reference to the amateur filmmaker's *Shadow Over Angkor*, which was released in 1968 and was based on the events surrounding the Dap Chhuon plot. In it, Lansdale is well represented as the quintessential ugly American.[67]

Sihanouk contends that Lansdale, along with General Lawton Collins, actually met with Chhuon in Siem Reap on 17 February 1959, even signing a guestbook. Sihanouk also claims that Admiral Harry D. Felt of CINPAC also visited ten days prior. Admiral Herbert G. Hopwood, commander in chief of the Pacific Fleet also stopped by to view the temples and share "a whiskey-soda with Dap Chhuon."[68] While impossible to substantiate these claims, Cecil B. Currey in his autobiography of Lansdale attempted to corroborate the dates of travel for the Anderson subcommittee, of which Lansdale was a member. This subcommittee was tasked with studying foreign aid and military programs of Southeast Asia.[69]

According to Currey, the Anderson subcommittee visited Thailand from 6 to 8 February, Laos from 8 to 10 February, Cambodia from 10 to 12, Burma from 13 to 14, and Indonesia from 15 to 20. Currey posits that "it was at least possible for Lansdale and Collins to travel briefly to Cambodia apart from the rest of the group. . . . The Anderson subcommittee spent more time in Indonesia than at any other stop . . . more than enough time for Lansdale and Collins to absent themselves for a time. It was also possible for CINCPAC [Commander-in-Chief, Pacific Command] and CINCPACFLT [Commander, US Pacific Fleet] to travel from Honolulu to Angkor; both men had authority to arrange for flights wherever they wished to go." Was the subcommittee created for more nefarious acts? If so, signing a guestbook would provide good misdirection, as no one would suspect an undercover agent of committing the act of a tourist.[70]

Lansdale had, at a minimum, made an impression on Sihanouk. With discussion in the air that Lansdale would return to the region, Ambassador Trimble cabled the secretary of state on 28 November 1960, and recommended "that General Lansdale not (repeat not) visit Cambodia." Phnom Penh officials were wary of Lansdale's supposed connection to the "Bangkok plots in late 1958 which they consider as precursor to Dap Chhuon uprising in February 1959." Any visit by Lansdale "would undoubted[ly] be linked by them to some similar type US intervention in Laos and revive their suspicions of him and of us."[71]

If US intelligence was not actively involved in the coup attempt, American officials certainly had foreknowledge. As early as August 1958 the embassy in Phnom Penh was aware of contacts between Thailand and Chhuon and passed this information along to the State Department.[72] President Eisenhower was informed of the plot as far back as 5 November 1958 when it was pegged as a South Vietnamese-supported operation. By January the CIA had confirmed both Saigon and Bangkok participation as well as the name of the principal instigator, Chhuon. Khmer Serei and Khmer Krom, who would later be explicitly tied to both US intelligence and American Special forces, were to provide martial support for the coup.[73]

Another key figure was Slat Peau, Chhuon's brother and a member of the Cambodian legislature. In the fall of 1958 he traveled to the United States, where, according to Trimble, some initial contacts in the American government were made. He was captured in Sihanouk's raid along with the two Vietnamese radio operators.[74] Sihanouk agrees that it was during the fall of 1958 that Slat Peau made substantial contacts with US officials. He also claims that Peau was "a very close friend" of Matsui, and acted as "a natural link between Matsui, Ngo Trong Hieu, and Dap Chhuon."[75] Chhuon had, in fact, been in contact with Strom through Slat Peau.[76]

French officials in Phnom Penh had informed Sihanouk of the Sam Sary affair, as did the communists. The French were also likely involved in the Cambodian government's move against Chhuon. The French ambassador to Cambodia Pierre Gorce was, in fact, on the scene when Sihanouk's forces apprehended Chhuon in Siem Reap. American officials would later grow concerned that French representatives not only believed that a US "special service" was supporting dissident elements in Cambodia, but were informing the Cambodians of this as well, despite American denials.[77]

In its aftermath, suspicions of American involvement were rampant. Sihanouk approached Ambassador Strom following the breakup of the Dap Chhuon plot. Although Strom was conscious that there had been some contact between Chhuon and American officials (notably himself), he maintained he was unaware of any specific messages or money being sent to Chhuon, and denied US involvement to Sihanouk.[78] Despite breaking up the coup attempt, Sihanouk remained flummoxed. To Strom he emphasized that trouble remained for Cambodia, and that dissident forces were massing on the Thai and South Vietnamese borders to continue harassment.[79]

The secretary general of the United Nations Dag Hammarskjöld was also suspicious of American involvement in the plots to overthrow Sihanouk, making a "passing reference to *The Quiet American* when mentioning that Cambodia was full of 'agents.' " He also stated that the Vietnamese and Thai governments were clearly involved and that the United States, at a minimum, should have informed Sihanouk of the existence of such plotting against him.[80] While the State Department continued to deny America's role, it did acknowledge to its British counterpart that the Saigon and Bangkok governments were "deeply involved."[81]

An unnamed high-level Cambodian official stated in private that while he did not implicate the US government in the coup plots, he was convinced that "individual Americans were involved." He went on to remark that Americans had been seen training dissident Cambodians in South Vietnam and that American money had financed various anti-Cambodian articles in Thailand in September 1958.[82]

In March 1959, during his briefing in Washington to take over for Strom, Trimble learned that Sihanouk had found messages to Slat Peau indicating foreign intervention (evidently Peau had been instructed to burn them, but failed to do so). Sihanouk fumed and accused the South Vietnamese of being complicit in coup plots. He implied an American connection as well.[83]

Thành, for his part, denied any involvement in the infamous "Bangkok plot," stating "I was in Saigon at that time."[84] David Chandler claims that, after fleeing to Thailand, Sary did indeed made contact with Thành. Whether the two did or not, it is understandable that Sihanouk would link Thành with the plotting. Milton Osborne believes that Thành likely provided the necessary contacts to Thai, Vietnamese, and American officials to get the coup off the ground.[85]

Later that spring, the Cambodian Ministry of Information created several posters depicting an unnamed giant, representing the United States, with three dogs on a leash, captioned Sam Sary, Dap Chhuon, and So'n Ngọc Thành. Although Son Sann, acting premier with Sihanouk out of the country, protested that the posters were commissioned without his knowledge or approval, the image the posters displayed was undoubtedly one that either many Cambodians believed or that Sihanouk wanted them to believe.[86]

So what is the reality? Was the United States involved in the Bangkok Plot and Dap Chhuon's attempted coup? Perhaps the truth was revealed years later, in a telephone conversation between President John

F. Kennedy and the assistant secretary of state for Far Eastern Affairs Roger Hilsman. In perhaps the most glaring example of the chasm that existed at times between different segments of the grand foreign policy apparatus of the United States, it is revealed that President Kennedy himself was unaware of prior CIA involvement in Cambodia. In a 20 November 1963 discussion of Sihanouk cutting off American aid, Hilsman stated that it was due to the continued antagonism of the Khmer Serei and fear of assassination. Hilsman informed Kennedy that "There's a history, during the administration of President Eisenhower, where the agency [CIA] did play footsie with opposition groups."

"Was that a true story about the '59 or something?" Kennedy asked, in reference to Chhuon's failed coup attempt.

Hilsman responded, "Yes sir, it is true."

"CIA did do it?" inquired the president.

"Sure. They supplied some money, and, uh, they were involved in a plot against Sihanouk back before this administration," replied Hilsman. He went on to say that "The agency in those days wasn't responsible to the State Department. They did things they probably didn't know about."[87]

With this it is clear that while some details remain murky, the United States was involved in the Bangkok Plot and Dap Chhuon Affair. The above conversation also highlights the seeming disconnect between members of the traditional diplomatic corps, be they ambassadors, embassy staff, or the State Department, and that of the intelligence community.[88] Many of the opinions cited in this chapter by key players in the Cambodian-American relationship hint at much the same. Sihanouk's own memoirs are titled *My War with the CIA* for this very reason. Eisenhower's "New Look" foreign policy included intelligence operations as one of the important means of deterrence in the Cold War, as opposed to Truman's more traditional containment policy. Cambodia in 1959 is, in many ways, symptomatic of the trappings of such a policy. It was here that future problems between the two countries emanated. And there was more to come.

The CIA reported in May 1959 that South Vietnamese and Thai officials planned "future covert operations against the Sihanouk regime in Cambodia." Governments in both Bangkok and Saigon "have continued to assist Cambodian dissidents, led by expatriates Sam Sary and Son Ngoc Thanh in anti-Sihanouk activities following the abortive Dap Chhuon plot last February." These efforts included anti-Sihanouk broadcasts over mobile clandestine radios and the distribution of revolutionary pamphlets. According to the CIA estimate, such interference has had the detrimental effect of "further consolidating Sihanouk's position and increasing his tendency to turn toward the Communist bloc," yet they continued unabated.[89]

From 3 to 5 August 1959 Sihanouk visited Saigon to meet with Diem and other Vietnamese leadership. With hopes of reconciliation, both Cambodian and Vietnamese officials expressed satisfaction with the results and the pleasant atmosphere of the talks. Many subjects were discussed, with the Cambodian rebel forces getting raised only briefly by Cambodian representatives, who did not belabor the point. Two days later, after several days of silence, Khmer Serei broadcasts resumed.[90] The antagonism of Sihanouk by his neighbors was evidently to continue, and events would literally explode at the end of the month.

On 31 August 1959, two suitcases supposedly containing gifts were delivered anonymously to Sihanouk's palace. While Sihanouk was in an adjoining room, one of the cases was opened, the blast killing a member of the palace staff and Prince Vakravan. The South Vietnamese government had been behind the assassination attempt. Ngo Dinh Nhu, brother of South Vietnamese president Ngo Dinh Diem and counselor to the president, had hoped to bring Thành to power with Sihanouk dead. Thành had been receiving a monthly retainer of three hundred thousand piasters from the Vietnamese.[91] Prior to the bombing, a special security police officer who worked in the office of the prime minister reportedly received a letter warning him to abandon his post, "as we are about to do away with him and his whole family." The letter was signed by the "Free Khmers Movement."[92] Following the bombing, a man was quickly arrested after being identified in a lineup by a servant to whom he had delivered the package.[93]

Hugh S. Cumming Jr., the director of the Bureau of Intelligence and Research, wrote a memo pinning responsibility of the bombing on "a communist instigated effort to discredit South Vietnam, Thailand, and the US, a politically motivated act of revenge, or a combination of the two." Although he admitted that "the identity of those guilty is not known," it was felt that "communist elements . . . instigated the assassination attempt in the hope that suspicion would be directed to Cambodia's neighbors and the US." Cambodians, on the other hand, were inclined to believe that either Thành or Sary bore responsibility. Long suspicious of US tacit support for South Vietnamese or Thai plots against the prince, Sary or Thành fit the mold.[94]

While this assassination attempt failed, Thành remained on the South Vietnamese payroll in their hope of fermenting a friendly government to the west. As stated in a report on covert actions in Vietnam on 18 April 1962, "Son Ngoc Thanh, Cambodian dissident, was being provided limited material and training assistance by Tran Quoc Buu, head of the CVTC [Vietnamese Confederation of Christian Workers] Labor Federation. The aid was limited to Vietnam, however, and primarily designed, with Ngo Dinh Nhu's approval, merely to keep Thanh on a string in case the political situation in Cambodia were to deteriorate."[95]

On 30 September 1959 Slat Peau was sentenced to death for his role in the coup attempt. During his testimony Slat Peau claimed that he was the contact man between Chhuon and both South Vietnamese officials and US intelligence.[96] He also implicated Matsui by name.[97] While his testimony was undoubtedly given under duress, his statements corroborate other evidence previously cited. Behind closed doors, a military tribunal sentenced sixteen men in total to death for their complicity in the plot.[98]

Following the public trial of supporters of Chhuon's aborted coup, Sihanouk called on all Cambodians to "choose between" his leadership and that of rebel leaders Thành and Sary in another referendum. According to Sihanouk, Thành and Sary were advocates of joining SEATO and were supported by "certain foreign powers," and he accused South Vietnam and Thailand of supporting the coup attempt. The prince stated that if he were to win the referendum, all nations that continued to support Thành and Sary "will be considered a nation hostile to the Cambodian people." By making these charges in public, the possibility of renewed tensions between Cambodia and the troika of the United States, Thailand, and South Vietnam once again grew.[99]

On 22 September 1959, Ambassador Durbrow proposed that he inform Diem that the United States has "compelling reasons to believe Free Khmer Radio located in VN and . . . [would] be glad to help find it so GVN [Government of (South) Vietnam] could put it out of business." Sihanouk was already convinced broadcasts emanated from South Vietnam.[100] As before, little was done in response.

On 25 September 1959 the director of Southeast Asian Affairs Daniel V. Anderson prepared a briefing memorandum for the assistant secretary J. Graham Parsons for Parsons's meeting with the foreign minister Son Sann and Ambassador Nong Kimny to take place the next day. While much of the briefing focused on the Cambodian five-year plan for economic development, Anderson did highlight the recent bomb

plot, recommending that Parsons "once more . . . express our condemnation of the recent attempt on the lives of the King and Queen" and
sympathies to the royal family, but to reiterate that the United States
had no information as to the perpetrators of the plot. Furthermore, "if
it was other than the work of a madman, it must have been at the insti-
gation of the Communists, who are the only ones who could conceiv-
ably benefit from the death of the Monarchs."[101]

In a 25 November 1959 background paper prepared for the acting
director of the International Cooperation Administration Leonard J.
Saccio, it was noted that the "Cambodian conviction that Thailand and
Vietnam are lending support to anti-Sihanouk Cambodia dissident elements, superimposed on long-standing fear of Thai and Vietnamese
territorial ambitions" have combined to be a great agitation for Phnom
Penh. It also noted that "Cambodia's vulnerability to Communist penetration under Sihanouk's neutrality policy seriously disturbs the out-
spokenly anti-Communist governments of Marshal Sarit (Thailand)
and President Diem (Vietnam), who fear that Communist subjugation
of Cambodia would expose their countries to greatly increased danger."
The Americans shared this concern, "but believe that Prince Sihanouk
earnestly seeks to maintain his country's independence and that he represents the best hope for stable government in Cambodia."[102]

That same day, the Thai newspaper *Sarn Seri* (Free Press) stated that
leaflets (which were under the imprint of the "Free Cambodian Movement" and printed in French) were distributed to both diplomatic
agencies and the press in Bangkok. The leaflets accused Sihanouk of
"political treachery" and praised Thành.[103] According to the Australian embassy, Sary and Thành were believed to be in Thailand, but
that "their only contacts with Thai officialdom had been at a low level
and with police officers who were concerned with keeping them under
surveillance."[104]

In a year-end summary of 1959, which it deemed the "Year of Troubles," the US embassy noted that although tensions had eased and relations had improved since the "low point" surrounding the previous
coup attempts, "US relations with Cambodia are determined in large
measure by the state of Cambodia's relations with Thailand and Viet-
Nam." "The situation again deteriorated in September with publication of Slat Peau's testimony incriminating Matsui. The embassy notes
that the importance of this development in shaking Cambodian confidence in US motives cannot be over-emphasized." Much of the renewed
goodwill between Cambodia and the United States was contributed

to the American efforts to "restrain Thailand and Viet-Nam." The embassy recommended continuing this effort and remaining patient with Sihanouk.[105]

Years later, Thành recounted the introduction of American aid to his Khmer Serei forces as occurring during this period. According to Thành, his forces located in South Vietnam began to receive military training from the United States in 1958. Many Khmer Serei were recruited into the "Mike Force," or mobile strike force. The general Paul D. Harkins organized the operation. According to Thành, the Khmer Serei received financial backing from the Americans, as well as all of its weapons from the late 1950s to the early 1960s.[106] The Prachinburi province in Thailand served as the headquarters for the Khmer Serei during this period.[107] From here the next phase of his rebellion would spring.

Chapter 4

The Breaking Point, 1960–1964

The dawn of a new decade brought with it the possibility of a rapprochement of sorts between the United States and Cambodia. While the Eisenhower administration's begrudging acceptance of Sihanouk shifted to John F. Kennedy's optimism, severe tensions between Cambodia and its Thai and South Vietnamese neighbors remained.[1] Sơn Ngọc Thành was an instrumental figure in the relationship between Cambodia and the governments in Saigon and Bangkok. The Republic of China became involved with Thành's crusade against Sihanouk as well. To Sihanouk, it seemed that the so-called Free World nations of the region had two things in common: they were against him, and they were allied with the United States. As Sihanouk in turn shifted further toward China, relations with the United States swung to the breaking point. While never the central figure in the frayed relationship between Cambodia, its neighbors, and the United States, Thành was nonetheless an essential element in understanding both how Sihanouk positioned himself politically inside Cambodia and portrayed himself to the wider world. As the record shows, as Cambodia moved toward a break with the United States, the mysterious Thành was never far from the minds of Sihanouk or American officials.

On 1 January 1960, Foreign Minister Son Sann met with the Japanese ambassador Chuichi Ohashi. Ohashi stated with conviction that the United States was working tirelessly to bring about a rapprochement between Cambodia and its neighbors. Sann replied that the failure of the United States to inform Sihanouk of the "Bangkok Plot" was not only irksome, but left the prince confused as to American motives since the United States was "undoubtedly in possession of such information." Sann also stated that the arms seized during the Dap Chhuon affair were of American origin, as was the bomb used in an assassination attempt against the queen.

Ohashi relayed this information to Ambassador William C. Trimble in a 12 January meeting. Ohashi stated that he deplored the reluctance of Cambodia to recognize the great importance that American aid has had in the country. As Trimble recalled, "He described the Cambodians as children who seemingly are unable to differentiate between their true friends and their real enemies. . . . A mature people would never dare to criticize the United States as Sihanouk is doing."[2]

Four days later the Indian newspaper *Blitz* published what was purportedly a letter dating back to the previous September from an exiled Sam Sary to Edmund Kellogg, a former counselor and the deputy chief of mission at the US embassy in Phnom Penh. The letter implied American support for Sary and his goal of deposing Sihanouk and personally implicated the ambassador. *Blitz* quickly sent copies of the letter to Phnom Penh, where they were prepared for publication in both private and quasi-state-run newspapers.[3] Trimble flew to Siem Reap on 3 February 1960 to meet with Sihanouk and discuss the *Blitz* incident. He denied to the prince any US association with Sary. Sihanouk promised to take this into account in the semiofficial publications *Réalités Cambodgiennes* and *The Nationalist* (both of which were seen by American officials as mouthpieces for the government), although he stated he could not control what other newspapers might say.[4] By 5 February several leading newspapers had reproduced it in full.

Once the newspapers hit the stands, American officials knew they had yet another crisis on their hands. The following day's *Réalités* clearly implied a belief in the authenticity of the Sary letter and, therefore, the implication of US participation. It accused two officials in the US embassy of supporting the nefarious movement, and it concluded with the unmistakable insinuation that the United States had attempted to overthrow Sihanouk.[5] Stapled to the front page of that same 6 February issue, however, was an apology by the prince that explained he received the American version of events too late to stop publication of the article. He asked readers to "regard as without foundation that which has been written concerning a rupture in Cambodian-American friendship," and to excuse his error.[6]

Realistically, Sihanouk could have stopped publication of the editorial following his 3 February meeting with Trimble before it hit the streets three days later. Sihanouk had remained suspicious of the United States since the initial Sary incident, and while some aspects of the editorial were dubious at best, by allowing publication he was sending a message to Cambodians that he wanted them to hear. His amending letter was likely intended to placate American officials.

In a 16 February 1960 memorandum for Hugh S. Cumming Jr., Charles N. Spinks, the office director for Asia of the State Department's Bureau of Intelligence and Research, discussed Sihanouk's reaction to the *Blitz* incident. He dismissed Sihanouk as having a "devious mind," "being cynical and unscrupulous by nature," regarding "self-interest as outweighing all ethical considerations," and possessing a "complete misunderstanding of US policy in Cambodia." He continued, commenting on Sihanouk's "conviction that different branches of the US Government are able to operate simultaneously in different directions with no apparent inconsistency or conflict of purpose. Thus in his mind there is nothing incongruous in sincere declarations of respect for Cambodian neutrality by the President and Secretary of State while other US officials work to bring about his overthrow."[7] As we have seen previously, perhaps Sihanouk's appraisal was correct. Although questions related specifically to the validity of the Sary letter remain, the results of American intervention in Cambodia up to this point prove much of its assertions factual.

By spring 1960 the United States came to the belated conclusion that it would have to conduct Cambodian foreign policy with Sihanouk as a major figure. Previously, the policy had been to "encourage noncommunist elements whether or not they are opposed to Sihanouk." The latter group, those noncommunists opposed to Sihanouk, had gained some power and prestige of late "from the abortive coup plots and subsequent subversive activities mounted against" the prince during 1959. Sihanouk had since adroitly sapped their strength and had many of them "eliminated." Along with that came the troubling aspect that the "revelation of their real or fancied association with the United States and other free world countries undermined Cambodian confidence in U.S. motives and became an obstacle to the pursuit of our objectives." Sihanouk, by this point, had also provided new "evidence of political astuteness in the domestic arena, has displayed increased alertness to communist subversion, and has shown no inclination to tolerate any challenge to his pre-eminence." US policy had to change. It now had to "be directed conspicuously and specifically at the problem of dealing with Sihanouk, by all odds the major single factor in Cambodia."[8] Events on the ground would soon dictate this American estimate of events on the ground in Cambodia to be an accurate one.

On 3 April 1960 King Norodom Suramarit finally succumbed to a long illness. Three days later the Crown Council met to address the issue of succession. The task at hand was a difficult one. In theory, any one of several hundred descendants of King Ang Duong were eligible to succeed Suramarit. Sihanouk asserted that the problem was so difficult that "it could create disunity and even lead us to civil war," as one group was "doing everything it can do to divide the Royal Family in order to weaken it and on its ruins establish a Republic of which Son Ngoc Thanh would be President."[9] His next moves would be made with the goal of not only solidifying his own political position in the country but also sidelining Thành's.

Sihanouk appointed Prince Monireth to stand in place of the departed monarch until a permanent successor could be found. Monireth urged Sihanouk to select Sisowath Kossamak as the new queen, which would require the constitution be amended to allow for a female monarch. Sihanouk was reluctant to take this step, however, as he viewed his mother as "a painful brake" on his political aspirations. "Only God understands the reasons why I do not want my mother to ascend the throne," he stated in a speech shortly after his father's death.[10] Around this time, a small demonstration took place in Battambang that promoted the queen's ascension to the throne. Sihanouk, perhaps seeing it as an excuse to pass on selecting his mother, chose to view this as a new Thành-led attempt to sow dissent in the countryside.[11]

Sihanouk created a regency council to deal with the constitutional crisis. Several associates turned down the position of prime minister, and Sihanouk himself refused the position. He eventually named Chuop Hell the head of the National Assembly and chief of state pro tem. Sihanouk, wanting to rid himself of the ceremonial rigors associated with the monarchy but retain the constitutional powers inherent in it, called for a referendum which, according to David Chandler, "in effect dismantled Cambodia's thousand-year-old monarchy. . . .

Motivated by a mixture of patriotism, gamesmanship, and self-concern, Sihanouk acted as if the monarchy were his to foreclose, deconstruct, and disarrange."[12]

The referendum pitted Sihanouk against his old bête noir, Thành. That he was even included as an option shows how much influence Thành maintained. Even more so, it demonstrates Sihanouk's laser-like focus on the man who had been conspiring against him for the past decade. Voters had a choice of four ballots: one containing Sihanouk's photograph; one Thành's; a red ballot, indicating communist allegiance; and one inscribed with a question mark, indicating voter indifference or confusion. Rejected ballots were to be handed in to members of Sangkum acting as poll workers. Such a public display of discarding Sihanouk's photograph was enough to dissuade many a voter from casting an unfavorable ballot.[13]

The Khmer Serei responded to Sihanouk's proposal in the form of a manifesto. While its contents do provide a glimpse into the political mindset of the group, it mostly consists of political propaganda similar in many ways to that of Sihanouk himself. It refers to the referendum as "Machiavellian," and that it was "proposed without legal basis and contrary to all principles of democracy and all the basic rules of morality." It argued that Sihanouk, following global condemnation, was forced to "succumb in silence" and let an earlier proposal for a referendum disappear. The manifesto went on to hint that International Arms Control Commission (CIC) officials, foreign observers, and journalists were bribed by the government with royal reception, travel, and "copious princely banquets."[14]

Thành, for his part, wanted nothing to do with the proposed referendum, it being "unworthy of an honest man." Current political conditions in Cambodia were absent of "freedom, justice, peace, honesty and harmony," which tarnished the reputation and dignity of Cambodians in the eyes of the world, according to the manifesto. The Khmer Serei encouraged Sihanouk to follow two courses of action. First, "instead of wasting time slandering and persecuting the Khmer Serei and Son-Ngoc-Thanh," he was encouraged to "withdraw completely, without fanfare, from the political arena of Cambodia, leaving others to repair" his mistakes and lead the nation to recovery. Second, leave the choice of the leadership of Cambodia to the people and allow them to choose between the president of the Regency Council Sisowath Monireth and Queen Kossamak, as supposedly stipulated in the Cambodian constitution of 1947.[15]

In closing, it stated, "The Khmer Serei Movement sincerely hopes that the entire Khmer [nation] will soon distinguish right from wrong, to separate the errors from truth and see clearly through the internal difficulties and external tensions, the right path that will actually lead Kampuchea and the Khmer in peace, harmony, understanding between peoples and the reconstruction of Cambodia in freedom, democracy and abundance. . . . Long Live Kampuchea!"[16]

The sham referendum went off as scheduled, with Sihanouk receiving close to two million votes of confidence. Thành and the communists collected a paltry 133 each. As *Réalités Cambodgiennes* recounted, "The wind blew, and bore away along the streams and gutters [all the] ballots for Son Ngoc Thanh, for Communists, and those with question marks." All of this was unnecessary, as it is hard to fathom how Sihanouk could have been defeated by anyone in a fair election. That being said, nefarious or not, Sihanouk had his mandate. The constitutional crisis was finally resolved when the National Assembly elected Sihanouk as head of state on 14 June.[17] With political power solidified, Sihanouk again turned his attention toward external threats to the nation.

On 20 June 1960 the Cambodian government issued a confidential circular that claimed dissident rebels supported by neighboring countries planned an imminent invasion of Cambodia. The US embassy in Phnom Penh approached the Cambodian government soon after, attempting to reassure it "in most categorical terms of firm United States opposition to any rebel activities directed against the Cambodian Government from foreign countries." US officials vowed to consult with the Cambodians, if they so desired, "on the extent and nature of the alleged threat, as well as on means to counter it."[18]

Additionally, their American counterparts in Saigon and Bangkok approached those respective governments with the not-so-veiled suggestion that they cease and desist support for Cambodian dissident forces. The Americans felt that it was a great opportunity for a rapprochement, if only Thailand and Vietnam responded positively to the charges levied against them. The Americans feared that the "failure of the Royal Thai Government and the Government of the Republic of Viet-Nam to respond with positive assurances could possibly be used as an excuse by the Cambodians to invoke formal protection of the Peiping regime."[19] Sihanouk reiterated as much in a 10 August 1960 speech that if Cambodia's existence continued to be threatened by South Vietnam or Thailand that he would likely be looking toward Peking for help as opposed to the West.[20] By the end of the year, Sihanouk declared his intention (on 15 December) to formalize a nonaggression and friendship treaty with communist China.[21] At the same time, Cambodian and Thai officials held talks at the United Nations between 15 and 23 December that resulted in an agreement to strive for more cordial relations between the two nations. Although the latter rapprochement would be short lived, there appeared to be an opportunity for reconciliation between Phnom Penh and Washington. American aid to Cambodia in its continued confrontations with Thailand and South Vietnam would symbolize the prospects that the two countries had to form a closer relationship, and perhaps a missed opportunity.

When the International Court of Justice held hearings in April 1961 on the rightful ownership of the disputed Preah Vihear temple complex, situated on the Thai-Cambodian border, the former secretary of state Dean Acheson served as lead council for Cambodia. Thailand saw this as tantamount to an American expression of support for Cambodian claims, although it should be noted that Thailand had a prominent American lawyer as its lead attorney as well (the case would not be settled until June 1962 when the court ruled in Cambodia's favor).[22] On 15 June the American embassy in Vietnam urged the State Department to exhibit a stronger "effort [to] convince Diem he should really do something more about the [border] problem than he has in the past."[23] Such efforts, among others, were not only an attempt to settle long standing regional issues between neighboring countries, but to pave the way for a smooth meeting between the Cambodian and American heads of state.

On 22 September 1961 Sihanouk expressed his openness to a "summit meeting" among Thailand, South Vietnam, and Cambodia to attempt to arrive at a mutual understanding.[24] Three days later Sihanouk met with President Kennedy in New York. The men discussed the crisis in Laos, the Southeast Asia Treaty Organization (SEATO), and Cambodia's relationship with its neighbors, among other topics. When asked about the deteriorating relationship between Cambodia and South Vietnam, Sihanouk replied that much of the tension between the two is a result of the poor treatment of the Khmer minority population residing in South Vietnam. There were also altercations arising over borders, disputed islands, and the Vietnamese accusation that Cambodia was acting as a harbor for Vietcong guerillas.[25] As recalled in a memorandum of the conversation, Sihanouk referred to the "600,000 Cambodians who were resident in Viet-Nam who were not accorded the normal freedoms, such as use of their own language, to be able to use their own script in writing and the denial of the right of Cambodian schools for

FIGURE 4.1.   Prince Norodom Sihanouk meets President John F. Kennedy, 25 September 1961. Courtesy of the John F. Kennedy Presidential Library and Museum.

their children." The Khmer Krom were also blamed for harboring the Vietcong.[26] All of these would remain points of tension for the next decade.

Sihanouk was greeted with a cheering throng when he returned to Cambodia on 8 October 1961. He delivered a two-and-a-half-hour speech detailing the accomplishments of his trip. His overall message was to recount the success he had in winning increased world esteem for Cambodia, and a newfound respect for his policies. He remarked on the Conference of Heads of State or Government of Non-Aligned Countries in Belgrade, his calls for a settlement in Laos, and his attempts to bring world attention to the plight of the Khmer Krom in South Vietnam. He spoke favorably of his discussion with Kennedy, although he remarked that "American people not very pleasant to colored people." Tensions with Thailand, however, remained high, and the omnipresence of Thành in the Cambodian-Thai relationship was a continuing factor.[27]

On 23 October, Sihanouk delivered a charged, emotional two-hour speech in front of the National Assembly, where he requested, and was granted, unanimous consent for the Cambodian parliament to sever relations with Thailand. He warned of a coming invasion and instructed Lon Nol to prepare defensive plans in case Thailand attempted to regain its lost provinces. He claimed that Sarit said Sihanouk had been "running around like a mad pig." He turned to Cambodia's relationship with the United States, saying that he had been fooled in 1958 by Eisenhower's charm while Dulles covertly supported Dap Chhuon and the Issaraks. Two days after the speech Thailand closed its border with Cambodia.[28]

Sihanouk also accused American "operators," such as Victor Matsui, as being involved with the Chhuon, Sary, and Thành plots against him. Sihanouk claimed that while he was meeting with Eisenhower in September 1958 that "agents of Mr. Allen Dulles were succeeding at [the] same time in New York in corrupting and buying the treason of one of our delegates to [the] 13th session of U.N." The delegate in question was Slat Peau, Chhuon's brother. Sihanouk went on to accuse him of playing a major role in subsequent plots against him, and that "before court martial, made a disturbing and complete confession involving a certain American organization." The prince stated that he hid the revelations "to safeguard our friendship with U.S., and out of gratitude to American people" for the aid Cambodia received.[29]

While thankful for American aid, Sihanouk stated that with it came certain "humiliations." Additionally, it "incites certain American activists to ignore policy lines . . . of [the] U.S. and to consider themselves free to undertake from Bangkok, Saigon and even Phnom Penh action against our sovereignty and territorial integrity." He went on to lament Cambodia's current weak state in comparison to its neighbors, which left it open to border incursions. He recounted recent invasions on Cambodia's eastern border by South Vietnam forces, Saigon's claims to coastal islands, and "attacks of Khmers-Serei of Son Ngoc Thanh, [and] Dap Chhuon." All of these issues were forcing him to turn toward China for help.[30]

Sihanouk went on another diatribe in a speech in Kompong Speu, likely in response to a *New York Times* editorial that accused him of acting with "characteristic emotion and arrogance" in the breaking of relations with Thailand. Trimble opined that, with the behavior Sihanouk was displaying, he might be "temporarily mentally deranged." Trimble stated that he felt "strongly that we must not ignore this outrageous and completely unclassed [sic] for attack on U.S. To do so would cause us to lose great face here, as well as in neighboring countries, but also would lead Sihanouk [to] feel [that] we will take anything from him." While he did not recommend an end to economic or military aid, he did suggest the United States should "go into slow motion in dealing with Cambodia."[31]

The US ambassador to Thailand Kenneth Todd Young saw things differently. He sent a telegram to the State Department detailing his interpretation of events in Cambodia. Young felt that Sihanouk's behavior, while "premeditated if rampant," was a "calculated policy related to his presumption either communists will win all of Laos and Vietnam or US and SEATO [were] about to intervene militarily in Laos and Vietnam. In either case Sihanouk is disengaging himself from US and American-back neighbors to placate Peking and Hanoi." Young consulted with the Belgian and Israeli ambassadors, and all agreed that "Sihanouk wants break with west and has purposely gone beyond point of reconciliation."[32]

The Far Eastern Bureau was of a different view, however. Robert H. Johnson of the National Security Council staff penned a memo for McGeorge Bundy detailing some divergent viewpoints on how to proceed with Cambodia. He felt that Sihanouk's recent outbursts were not part of a larger grand strategy, but instead "a typical emotional reaction to outside criticism." It urged calm and gentle prodding of Thailand's Sarit Thanarat since he "bears a considerable measure of the responsibility for the Thai-Cambodian situation." Sihanouk was said to be "terribly sensitive to criticism and to the possibility that the traditional enemies of Cambodia, Thailand and Viet Nam are plotting against him." For Sihanouk, his worst fears had been confirmed by the 1958 coup attempt where "the U. S. seemed to be [*less than one line of text redacted*] using Thailand and Viet Nam as bases from which to launch an effort to overthrow him." To Sihanouk, the parallels between 1958 and 1961 were concrete. The bureau urged a presidential reassurance, mediation through the UN of the Thai-Cambodian border disputes, and a "strong demarche" to Sarit.[33]

When the South Vietnamese government made overtures to Cambodia to express regret over an attack on a Cambodian village, Trimble urged the Saigon embassy to refrain from mentioning to the press that "US advisers participated in [South Vietnamese] operation in accordance with normal practice," that any Americans present were there "only in routine observer capacity." His concern was that such participation would be reminiscent, in Sihanouk's mind, of the Dap Chhuon affair and had the potential to rekindle animosity between the two countries.[34]

Beginning in March 1962, Sihanouk's speeches and reports in the press began focusing in on subversive actions being taken by Cambodia's neighbors in the recruitment of Cambodian dissidents for insurgent operations against the prince. Numerous editorials and press reports asserted the existence of coup plots.[35] Thành's name was never far from such reporting.

By summer 1962 it was clear that both Thailand and South Vietnam had stepped up support for anti-Sihanouk dissidents with the goal of forcing him from office. For months these forces had been trained in Thailand and South Vietnam with those respective governments not only tolerating it, but likely encouraging it. The State Department worried that "movement of dissidents into Cambodia may be imminent." Secretary Dean Rusk fired off a telegram to the embassies in Bangkok, Saigon, and Phnom Penh on 1 June detailing the State Department's concerns with these developments, which it considered "unrealistic and dangerous to Free World interests." Rusk doubted that such plans would be successful and would only drive Sihanouk closer to the communist bloc. Rusk felt that "in view of [the] contribution which US [is] making to Thai and Vietnamese security, we have right to expect they will refrain from and prevent any activities on their soil which might greatly weaken" America's position in the region. He instructed the Bangkok and Saigon embassies to press their respective host countries for additional information and to make known the American position on the situation. Admitting that the United States in fact knew about the Dap Chhuon plot ahead of time but failed to inform the Cambodian government, Rusk worried that a repeat of such a failure would exacerbate the tense relationship that already existed between the United States and Cambodia. He suggested that it might become desirable to secretly inform Cambodian officials of the reports he had been receiving and indicate American disapproval of such plots.[36]

Two days later, in a toast at a dinner to honor Trimble (who was leaving his post as ambassador), Sihanouk made known that he was aware of such plotting himself. As Trimble recounted in a telegram to the State Department, "Sihanouk made thinly veiled accusations against neighbors for plotting against Cambodia and even alluding to possibility that Cambodia might be [the] victim [of an] unjustified at-tack."[37] This indicates that Sihanouk's intelligence services were quite astute.

On 5 June Trimble attempted to assure Sihanouk that the United States would "do everything it could to quash such activities." Sihanouk expressed his gratitude, and informed the ambassador that a Cambo-dian representative in Saigon had recently reported back that dissident designs on a government overthrow were being orchestrated under the leadership of Thành and his brother Sơn Thái Nguyễn, with support from the Saigon government. Sihanouk stated that Thành hoped to replace him and that he should return to Phnom Penh and make an ap-peal to the Cambodian people. As would become a common pattern, if the people so desired, the prince stated he would retire and live in exile; he claimed he had no thirst for power, just the desire to do good for the country, but the South Vietnamese government was almost pushing him into the arms of the communists. This was mystifying to Siha-nouk, as neither he nor the Cambodian population held sympathies for the communists.[38]

Throughout the spring and summer months, the Cambodian press hammered away on the links between the Khmer Serei, South Viet-nam, and (sometimes) the United States. The Cambodian newspaper *Neak Chiet Niyum* (Nationalism or People's Nationalism) reported on 1 April 1962 that Khmer Serei based in Thailand made the decision to recognize Thành as their chief over Sary, of whose whereabouts they were unaware.[39] *Neak Chiet Niyum* reported on 27 May 1962 that Thành and Sary established their headquarters in the home of Chau Bory, just outside Saigon. According to the paper, the Diem regime and the Amer-icans ordered Thành and Sary to rally the Khmer Krom and combine forces with Chau Bory's military for the purpose of assassination of local Vietnamese. Blame would then be attributed to the Cambodian armed forces. This is in reference to the attack on the village of Vinh Lac on 20 April, where over two hundred armed men crossed over the Cam-bodian border and raided the village, killing fifty-two. Survivors did, in fact, blame it on Cambodian forces, as did the Vietnamese government. American officials felt it more likely the raid was carried out by Khmer Krom, long frustrated with the discrimination they faced in Vietnam.[40] *La Dépêche* reported on 10 June 1962 that "students and young people" were "forced" to participate in a Khmer Serei civic action program. Some were sent to Buôn Ma Thuột in Vietnam's central highlands for training after which they were ushered back to the frontier to conduct

actions against Cambodia. *Neak Chiet Niyum* reported the same day that
So'n Thái Nguyễn was recruiting regional cadres for the purpose of political education of Khmer Krom.[41] Radio Nationale Khmère reported
on 25 July 1962 that 570 armed Khmer Serei had formed a base camp
in Tan Chiet, Binh Long Province, South Vietnam, just eleven kilometers from the Cambodian border.[42] On 6 September *Sangkum Monous*
reported that ARVN (Army of the Republic of Vietnam) and the Khmer
Serei were essentially receiving the same military training.[43] And on and
on they went. The quasi-state-run media's obsession with Thành and
the Khmer Serei would only be tempered when renewed tensions arose
with Thailand over the disputed Preah Vihear temple.

In talks with Ambassador Frederick Nolting, Diem, for his part, categorically denied promoting or aiding any group with aims on attacking Cambodia. Diem maintained his government had nothing to do
with the previous Dap Chhuon plot, despite concrete evidence to the
contrary, leaving a sour taste in the mouths of American officials.[44] Sihanouk also expressed anxiety to Ambassador Trimble over the subversive intentions of his neighbors.[45]

In early June, following approval from the director of the presidential security service of the government of Vietnam Tran Kim Tuyen,
Thành "AKA Shan Yu-Ch'eng," flew to Taipei aboard a Thai International Airlines flight after a request by the National Security Bureau
(NSB) of the government of the Republic of China for him to visit. Two
associates joined him. Tuyen had long been in contact with the NSB,
discussing, according to the CIA, "plans for political action against the
Sihanouk government." As it stood, the plan "was to use Son Ngoc
Thanh's popular appeal with the Cambodian people to overthrow Sihanouk's political power, and would be carried out by Nationalist China,
South Vietnam and Thailand, or only by Nationalist China and South
Vietnam." The Thai government had already approved the supplying of
"ammunition, bombs, and explosives" to the plot, and South Vietnam
advocated using Thành's Khmer Serei "as infiltrators into Cambodia
to conduct political warfare operations," but there was concern that
keeping such a plan secret would prove difficult. Tuyen was aware that
the United States had sniffed out the plan and that Ambassador Nolting had attempted to dissuade Diem from engaging in such actions.[46]

That Taiwan would lend its support to a rightist revolutionary such
as Thành should come as no surprise. In 1950 the remnants of Chiang
Kai-shek's mainland nationalist army fled approaching communist
forces into Burma. This covert Kuomingtang army received support

from the Republic of China and occasionally from the CIA. In addition to wreaking chaos in Burma, it fought as mercenaries in Laos in the early 1960s and as strongmen for the Thai government against communist insurgencies. Taiwan's support for Thành must thusly be seen in the context of the regional political goals of creating the conditions for anti-communism to thrive.[47]

Tuyen informed Taipei that he agreed on a joint operation and that he had already presented the plan to Diem. All that was needed now was his approval, but Tuyen worried that the Thais might be bluffing and be unable to guarantee engagement without Vietnamese participation. The CIA reported that "the Chinese Nationalists felt that there were differences of opinion between Thailand and South Vietnam . . . and therefore considered it wise to work with the GVN [Government of Vietnam, or South Vietnamese government] and the Thai government separately. . . . Discussions were to continue between the GVN and the GRC [Government of the Republic of China] on the part that Son Ngoc Thanh would play in the operation, and also on the way in which the over-all plan should be drafted in order to insure approval."[48] It was also reported that around this same time Thành, under the alias Kien Veen, was spotted departing the Saigon airport for Hong Kong via Cathay Pacific Airlines, with Bangkok as his likely next destination.[49]

The State Department's annoyance with its Asian allies continued, as it spelled out in a telegram on 13 August 1962 to the embassies in Bangkok, Saigon, Taipei, and Phnom Penh. It bemoaned the "continuing reports of Thai and SVN [South Vietnamese] support for possibly imminent action against Sihanouk by Son Ngoc Thanh." The State Department categorized such plots as "highly unrealistic in view [of] Sihanouk's popular support, undesirable because [they would] likely lead Cambodia into alignment with [the communist] Bloc, and dangerous in view [of] present situation [in] SEA [Southeast Asia]." Thành had been steadily increasing his activities since April, although his group of supporters remained relatively small. By August, the State Department was aware that Thành had contacts with low-level representatives of South Vietnam, the Republic of China, and Thailand, and "had contact with senior GVN and GRC intelligence officials." He had received material assistance from Vietnam and possibly Thailand. Discussions between Thành and the three nationalist countries continued for the purpose of coordinating support for further activity. Possible courses of action at this point included "armed dissidence and possibly assassination."[50] That same day, Lon Nol told an American embassy official that several Khmer Serei agents, under the orders of South Vietnamese authorities, had recently infiltrated Cambodian territory and had turned themselves over to Cambodian forces.[51]

Strategically, Sihanouk continued to play both blocs against each other, and he courted each with vigor. On 1 August 1962 Sihanouk announced that the Soviet ambassador pledged support from the Soviet Union if the Thais or Vietnamese went through with an attack.[52] Three weeks later, on 20 August, he wrote to Kennedy requesting his aid with the "very serious threat that has for years been hanging over [his] country."[53]

On 24 August Sihanouk threatened to sever diplomatic relations with South Vietnam for repeated aggressive action which had "backed Cambodia up against wall." The new American ambassador to Cambodia Phillip D. Sprouse reported from Phnom Penh that up to that point there was "no proof for charge Cambodians have actually harbored Viet Cong or permitted Viet Cong establish bases on Cambodian territory." He felt that, while unlikely for economic reasons, severing relations between the two countries would only push Cambodia toward the communist bloc.[54] Former ambassador Trimble, for his part, agreed with Sprouse's assessment on the lack of communist bases on Cambodian territory.[55]

In an effort to get Taipei to restrain itself from further assistance to Thành, the State Department directed Admiral Alan G. Kirk, ambassador to the Republic of China, to lay out to Chiang Kai-shek America's position on "various mischievous anti-Sihanouk activities being conducted by certain Southeast Asian countries." It stated that Sihanouk held "essentially anti-communist, nationalistic motivation[s], which emphasizes independent stature for [the] Cambodian nation," and was a "positive benefit [to the] free world."[56] This was a sharp departure from past language, and possibly a ploy to assure no further Taiwanese assistance to the Cambodian dissidents. The American embassy in Phnom Penh wrote to the State Department, stating that "any actions by US allies in the area in support of dissident movements against the present Cambodian regime would . . . be contrary to US national interests."[57]

Despite concerns with Thailand, South Vietnam, and the Republic of China, Sihanouk had been riding a wave of domestic success over the past three years. But initial cracks in the façade became visible with a small student uprising in Siem Reap in late February 1963 while Sihanouk was away in China. Police responded brutally, killing one student.

When authorities failed to investigate, over one thousand students stampeded into police headquarters, tearing down Sihanouk posters and photographs in the process. Several more students were killed, and the police, unable to restore order, had to call in the military for assistance. The cabinet accepted responsibility for the revolt and resigned, allowing Sihanouk to save face.[58]

When Sihanouk returned, Lon Nol supplied several dossiers which implicated "certain elements" within the student population that were allegedly followers of So'n Ngọc Thành, although the American Embassy suspected communist influence. Having just returned from a lavish reception in China where on 27 February 1963 the PRC proclaimed its intention to sign an international guarantee of Cambodia's neutrality, Sihanouk was hesitant to blame communist agitators for the uprising, at least initially. In actuality, he and Lon Nol had already been preparing dossiers on leftist subversives who were soon tacked onto Sihanouk's ever-growing list of enemies[59] American officials expressed concern that China plied Sihanouk's always fragile confidence with the specter of new plots by Thành against the Cambodian government. His fears likely reinforced, Sihanouk continued to drift from the West and his neighbors to the point that the prince brushed off the possibility of rapprochement with the current Thai and South Vietnamese regimes.[60]

Following his return from trips to India and China, Sihanouk stated that "eminent friends inform me that our neighbors have recently put Son Ngoc Thanh back into business naturally on the enlightened advice of certain big imperialists whom it is not necessary to name but who are behind all the machinations against Cambodia. Once again our enemies desire to launch a coup d'état or, failing that, to assassinate me. Son Ngoc Thanh has lately spent some time in Taiwan, travelling by Hong Kong, to work out plans for this undertaking with specialized agents of Chiang Kai-shek."[61]

In a one-and-a-half-hour speech on 3 March 1963, Sihanouk lashed out at, on the one hand, leftist elements for subverting student groups and sowing discontent with his government, and, on the other, the Khmer Serei for its close association with Thành and working against Cambodia's national interests. He slighted various leaders like Chau Seng, Lon Nol, and Sann as incapable or unwilling to take on the responsibilities of prime minister, and intimated that he would have to resume the job himself.[62]

The snub to Lon Nol may have come as a surprise, but there were rumblings in Cambodian and American circles that Sihanouk had grown suspicious of Lon Nol's ambitions. Cambodian leftists at the time promoted the theory, which also had Lon Nol consolidating his relationships with the West and the United States. Reports claim that Chinese president Liu Shaoqi sent Sihanouk a letter advising him to be wary of disloyalty in the government, especially in the armed forces. French sources claimed that the queen was so concerned that while she ostensibly advised Lon Nol to travel to France in July 1963 for medical treatment (which he was in need of), her real hope was that Lon Nol's absence would allow Sihanouk time to calm down.[63]

The announcement on 25 July 1963 by the Thai general Thanom Kittikachorn that Thailand planned to send troops to the Thai-Cambodian border region for "training and patrol" did not help matters.[64] In response, on 1 August 1963, an official state announcement from Phnom Penh stated that Thailand was now a direct threat to Cambodia, and that the Cambodian government reached out to the UN and "all peaceful countries" for aid in stemming this perilous situation.[65]

On the opposite border, in mid-August 1963, Khmer Serei radio broadcasts resumed from Vietnam. On 23 August, Cambodian officials claimed that two South Vietnamese aircraft gunned down a Cambodian provincial guard in Kuak Tek. Four days later Cambodia declared an official break in diplomatic relations with the Saigon government.[66] Numerous Khmer Krom professed their loyalty to Diem, which Sihanouk denounced as forced. Sihanouk mounted a campaign to discredit anyone or anything that opposed his rule. Chief recipients of his ire continued to be the Khmer Serei, which were now being overtly connected to the CIA in both the press and by Sihanouk. By ramping up the public pressure, Sihanouk hoped South Vietnam and Thailand would discontinue their support for the rebel group.[67]

The US embassy in Phnom Penh reacted harshly to an October Sihanouk editorial in the *Neak Cheit Neyun* in which the prince accused the United States of supporting the movement to overthrow his government. Sprouse recommended to Rusk that Nong Kimny be called in for a sharp rebuke rather than confronting Sihanouk personally, "which would involve loss of face for him and might lead to unpredictable reaction." He also suggested Bangkok and Saigon be contacted and urged to halt Khmer Serei activities on their land.[68]

Thành later revealed that in October 1963 Sihanouk made overtures for him to return to Cambodia and attempt to work within the existing government. Thành recounted that his reply to Sihanouk was that his return was not important, and what really mattered was the liberalization of the economy, a shift from Sihanouk's anti-Western neutralist stance, and for the prince to return to the throne to allow political parties to function more freely. Thành repeatedly characterized his clash with Sihanouk as one simply between Cambodians, and that he longed to avoid the involvement of other countries in it, including the United States.[69] If there was any sincerity to Sihanouk's proposal, it may have been as a last-ditch effort to avoid a rise in tensions with the United States, which was beginning to look inevitable.

The harsh tone of Sihanouk's rhetoric was slightly dampened when on 21 October he attributed Khmer Serei support to American "services," a not-so-veiled reference to the CIA, as opposed to the United States government. Four days later *Réalités Cambodgiennes* also made the distinction between the American government and its intelligence apparatus, stating, "We think it likely that White House and Department of State not aware [of] all criminal activities in which [it] has engaged in Far East," but expressing certainty that the CIA was collaborating closely with Thailand and South Vietnam in support of the Khmer Serei.[70] On 28 October Penn Nouth relayed a message from Sihanouk to Spivack that any recent accusations made were strictly levied against the CIA and did not apply to the US government. He stated that while Cambodia remained grateful for US aid, the Cambodian government had concrete evidence of CIA involvement in the Dap Chhuon plot and subsequent Khmer Serei activities. Cambodia, Nouth said, had no desire to turn toward the communist bloc for support but felt it was the only option to sustain survival in the face of aggressive actions by its neighbors and failure of the United States to reign in its allies.[71]

To allay Sihanouk's fears, some protocol had to change. In years past, presidential messages of congratulations were not sent for Sihanouk's birthday on 31 October. In 1963, Kennedy sent long messages commemorating it with the hope that it would allay Sihanouk's delicate psyche. Any relief Sihanouk may have felt from the letters was short-lived. Days later, on 3 November, Diem and Nhu were assassinated[72]

Following Diem's assassination, there was brief hope on the part of US officials that Sihanouk would temper his stance vis-à-vis South Vietnam and offer a conciliatory gesture to improve relations. That did not occur. He immediately set conditions for a resumption of diplomatic relations between the two, which would be extremely difficult for Saigon to accept. As always, South Vietnamese support for the Khmer Serei was high on his list. As Spivack stated in a telegram to Rusk, "no real improvement [in] Cambodian-SVN relations possible unless border violations and Khmer Serei activities halted."[73]

On 5 November 1963, Sihanouk declared that he would renounce American aid if the Khmer Serei radio station based in South Vietnam was not shut down before the end of the year. Sihanouk attributed much blame to the United States for various acts of "pro-Western" subversion.[74]

Sihanouk also delivered an ultimatum that if Khmer Serei broadcasts were not suspended by the new year that he would suspend Western aid and turn to communist China for assistance. This left the United States in an awkward position. If the broadcasts were stopped, Sihanouk could claim it was a result of the pressure he applied and proved his charges correct. If they continued, he could say the United States was given fair warning. A perhaps uncalculated layer of such a demand left the Khmer Serei itself with tacit veto power on the continuation of Western aid. If the Khmer Serei wanted it to cease, it simply had to continue broadcasting. If Sihanouk then did, in fact, turn to China for aid, it would support the long-stated claims of Bangkok and Saigon that Sihanouk's plan all along was, in fact, to bring Cambodia into the communist camp. It was a complex, precarious situation on all fronts. Additionally, Diem's assassination in Vietnam by a supposedly supportive military likely left Sihanouk feeling more vulnerable than ever.[75]

Traditionally, felicitations marking Cambodia's Independence Day on 9 November were strictly routine and brief in nature. For the celebration in 1963, Kennedy sent a much longer message, just as he did to mark Sihanouk's birthday the week prior. He also expressed American support for the prince's neutralist policy.[76] The conciliatory tone was not reciprocated days later when on 12 November Sihanouk gave an unscripted, blistering three-and-a-half-hour speech. In it, he insisted that his actions were not solely a result of the Khmer Serei. American aid in general, he stated, "irritates me and Cambodians of all persuasions more and more . . . I must admit clearly that withdrawal of this aid will be immense relief for us."[77]

That same day the Cambodian National Assembly met to discuss the latest developments during which the idea was floated that if Khmer Serei broadcasts continued, Sihanouk would leave the country for one month to allow the Khmer Serei to enter Cambodia and attempt to establish a government of their own. The theory was that the Khmer Serei would look foolish and inept in the process. It is doubtful this plan was ever given much serious consideration.[78]

Rusk felt that the "immediate cause of Sihanouk's irritation at the Khmer Serei has been comparisons between Son Ngoc Thanh's record as Cambodian nationalist and that of Sihanouk's, with invidious references to Sihanouk's less consistent position," a charge that Thành and his supporters had long been making. As for the Khmer Serei itself, Rusk felt they constituted "no significant military or political threat to Cambodian government," but that the United States had "no means of controlling broadcasts" and, in fact, did not even know the location of the transmitter.[79] For their part, the Thai deputy prime minister and defense minister Thanom, foreign minister Thanat, the SEATO secretary general Pote Sarasin, interior minister Praphat, and the principal advisor to the prime minister Ptya Srivisar all publicly denied any responsibility on the part of the Thai government for the Khmer Serei broadcasts.[80]

As Sprouse noted, Sihanouk's "principal source [of] recent anger and irritation are scurrilous personal attacks on him and on [the] royal family, bitter criticism [of] his policies and rule, and predictions [the] Khmer Serei will shortly overthrow him." Additionally, "Thanh's long-term claim to have been original leader [of] Cambodian independence movement is, of course, and has been for many years perennial source of irritation and has long been target of Sihanouk's counterattacking speeches and writings."[81]

In a press conference on 16 November Sihanouk attempted to clear up any "confusion in [the] minds [of] Anglo-Saxon correspondents and [the] American Embassy." He stated, again, that if Khmer Serei broadcasts continued past 31 December that all aid from the United States would be terminated, but if the broadcasts ceased, aid could continue on an unconditional basis. He also made reference to a statement by Kennedy on Cambodia's independence. Sihanouk responded by boldly stating, "I have no lesson to receive from anybody so far as national independence in concerned. All my life I have fought, am fighting, and will fight for the independence of my country. . . . I would like to suggest to President Kennedy that he not give such lessons to Sihanouk but to Sarit, Chaing Kai-chek [sic], and South Vietnamese leaders because they need such lessons; I don't."[82]

In a speech given that same day Sihanouk stated that his government knew the location of the Khmer Serei radio transmitter in South Vietnam as it had been spotted a number of times by General Ngo Hou, the chief of staff for ARVK (Royal Khmer Aviation) from the air. The transmitter was supposedly located near the Cambodian border, and

Khmer Serei guerillas sporting American uniforms were seen in the area, as were South Vietnamese and US soldiers. Sihanouk concluded his speech by saying that the Khmer Serei attacks on him have left him sleepless, physically sick, and unsure if he had the strength to go on if they were to continue.[83]

Rusk stated in a 16 November telegram to the Saigon embassy his feelings that while "Sihanouk [had] gone far toward destroying opportunity presented by new Government in Viet-Nam for improving relations between Cambodia and Viet-Nam," that the South Vietnam government should nonetheless be urged to do all it can to end Khmer Serei activities in an effort to placate Sihanouk. He also noted that Khmer Serei activities "do not in any way serve or involve [South Vietnamese] interests. Objectively they represent at best pinpricks against Sihanouk, but he reacts to them in manner which may create serious world crisis in SEA." If the new Saigon government wanted Cambodian cooperation in ending border crossings by the Vietcong, a cessation of Khmer Serei activities would go a long way toward making that happen. It would also make a demonstrative "switch from methods of intrigue and plotting which characterized [the] Diem-Nhu Government in its external as well as in its internal operations." Rusk closed by stating "it would be helpful also for new GVN overlook Sihanouk's statements to extent of making some conciliatory gesture toward Cambodia."[84]

Rusk also sent a telegram to the embassy in Phnom Penh in which he urged caution with Sihanouk, "who evidently [is] in highly disturbed state of mind." Rusk felt it inconceivable "that Cambodia should be led [to] commit national political suicide in response to activities of small dissident group that has no popular support in Cambodia and represents no threat to RKG [Royal Khmer Government], no matter how irritating its propaganda may be." He continued his assessment in a broader, global, Cold War context, stating:

> Cambodia would be foolish [to] think that Chicoms [are] prepared [to] assist Cambodia to extent needed and still leave Cambodia independent, and [the] final result would be [the] loss of identity as a nation and acquisition of unenviable satellite status. . . . The Cambodians might also be stimulated to consider the implications of in effect threatening establishment of a Chicom base of operations deep behind Free World lines. It should be clear that any action by Sihanouk tending in this direction would be based on a major miscalculation of the extent of US

determination . . . and ought to be avoided. Accordingly, we hope Sihanouk will set aside his unwarranted threats and turn his attention to solving problems with his neighbors.[85]

That same day, Khmer Serei radio broadcasts resumed after a period of dormancy.[86]

Sprouse stated in a telegram to the State Department that Khmer Serei activities "are not relevant to our aid programs and we are not responsible for or involved in them." He recommended continuing to "make clear we oppose and deplore KS [Khmer Serei] activities and would do what we could to put an end to them insofar as it lay within our capabilities." Sprouse then thanked the State Department's "efforts to put an end to [Khmer Serei] activities," which he hoped could allow for moderate voices to begin to influence Sihanouk.[87] Sprouse attempted to reassure one of these potential moderate voices when he insisted to acting secretary of state for foreign affairs and Sihanouk's cousin Norodom Phurissara of the American desire to be of help with respect to Khmer Serei activities and locating their transmitters. Sprouse had somewhat tempered hopes that these overtures would be reassuring to Sihanouk.[88] That pessimistic outlook was reinforced when that same day, Cambodian National Radio relayed rumors from the press in Saigon that a "coup d'etat" was "imminent," although the US embassy in Phnom Penh was unaware of any substantive rumors.[89]

The British embassy informed the State Department that it would encourage South Vietnam to recognize the importance of reconciliation with Cambodia, a prominent feature of which would be discouraging Khmer Serei activity. The embassy considered Thailand's support of the Khmer Serei to be a more difficult obstacle to overcome and urged the United States to pressure Thai authorities to do more.[90]

Severely backpedaling from his angry pronouncements of the past days, Sihanouk wrote a very gracious letter to Kennedy on 17 November, thanking the president for his warm wishes on the occasion of the tenth anniversary of Cambodian independence. His tone was warm throughout, and he assured Kennedy that he "never had any doubts about the sincere support given by your Excellency to our foreign policy and to our efforts to develop and to modernize our country. This is also the feeling of the people of Cambodia, who are deeply grateful to the American people and their president for the aid furnished them since the return of independence." In days, however, that tone would change strikingly.[91]

Thành perhaps saw that the tense relationship between the United States and Cambodia opened a potential window for him. On 18 November a representative of the Khmer Serei reached out to an employee at the American embassy in Saigon with a message for Henry Cabot Lodge, who had replaced Nolting as ambassador to South Vietnam. While the request for an urgent meeting between Thành and the ambassador was rebuffed, to American officials it nonetheless was symbolic of the "boldness with which he is acting."[92]

A "special congress" was announced for 19 November 1963 for what many expected to be Sihanouk's announcement of new economic reforms. A large crowd gathered, as did a number of foreign journalists. After declaring the session open, Sihanouk informed the waiting crowd that two Khmer Serei rebels were among them. One, Preap In, was referred to as a "political commissioner" for the group. Sihanouk relayed that In had informed him that Thành resided in Saigon. Thành's brother, Sơn Thái Nguyễn, headed the general staff for recruitment, which met in the local Cambodia pagoda in the South Vietnamese capital.

While the number of active collaborators were claimed to be small in number (around fifty), they were supported by the local Khmer Krom population and recognized by the South Vietnamese government. It was here, living among the strategic hamlets that they were allegedly furnished with American weapons, radio transmitters, and equipment. Dollars and arms flooded in from both American and South Vietnamese as reward for success in battle against the Vietcong. Some segments were under direct American supervision and control, some units incorporated into the South Vietnamese military. Thành himself issued laissez-passer to Khmer Serei members, which bore the visa of the South Vietnam government. Thành's reach, according to In, extended throughout the former Cochinchina wherever Khmer Krom resided.

As In recounted, the Khmer Serei fashioned itself as the barrier to Chinese and communist political domination of Cambodia. Its two goals were maintaining independence and providing for shelter, food, and clothing for the country. Sihanouk opined that in reality, it had succumbed to the political will of the Saigon and Bangkok governments to bring Cambodia into the Free World camp. This evidence of American collusion, as it were, persuaded the congress to unanimously reject future economic, cultural, and military aid from the United States.[93]

Alarmed at the increased amplification of Sihanouk's threats to cut off aid, the State Department recommended to Kennedy that he send a "special representative" to Cambodia to engage in high level discussions with the goal being a cessation of anti-American rhetoric and a return to a cordial diplomatic relationship between the two countries.[94]

Kennedy quickly wrote to Sihanouk expressing dismay at the turn of events. He proclaimed that Sihanouk was misled and misinformed on charges of American support for the Khmer Serei. Kennedy emphatically stated that the US "government is not supporting the Khmer Serei group in any way," although in a draft version of the letter that sentence concluded with the crossed-out phrase "nor is any of its Agencies so doing." Kennedy emphasized America's support for Cambodian neutrality and the importance that American aid played in "supporting [Cambodia's] independence and assisting in its development." He concluded with an offer, following the suggestion of the State Department, to send Dean Acheson as his personal envoy to further discuss the situation.[95]

Rusk then urged the embassy in South Vietnam to make known to South Vietnamese officials that any retaliatory measures taken against Cambodia, such as closing off the Mekong, "could complicate situation irretrievably." He emphasized the importance of a cessation of Khmer Serei activities on South Vietnamese soil, and suggested informing the government of South Vietnam of Thành's overtures to the United States "as proof his presence in South Vietnam and example boldness with which he is acting."[96]

Sihanouk, full of bluster and bravado, spoke before the National Congress that same day requesting a termination of American aid. As reported by the Agence Khmere de Presse (AKP), Sihanouk rhetorically asked,

> Now that we have from very mouth of political commissar of Khmer Serei movement . . . irrevocable proof of support and patronage accorded this movement by South Vietnamese and American governments, should our country continue [to] accept aid from USA, from this government which gives to us with one hand and stabs us in [the] back with other? Could we from now on receive from USA one single dollar without our nation and our country being dishonored thereby?[97]

American intelligence noted that Sihanouk's suspicions of Khmer Serei plots to overthrow him "underlie his announced refusal to accept further US aid," and that they were intensifying. At a massive rally that day in Phonm Penh, two alleged Khmer Serei agents who supposedly confessed to receiving American and South Vietnamese aid in support of operations against the prince were used to whip up support for his demand for the withdrawal of American advisors, both military and civilian, from Cambodia, and for his rejection of additional US aid. "The Americans are noted for their habit of buying the conscience of other persons," Sihanouk bellowed to the crowd. "They have bought such running dogs as Sam Sary, Son Ngoc Thanh, and the Khmers Serei, the Vietnamese, and the new Vietnamese government." Rumors floated in Saigon that a coup was imminent, which possibly triggered Sihanouk's reaction. Despite his projections of concern, according to the CIA, "the Khmer Serei in reality appears to have little capability for action against Sihanouk's regime."[98]

The next day, as the Chinese government issued a statement that declared Peking's "all-out support" for Cambodia in the event of an American instigated armed invasion by its neighbors, Norodom Phurissara called Sprouse to inform him that Cambodia was requesting a termination of US economic, technical, military, and cultural aid due to American support for the Khmer Serei. Sprouse reiterated past American rejections of such charges and, speaking in a frank and personal tone, stated that he was fully convinced that the US government had no contacts with the Khmer Serei. Just before this conversation a Khmer Serei agent gave testimony before the Cambodian National Congress that three thousand Khmer Serei were operating within the Vietnamese army. Sprouse speculated that it was possible American military personnel stationed in South Vietnam could have come into contact with Khmer Serei units without knowledge of their identity.[99]

Phurissara also detailed Cambodia's complaints against the United States. According to Phurissara, an emissary for the Khmer Serei provided proof that American agents had in fact been the suppliers of aid, arms, and propaganda materials to the movement. As stated in his note, "from now on the Cambodian people cannot understand how official American declarations of respect for our sovereignty and our national policy can find expression in such flagrant American participation in a plot against our people and our liberties." To retain its dignity, the royal government had no choice but to demand a cessation of American aid. After expressing thanks for past support, the note expressed hope that the United States "will understand that a sovereign state such as ours cannot tolerate in silence the intrigues of American officials and agents working relentless [sic] to undermine its independence." Cambodia maintained diplomatic relations "because our friendship for the American people remains intact."[100] By now it was no secret that

Sihanouk had felt burned by American actions.[101] The prince may have felt burned, but his passions were buoyed.

In a telegram to the Department of State, Sprouse quickly relayed that it was his belief that "we should do everything we can to pick up pieces and start rebuilding in a way designed to minimize damage to U.S. prestige and repair and improve U.S. image. . . . Otherwise our image in this country will be tarnished and our position adversely affected for a long time to come."[102]

Roger Hilsman immediately called on the Cambodian ambassador Nong Kimny to explain the sweeping and dramatic changes in the two nations' relationship over the past days. Hilsman repeated that the United States had no complicity in any Khmer Serei plots and that South Vietnam and Thailand were not subject to American control. He urged Kimny to allow the new government in South Vietnam (which came to power following the coup that resulted in the arrest and assassination of Diem) to establish itself and potentially foster a new relationship between the Southeast Asian neighbors. Kimny espoused optimism for the future of Cambodian–South Vietnamese relations as long as existing problems could be resolved. He dismissed the Khmer Serei as negligible, but in the context of multiple plots to overthrow Sihanouk over the previous years, the prince was shaken. Kimny stated that the suspicions of Cambodians were that instructions from Washington were not being followed at the lower, local levels. Hilsman emphatically denied this. Despite differences in approach and method, Kimny insisted that Cambodia and the United States indeed had the same goals, Cambodia was in no way moving closer to the communist bloc, and Cambodia would be the last country to fall to communism.[103]

With the dramatic shift in American-Cambodian relations as the backdrop, Melvin L. Manfull, the counselor for political affairs at the American embassy in Saigon, met with the South Vietnamese foreign minister Charles Trần Văn Lắm to discuss the new government's stance toward Sihanouk and Cambodia. Lam stated that Vietnam hoped to work together with Phnom Penh to create the conditions for an improved relationship. As for the Khmer Serei, Lam stated that both he and the prime minister Nguyễn Ngọc Tho' were unaware of current government support for their activities. He stated that he had never met Thành and was unaware of his current location. Manfull commented to the State department that based on this conversation, it was "highly probable GVN not now aiding or abetting Khmer Serei activities." It remained possible, however, that some "Khmer Serei agents trained by Diem regime may still be operating without knowledge of, or any connection with, new government."[104] The Peking government protested otherwise when it issued a statement the following day, declaring its "all-out support" for Cambodia in the event of an American instigated armed invasion by its neighbors.[105]

In what was to be the last time he ever saw him, Roger Hilsman met with President Kennedy on 20 November 1963 to discuss the situation in Cambodia.[106] Hilsman attributed Sihanouk's outbursts and threats to cut off American aid to his paranoia with the Khmer Serei. Hilsman stated that the United States had nothing to do with the Khmer Serei, and that Sihanouk had been given assurances about this. Hilsman informed the president that during the Eisenhower administration "we did pay [sic] footsie" with the Khmer Serei, and that "there was money involved." All this seemed hard for Kennedy to believe. He did not know why a group he had never heard of could be wreaking havoc on America's relations with Sihanouk. He asked Hilsman to explain what the Khmer Serei was. Hilsman informed the president that the group "does not number more than 300 or 400 people. It has one or two transmitters that they carry around in a cart in Thailand. You have to be within ten miles to detect them." He stated that Sihanouk and Sarit's relationship had deteriorated to the point that the latter refused to do anything to stop Khmer Serei broadcasts. In the aftermath of Diem and Nhu's assassinations, Sihanouk also felt that he could be next, which added another layer of tension to his position.[107]

Later that day Kennedy and Hilsman discussed the situation further, with the president stating that "we ought to be thinking about getting Acheson there in three or four weeks" and that he would give him a call. Hilsman, worried of a possible leak, suggested he hold off for a few days. Kennedy said that was fine and agreed to wait until the weekend to make a decision. It was a Wednesday. Kennedy would not live to see that weekend. Two days later the president was dead.[108]

In early December Hilsman wrote to Thomas L. Hughes, assistant secretary of state for intelligence and research, about the "ambivalent attitudes toward aid that have been developing in Cambodia." He also expressed concern that Sihanouk could "at any moment launch further half-baked schemes, such as recognition of North Viet-Nam." He stated that the State Department was "seriously sending Dean Acheson to Cambodia with broad authority to negotiate on both aid neutrality proposals. If he is to do any good he must go soon."[109]

By then it was too late. On 8 December Sarit died. Two days later, Sihanouk triumphantly declared that "the three enemies of Cambodia," referring to Diem, Sarit, and Kennedy, "are now in Hell to pursue their SEATO meetings."[110] This outburst exacerbated tensions between the two nations greatly. A plan was crafted whereby Acheson would be dispatched to Phnom Penh to attempt to calm relations, but it failed after Sihanouk denied using Kennedy's name in a celebratory manner (which was literally true), and then insisted that the United States, in fact, owed Cambodia an apology for describing alleged rejoicings at the deaths as "barbaric" and demanded once again that Khmer Serei radio stations be shut down. Washington demurred, and the Acheson mission was scrapped. The Philippine government, acting as a mediator, offered a blueprint for reconciliation whereby the United States dropped complaints over broadcasts rejoicing in Kennedy's death, and Cambodia dropped demands for the scuttling of Khmer Serei radio. While not officially agreed to by either party, both sides, for a time, tacitly accepted the formula.[111]

Years later, Thành would confirm Sihanouk's claims against Saigon, Bangkok, and Washington. According to Thành, his Khmer Serei received "millions of dollars" in assistance. All three antagonistic governments aided in the formation of eight battalions of mainly Khmer Krom anti-Sihanouk forces. Four of those battalions had made their way from South Vietnam to Thailand "with the help of the Thai police" via both sea and air, operating "between Surin and Aranyapraprathet [sic]," just along the Cambodian border. The other four remained in South Vietnam. Three battalions were stationed at Chau Doc in the delta, with the fourth further north at Ban Me Thuot. The clandestine radio station that caused Sihanouk so much grief was also supported by all three governments and "was run from a truck inside Thailand. It was a hand-cranked transmitter."[112] Sihanouk's intuition, not to mention his highly effective intelligence gathering apparatus inside Cambodia, was oftentimes correct.

As early as 1964 Peking began supporting communist, anti-Sihanouk forces in Battambang, in large part to offset the potential for Khmer Serei gains.[113] It was also reported in early 1964 that Thành, based in his headquarters in Saigon, remained in good spirits and confident that he would eventually take power in Cambodia, though he was worried about the rising influence of the communist Chinese on Sihanouk. Six new economic advisors, sent from China to aid in the implementation of Sihanouk's nationalization plans, especially concerned him. To

Thành, the Chinese were far more "realistic" than the French. They were simply biding their time until the Americans were driven out of the country, according to Thành, and were softly pushing Sihanouk down the path of communism. He predicted that it was only a matter of time before the Chinese either forcibly overthrew Sihanouk or turned him into a puppet. The only remedy, according to Thành, was to institute a free economic system where the feudal relationships that remained from the past were done away with.[114] That could only be accomplished with Sihanouk out of the picture. The next phase of Thành's career would see him laying the groundwork to attempt just that.

CHAPTER 5

Path to Power, 1965–1970

This chapter explores the history of Khmer Serei involvement with the US Special Forces and tracks the events that ultimately led to the overthrow of Norodom Sihanouk in spring 1970. While the rise of the communist Khmer Rouge was one of the most important features of this period, David Chandler, Ben Kiernan, and others have examined this in depth. This chapter will instead focus on another wing of anti-Sihanouk sentiment was also brewing during this period, and the rise of right-wing political elements in Cambodia, the Khmer Serei, the United States, and the coup that ultimately unseated the prince from power after nearly thirty years. So'n Ngọc Thành was an essential figure in all of these, and once again divergent approaches emerged between the State Department on the one hand and American military and intelligence services on the other. What is clear is that the Khmer Serei was a highly respected and utilized force under the direction of American Special Forces during the Vietnam War. Thành was crucial in recruiting Khmer Serei to the American cause and was also a key figure, along with American officials, in the coup that unseated Sihanouk. The exact nature of these relationships is examined in depth in this chapter.

While it has been discussed in brief in earlier sections of this book, a more detailed accounting of the American relationship with the Khmer

Serei and Khmer Krom minority in South Vietnam is warranted. When discussing Khmer minority groups and their association with the United States military or Special Forces in South Vietnam, there were, in fact, three distinct groups that contributed in three distinct ways: the Khmer Krom, the Khmer Kampuchea Krom, and the Khmer Serei. While in many ways quite different, these groups had a common connection to Thành.

The Khmer Kampuchea Krom, also known as the Struggle Front of the Khmer of Lower Cambodia, was a movement founded by "mystics who spent considerable time amidst the monks, hermits, healers, and sorcerers who for centuries ha[d] made their abode in the Seven Mountains . . . near the Cambodian border." In the 1950s a Khmer monk, Samouk Seng, created the Can Sen So, or "White Turban" movement (so named for the white scarves favored by its members), which developed into the Khmer Kampuchea Krom. Although small, the Cambodian government saw it as a rival to the Khmer Serei and lent it support. By 1961 it had formally changed its name, improved recruitment, and explicitly demanded greater rights and better treatment for Khmer in the region. Most importantly, it called for "Lower Cambodia" (the area situated in the Mekong Delta) and "Upper Cambodia" (Cambodia proper) to be reunited. At its height it boasted an army of 1,500 men, but when its leader, Chau Dara, was captured by South Vietnamese forces in November 1963, it began to lose support.[1]

Khmer Krom refers to the ethnic minority group of Cambodians born in South Vietnam, formerly a part of the sprawling empire of Angkor. From the early 1960s, American Special Forces were keen to tap into this group for recruitment into the Civilian Irregular Defense Group (CIDG). The Khmer Krom, along with the Khmer Serei and Khmer Kampuchea Krom, would supply the manpower for the Mobile Strike Force Command (MSFC or MIKE Force), a key component of Special Forces operations at the time.[2] The Saigon government attempted to assimilate the Khmer population into Vietnamese society by requiring them to either accept Vietnamese citizenship or register as aliens. Most chose to retain their alien status. They viewed themselves as Cambodian, and, through the CIDG, would fight for what they saw as Cambodian interests.[3]

The CIA conceived the CIDG in 1961 in response to Vietcong successes in establishing bases among the tribal peoples of the Vietnamese highlands, who were often referred to by the blanket term Montagnards, or "mountain men." It was, by design, a defensive program centered on denying the Vietcong access to exploitable populations. In this respect, it was similar to the much-maligned Strategic Hamlet Program, although resettlement was avoided. Due to the instinctive distrust between Vietnamese and Montagnards, it was initially an American, CIA-run project, with the Special Forces providing the troops.[4] On 1 July 1963, the CIDG reorganized under Military Assistance Command, Vietnam (MACV), removing the CIA from the chain of command.[5]

MACV recruited the Khmer Krom into the Mobile Strike Force Command (MSFC) and Mobile Guerilla Force (MGF) in III Corps, as well as into the border forces of IV Corps. In IV Corps, 70 percent of the CIDG forces were Khmer Krom. Those not recruited into the CIDG augmented the ranks of the Khmer Serei and the Khmer Kampuchea Krom. Following its formation in the late 1950s, the Khmer Serei primarily used the Thai border area as its staging ground. After the break in relations between South Vietnam and Cambodia, the Khmer Serei aggressively reestablished itself in the Mekong Delta.[6] Robert L. Turkoly-Joczik, a lieutenant colonel in the Special Forces at the time, remarked that "although having different long-range objectives [notably the Khmer Serei desire to reunify 'Upper' and 'Lower' Cambodia], Saigon and the Khmer Serei shared sufficiently similar intermediate goals to permit them to achieve a type of symbiosis through the CIDG."[7]

By 1964 the pacification program was in full swing in South Vietnam. In the Vinh Binh province, where about one-quarter of the population was ethnic Khmer, the Vietcong had made great progress in gaining the support of the locals. An MACV advisor noted, however, that "the exception is the ethnic-Cambodians who resist the Viet Cong and generally cooperate with the government whenever possible." He also felt that "these groups needed only organization and arms to mobilize a social movement toward the government of South Vietnam." Where better to stage such a movement than in Vinh Binh, Thành's birthplace? He and the Khmer Serei were popular in the area, which, in turn, made communist infiltration most difficult.[8]

But why return to South Vietnam? For the Khmer Serei, the main draw was the material and financial support that the Diem government could offer, especially following the severance of relations between Cambodia and South Vietnam in 1963.[9] The Mekong Delta was also home to a Khmer Krom population that was estimated to be between four and six hundred thousand, which provided great potential for recruits.[10] The Khmer Serei encouraged its members to join the CIDG, as recruits were then required to donate to the movement. As

Turkoly-Joczik recalled, "When the CIDG troops were mustered for monthly pay call, it was not unusual to note the presence of the Khmer Serei cadre, who were there to collect funds for the movement."[11]

The US Special Forces found itself in a fortuitous position with the influx of organized, seasoned rebels. In October 1963, the Border Surveillance Program was incorporated into CIDG, where newly recruited Khmer Serei would monitor border outposts in III and IV Corps.[12] The mission for the Border Surveillance Program was to:

> recruit and train personnel to serve in border surveillance and control units in populated areas; establish intelligence nets in the border areas to detect infiltration; direct psychological indoctrination and civic action programs in the border control zone; gain control of the international border little by little and gradually expand small secure areas until the border zone should be permanently under the control of the Border Command; and conduct guerilla warfare—long-range patrol activities to deny the border areas to the Viet Cong by detection, interdiction, harassment, and elimination of the infiltration routes parallel to or through the border zone.[13]

III Corps, between Saigon and the Cambodian border, was ripe with potential Khmer Serei recruits. Filtered into the CIDG through the Khmer Serei headquarters in a Buddhist complex known as "the Temple" in Saigon, these troops came with skill, training, and intelligence. Often, they were recruited in company-sized blocks complete with a built-in chain of command.[14] The military organizational structure of the Khmer Serei coincided with that of the CIDG. Men were organized into battalions, companies, and platoons.[15] The Khmer Serei also had the reputation of being a very hands-on group of soldiers. As Charles M. Simpson III recounts in his history of the Green Berets, "If a company of Cambodians performed badly, a call would go back through SF [Special Forces] channels, and one of the Khmer Serei leaders would be brought out from Saigon by helicopter. He would assemble the strike force, deliver a striking rebuke, perhaps replace a commander or two, and everything would be squared away."[16] The Khmer Serei was often tasked with intelligence gathering or espionage across the Cambodian border.[17] Both the Khmer Serei and the Khmer Kampuchea Krom were involved with the Phoenix Program and targeted political assassinations. As recounted by a senior Green Beret officer, the Khmer Kampuchea Krom "would fight anybody provided there was something in it for them."[18] Those Khmer Serei who pledged allegiance to Thành and his movement were adorned with a "serrated wheel" badge, the official symbol of the Khmer Serei movement.[19]

The Khmer Serei were, in many ways, a symbol of the vitriol that existed between Cambodia and its neighbors. Sihanouk's stance toward South Vietnam following continued border incidents in May 1964 could have "prompted a tougher anti-Cambodian line" on the part of the South Vietnamese. There was evidence that South Vietnam was prepared, in the summer of 1964, to increase its support of Thành, the dissident, anti-Sihanouk rebel.[20]

There was some confusion over how to handle such issues in dealings with Sihanouk. On 30 June 1964 the assistant secretary of state for Far Eastern affairs William Bundy wrote to the director of the Office of Southeast Asian Affairs William C. Trueheart asking if, in a backchannel message to Sihanouk, "we should say anything about the Khmer Serei or any other specific problem that has haunted our relationship." In seeking clarification, he added, "whether or not we put it in the letter, I wonder where we do stand about the [Khmer Serei]." Additionally, he asked for more general information about the Khmer Serei situation.[21]

It was around this time that the Khmer Serei, in fact, had been briefly operating without Thai or South Vietnamese support. Thành revealed in an interview that while his clandestine radio stations continued to operate, he no longer received aid from the Vietnamese or, indirectly, from the Americans. Songsakd Kitchpanich, a prominent Cambodian banker, had stepped into their place. The previous December 1963 he fled Phnom Penh with over $3 million and donated a great portion of it to the Khmer Serei.[22] This situation, however, was only temporary.

According to the CIA, in mid-July 1964 the Thai prime minister Thanom Kittikachorn and South Vietnam's defense minister Trần Thiện Khiêm scheduled a meeting in Bangkok to discuss "the resumption of joint aid to Cambodian dissidents." The CIA report noted that "The rebels have maintained daily propaganda broadcasts from transmitters located in Thailand since late last year," and that "Khmer Serei elements based in South Vietnamese territory along the Cambodian border received substantial support from the Diem regime."[23]

After the Khmer Serei broadcast criticisms of Sihanouk's personal life, he almost seemed to relish in them:

This radio accuses me of having numerous mistresses, including a beautiful Chinese for whom I have sold out to the People's

Republic. It is true that from 1941 until 1952, when I was king, still young and handsome, certain pretty specimens of the feeble sex liked my company and it came about that I sinned. But I am able to swear that since 1952, the year that there was taken from me the most dear and most affectionate of my children, my personal life has been beyond reproach. . . . I back China's legitimate rights, but not because of the beautiful eyes of a Chinese girl who exists only in the stupid and morbid imagination of traitors.[24]

On 16 September 1964 the Cambodian press reported on "a U.S. plot to assassinate Prince Sihanouk, disrupt the country from within, and attack at the same time from without by forces from South Vietnam and Thailand."[25] American officials were similarly hearing talk of a potential coup. A US memo on 16 October 1964 relayed that several reports from Bangkok and Saigon indicated "the existence of an active plot supported by at least some elements of the RTG [Royal Thai Government] and GVN [Government of Vietnam] directed at overthrowing Sihanouk." The plot centered around the Khmer Serei. American officials gave it little chance for success unless it included "massive and overt Vietnamese and Thai backing." The real concern was that, if the attempt were made, it would prove to be a serious impediment to improved relations between Cambodia and its neighbors, "and could greatly complicate the South Viet Nam struggle against the Viet Cong."[26]

In the fall of 1964, Sihanouk traveled to Peking in hopes of obtaining a renewed commitment of Chinese military assistance in the event of an attack from his Thai or South Vietnamese neighbors, but he received no new public assurances of support beyond the previous, vague promises.[27] At the time, American policy toward Cambodia was "to deny the area to the [communist] Bloc, to encourage a more genuine nonalignment on the part of Sihanouk, and generally to attempt to 'get along.'" Jack Taylor, formerly of the CIA, who deemed Cambodia "always a secondary consideration in our Southeast Asian strategy," urged a "strong" approach to Cambodia, as opposed to the "soft" approach he deemed the prevailing policy. He felt that such a shift could bring either "a change in the fortunes of war in Vietnam or a sign that China cannot be counted upon to assist Cambodia to the degree which Sihanouk has assumed." If "a serious politico-military setback for Sihanouk, in which China would prove unwilling or unable to be of assistance" could be manufactured, Taylor foresaw a potential split between the two.[28]

The first step for US officials was to consult with the South Vietnamese government concerning a complete blockade of the Mekong Delta "justified on grounds of military necessity." US personnel would also be withdrawn from the embassy "to deny to Sihanouk potential hostages." The resulting economic pressure on Sihanouk would, at a minimum, force him to shift tactics, and potentially cause him to change policy. Additional recommendations included hinting that the United States would cease pressuring Thailand and South Vietnam to refrain from support for the Khmer Serei was recommended.[29]

By the end of 1964, it was clear to many in Washington that American "patience with Prince Sihanouk [was] well-nigh exhausted." Alf E. Bergesen, the chargé d'affaires ad interim, wrote that "This is a reaction which we here also feel from time to time, especially because the Prince's words are amplified and rendered even nastier by local propagandists." While showing some sympathy for Sihanouk's position, Bergesen was dismayed that "it has not been possible to make some progress on the Khmer Serei issue." The Thai, according to Bergesen, felt that "they can do as they see fit, regardless of the fact that support of the Khmer Serei is a thoroughly stupid policy which has contributed as much as any single issue to the decline of U.S./Cambodian relations." While he understood Thai apprehensions over Sihanouk's ties to the communists and Thai reluctance to certify Cambodian maps delineating the contested boundaries, Bergesen could not comprehend or find justification for "armed raids into Cambodia by Khmer Serei from Thailand as has apparently taken place during the past week." The only result, he felt, was further strains on the American relationship with Cambodia.[30]

Incongruous with Bergesen's feelings on the matter came a draft prepared by Taylor of several contingency plans for Cambodia in the event Sihanouk broke relations with the United States, recognized North Vietnam, or attacked the South—all of which Sihanouk threatened to do if further "aggression" was brought against Cambodia. Among the most severe potential actions up for consideration was the plan to inform the Cambodian government that the United States would "no longer attempt to restrain Thailand or the GVN from supporting Khmer Serei operations against Cambodian territory." The action deemed having the most "vigor" was to "encourage the GVN to recognize the Khmer Serei as a Cambodian government-in-exile." While deemed "unrealistic," such a move "would be sure to infuriate Sihanouk, and for this reason would have a certain therapeutic value for the GVN. While it would be highly undesirable for the US to associate itself with such a move, there would be no reason for our opposing such action by the GVN."[31] That Sihanouk would undoubtedly link the United States with such a move was evidently not fully considered.

On 5 February 1965 an Australian Secret Intelligence Service (ASIS) station received approval for an operation in Phnom Penh. After Sihanouk severed ties with the United States in May, an undeclared ASIS officer took over the CIA's vast network of agents. With the American mission expelled from the country, by 1966 ASIS had begun working as a proxy for the CIA in Cambodia.[32] It was around this time that Thành renewed contacts with American officials.

According to Thành, it was not until 1965, in the aftermath of the Gulf of Tonkin incident, that his Khmer Serei began to receive large-scale support from the United States.[33] It was also around this time that the Khmer Serei openly proclaimed its opposition to Sihanouk and declared war on his government. Thành remained defiant, and even at the age of fifty-seven declared that he would ultimately prevail in his longtime battle with Sihanouk.[34] That summer, Thành made contact with an American official in Saigon and made it known that he wanted to "establish a dialogue." James C. Thomson Jr. of the National Security Council (NSC) staff noted in a memo to Bundy that "State is properly skittish as this guy has the political future of Harold Stassen but drives Sihanouk crazy. We are permitting one or two more 'contacts' with him—but we may be risking a further Cambodia blow-up."[35] American officials remained wary. Thành once again stood in between Washington and Phnom Penh.

US intelligence uncovered plans for a major buildup of Khmer Serei forces on Cambodia's northwest border with designs for a large-scale attack in the winter of 1965 to 1966. Once word reached the ambassadors Graham Martin in Bangkok and Henry Cabot Lodge in Saigon, under the directive of Dean Rusk the two men strongly urged the Thai and Vietnamese governments to end the continued support of Khmer Serei activities.[36]

Lodge broached the subject of Vietnamese aid to Thành with South Vietnamese prime minister Nguyễn Cao Kỳ and urged him to suspend it. Kỳ was receptive, and responded favorably, noting that weapons could also be withheld.[37] Despite this, support continued to flow to the Khmer Serei from Saigon and Bangkok. Later that month Rusk wrote to Ambassador Martin in Thailand of his concern that "Vietnamese and Thai authorities continue to provide active support to Khmer Serei

FIGURE 5.1. So'n Ngọc Thành and his wife Nguyen Thi Tri in Phu Quoc, Vietnam, 1966. Courtesy of Vann Ung.

action against Cambodia and that a major acceleration of this activity is now imminent." Although efforts had thus far basically been rebuffed, he wanted both Martin and Lodge to continue to lobby for a cessation of support for the Cambodian rebels.[38]

While the State Department continued its attempts to diffuse the situation, the Joint Chiefs of Staff (JCS) presented a different message to the Defense Department in a 12 November 1965 memorandum. There the JCS recommended that "US policy toward Cambodia should provide for GVN/US action which will result in minimizing Cambodian support of the VC [Vietcong]." To accomplish this, a number of courses of action were recommended, including "covert paramilitary operations into Cambodia to reduce the infiltration of personnel and materiel and to collect intelligence information" and the authorization of "GVN/US operations into Cambodia in immediate pursuit of VC [Vietcong] forces."[39] The Khmer Serei were an essential element in both of these types of offensive actions.

In December 1965, non-CIDG-affiliated Khmer Serei launched a series of attacks in Cambodian territory.[40] On 31 December a Khmer Serei clandestine radio broadcast claimed responsibility for attacks on several military outposts on the frontier in Cambodia. The operations in Ratanakiri, Stung Treng, and Battambang were ostensibly done to free the country from Sihanouk's "suicidal policies."[41] Cambodian officials were quick to point to Thailand as behind the "armed aggression," where a reported eight Cambodians were killed, and eight others, including the provincial governor and military commander of Oddor Meanchey, were wounded.[42] The arrival of the new year saw much of the same, as in February 1966 there was an uptick in Khmer Serei activity, in collusion with local groups of bandits, in Battambang.[43]

On 5 January 1966 Thomson Jr. wrote that Cambodia was "more gravely threatened than ever before—by a pincer movement with MACV on Cambodia's eastern frontier and the Thai/GVN-supported Khmer Serei on the western frontier. Sihanouk is properly scared." He went on to urge a continued attempt "to get the Thai and GVN to call off their dogs—an effort in which we have been so far markedly unsuccessful." At the same time US officials considered a push for a conference on Cambodian security. The Khmer Serei continued to be a problem in the State Department's goal of a thawed relationship between the two countries.[44]

A short time later, acting secretary of state George Ball drafted a top-secret letter to the secretary of defense Robert McNamara that addressed issues of communist infiltration and use of Cambodian territory. In it he stated that "unless there is a sudden and significant increase in the use of Cambodian territory by the PAVN [People's Army of Vietnam]/Viet Cong . . . a gradual and cautious response by the U.S. Government and by certain other friendly governments is appropriate and desirable." Ball agreed that the procurement of intelligence in Cambodia had to be increased and would request that Admiral William Raborn, the CIA chief, "ask USIB [United States Intelligence Bureau] to re-examine all possible assets to determine additional programs which might be developed to enhance our intelligence capability." He noted that the JICS "envisage as being included in a stepped-up intelligence collection program . . . covert ground cross border intelligence incursions by small teams into Cambodian territory. . . . In any proposal for this type of activity, I would wish to make certain that the full consideration is given to the political problems it may raise, particularly should there be any question of the use of Vietnamese or 'Khmer Serei'

Cambodians." He concluded by stating that although current diplomatic relations between the United States and Cambodia were "unsatisfactory, . . . it would be far worse . . . if Cambodia were pushed into active belligerency against South Vietnam and against U.S. armed forces or if control authority there were to collapse into civil strife and virtual anarchy as a consequence of border incidents and pressures from such elements as the Khmer Serei movement."[45] Once again, the State Department expressed its apprehension about using the Khmer Serei.

The sacred temple of Preah Vihear, resting high on a cliff on the Thai-Cambodian border, had long been a source of tension and was often the site of skirmishes between Cambodian and Thai forces. It was again in the spring of 1966, and served as another example of how the Khmer Serei were instrumental in driving a wedge between Thailand and Cambodia. The Khmer Serei, with its bases located so close to the temple, were accused by Phnom Penh of being behind the latest attacks. According to *Réalités Cambodgiennes*, Bangkok was behind the Khmer Serei attack on Preah Vihear. The Thai foreign minister Thanat Khoman on 4 April 1966 stated that "his government has 'never accepted' the judgment of the ICJ [International Court of Justice] making Preah Vihear" part of Cambodia, which was the purported impetus behind the latest attacks.[46]

The British embassy was quite concerned with the constant Khmer Serei antagonism and Bangkok's continued support for it. As one official wrote, "The Khmer Serei movement is not a genuine part of Cambodian political life. It is an *external organization* [emphasis added] covertly supported by the Thais and South Vietnamese Governments with the object of overthrowing the Sihanouk regime. Its chief methods are subversion and terrorism." The incursions from Thailand added "an additional strain . . . on the already patchy fabric of Sihanouk's neutralist policy." If these activities were to increase, the concern was that "there might emerge a state of open if undeclared hostility between Thailand and Cambodia." This could drive Sihanouk closer to the communist camp. Fielding felt the best course of action was to take joint Western action and press Thailand to cease support.[47]

A great source of information, and propaganda, for the Cambodian government came when Khmer Serei soldiers did, from time to time, surrender to government forces. According to the Cambodian Ministry of Information, between July 1965 and June 1966, for example, forty-two Khmer Serei were reported to have rallied to the Cambodian government. Chéa San, the information minister, paraded nine Khmer

Serei at a 4 June press conference. He reported that all but one were Khmer Krom who came from Tra Vinh or Chau Doc provinces in South Vietnam. They had received military training in South Vietnam and were then flown to the Thai border. Between six and seven thousand Khmer Krom served in the South Vietnamese army at the time. Khmer Serei forces numbered between two and three thousand in South Vietnam and six hundred and one thousand in Thailand. Of the nine men featured at the press conference, none claimed to have had contacts with American officials in Thailand, yet all stated that contacts did occur while in training in South Vietnam.[48]

On 13 June 1966, McNamara approved the organizing, training, and equipping of indigenous forces for cross-border operations into Cambodia, although the State Department attempted to scuttle it. They opposed such operations because "the Cambodian minority in Vietnam is strongly influenced by the Khmer Serei movement," and "should Prince Sihanouk learn that a force of Khmers was being formed for cross-border operations into Cambodia, he would interpret this as a serious threat to his regime and be more likely than ever to cast his lot with the Chinese communists." CINCPAC, the MAACV commander William Westmoreland, and the JICS wanted the program to proceed because "Cambodians who have lived in border regions are ideal for use in this type operation due to their familiarity with the area, language, and customs of the people." It simply recommended a stringent screening process to "minimize penetration of the operation by the Khmer Serei."[49]

Despite recent diplomatic tensions, President Lyndon Johnson believed in a path forward with Sihanouk. Early in 1966 he discussed the intrigue of the prince with his NSC staff. "Everything I hear about the Prince suggests we ought to get on well with him."[50] A memo from James C. Thomson Jr. of the NSC staff classified Khmer Serei activities as having "no chance of success and run counter to our national interests, [and] can only be turned off by a Presidential directive" and that "repeated lower level protests have simply not been taken seriously by the GVN or the RTG." Thomson recommended "That you direct the Department and CIA to press the Thai and Vietnam Governments to cease all support for the Khmer Serei rebels." Johnson approved, writing "Good & Strong!" in the margins.[51] Johnson also requested proposals from his NSC staff on ways to get closer to Sihanouk.[52] In the immediate aftermath, it seemed as though the diplomatic push had finally paid off. Aside from a small-scale clash in April, reports of Khmer Serei activity dwindled precipitously.[53]

More significantly, the evidence suggests that at this point the president himself ordered Americans not to contact or support the Khmer Serei.

By summer 1966, it seemed as though American pressure had been successful. As George Ball wrote in a memo to President Johnson, referring to the new approach to Cambodia that Johnson approved the previous week, the Thais had become "disillusioned by the demonstrated ineffectiveness of the Khmer Serei and are anxious to damp down tensions in the border area." They had even reached out to the UN secretary general, requesting observers on the Thai-Cambodian border. The secretary general expressed his support, to both the Thai and Cambodians, of a mediation of the ongoing tensions, to which Sihanouk was quite agreeable.[54]

That being said, Sihanouk remained more than willing to keep the pressure on Thailand. On 15 June 1966, Sihanouk was on hand for the grand opening of a railway construction site in Kampot province, where he condemned the continued aid the Khmer Serei and Thành were giving to Thailand in undermining Cambodian independence. That same day, the minister of information Chia Xan led representatives and press of foreign nations to where a locomotive was destroyed on the Poipet-Battambang railway, just 1.5 kilometers from the Thai border. Xan claimed the area had been infiltrated fifteen times since the beginning of the year for subversive activities by so-called puppets of American imperialism.[55] While the prince was open to mediation, he was happy to highlight such activities if they kept international attention on Thai intransience.

In a 9 September 1966 press conference, Sihanouk goaded Thailand regarding its harboring of the Khmer Serei. "I have read articles in the latest issues of U.S. papers and magazines which admit that the Khmer Serei movement is now in Thailand. Everyone knows that that is an open secret. . . . If the Thai want to keep the Khmer Serei in their country, let them do so." Instead of sending small bands of Khmer Serei over the border, Sihanouk suggested "that the Thai send all the Khmer Serei to Cambodia so that everyone can know it and that we can liquidate them once and for all," and then laughed. "Since the Thai do not want to admit their patronage, let them send all the Khmer Serei here and we will know how to welcome them."[56]

Sihanouk also referred to a bulletin prepared by Lon Nol detailing a joint Thai–Khmer Serei plan to create disturbances during a visit by the French president Charles De Gaulle, including "sabotage, mining, and destruction of our works of art and lines of communications, and attacks on our posts." Four detained Khmer Serei supposedly supplied this information. Two of the men surrendered in Battambang on 24 August and made the following "voluntary statements":

> During July 1966, The Thai authorities ordered the Khmer Serei to stand ready to attack Cambodia . . . and to leave Thailand and settle themselves in Cambodia prior to the U.N. observer's arrival in Thailand. After that, the Khmer Serei would try to draw the U.N. observer's attention to their presence on Khmer territory by staging demonstrations, and would also cause disturbances during General De Gaulle's state visit to Cambodia.

According to Sihanouk's version of the men's confession, around 30 July a group of around twenty heavily armed Khmer Serei, dressed in civilian clothes, were ordered to cross the border into Battambang province and detonate several bridges.[57]

Despite the continuous harsh public rhetoric from Sihanouk, there was some hope that tensions were easing between Phnom Penh and Bangkok. The Thai deputy prime minister Praphat Charusathien continued to take a hard stance in relations between the two. While he rejected a recent Cambodian gesture in July, his tone softened in a 14 September 1966 statement to the press, where he stated that Thailand had no objections to a resumption of diplomatic relations between the two countries. Praphat remained, however, a key figure behind Thai support of the Khmer Serei. Despite friendly overtures, Sihanouk was clear that a continuation of Khmer Serei activities was a detriment to any potential compromise.[58] That being said, toward the end of 1966, Sihanouk began to position himself as a moderating figure between two political extremes. When he spoke at a Buddhist congress around this time, he characterized himself as "neither Khmer Serei or a Khmer Red. I am pure Khmer." In doing so, he framed both as enemies of the state.[59]

While Sihanouk continued his political maneuvering, Cambodians in the American Special Forces continued to make a name for themselves. In December 1966, a U-2 reconnaissance plane crashed in the dense jungles along the Cambodian–South Vietnamese border. While the pilot ejected and was rescued, the plane contained a secret "black box" that had to be recovered. Unfortunately, the exact location of the downed craft was unknown, and aerial surveillance revealed nothing. The only option was to send in men on the ground.[60]

The task fell to Captain James G. "Bo" Gritz, commander of approximately 150 Khmer CIDG troops, whom Gritz referred to as his "Bodes."

Some Green Berets also assisted. As Westmoreland recounted in his memoirs, "For close to three days Bo Gritz, his Green Beret colleagues, and his 'Bodes plowed through the jungle, cutting paths through vines and elephant grass, wading streams, following elephant trails, plodding uphill and down, trying always to maintain some kind of pattern to insure [sic] full coverage of the vast area they had to search."[61]

After three days of searching and sporadic contact with enemy forces, the plane was found, although the black box had been removed. Suspecting that the prize was still in the area, Gritz and ten Cambodians spent the next two nights attempting to capture a prisoner, who after some convincing led the men to a Vietcong camp a few miles away. The Cambodians blasted their way into the camp, secured the black box, and made a hasty escape. They were extracted by helicopter the following day, which was Christmas, with a gift for the US Air Force. This is but one example that demonstrates not just how skilled, but how trusted the Khmer CIDG soldiers were to the American war effort.[62]

Due to concerns over North Vietnamese use of Cambodian territory, in 1966 MACV requested approval to conduct cross-border operations. By June the Fifth Special Forces Group was selected to carry out these operations. According to the official Department of the Army history, the objectives "were to develop timely intelligence on North Vietnamese Army infiltration through Cambodia, the Viet Cong and North Vietnamese Army bases in Cambodia, and Cambodian support to the Viet Cong and North Vietnamese Army." One of the units involved with the project was Detachment B57, a fifty-two-man outfit.[63]

Beginning in May 1967, MACV Studies and Operations Group (or SOG, the name was given to provide cover for the covert nature of its mission) began cross-border operations into Cambodia under the name Project DANIEL BOONE, later to be known as SALEM HOUSE (in 1971 the name was changed to Thot Not). These consisted of highly classified "special unconventional warfare missions . . . throughout Cambodia." Khmer Krom and Khmer Serei soldiers selected for their capabilities in jungle warfare and intense loyalty fought alongside US Special Forces.[64] This program was created without the knowledge of Congress. Thành was ferried to the various CIDG camps by a US helicopter. According to William Colby, "He was used as a recruiter. This certainly gave him the mark of U.S. approval."[65]

At this point, it is clear that Johnson's previous directive to cease contact with the Khmer Serei seems to have been altered or was being ignored. Marshall Wright of the NSC staff wrote a memorandum to

Walt Rostow to answer the question "what to do about Cambodia?" Among his recommendations were to "make use of the anti-Sihanouk Khmer Serei elements in South Vietnam and Thailand." Although there were risks in doing so, they were "dwarfed by the disadvantages of overt military action against Cambodia," a growing concern in the administration as Vietnamese communists continued to utilize the Cambodian frontier as a sanctuary. "If a rejuvenated Khmer Serei does nothing else, it might convince Sihanouk and others in the Cambodian Government that their own interests lie in trying to minimize Cambodia's availability to the Communists as a sanctuary." Evidently the concept that US support for the Khmer Serei, which threatened to overthrow Sihanouk, may have turned Sihanouk toward the communists was not considered at this point, as it had been eighteen months prior.[66]

Years later, reports surfaced which linked Thành to involvement in a "cloak-and-dagger 1968 murder trial involving the Green Berets and clandestine U.S. commando operations into then-neutral Cambodia." The trial was that of the former captain in the Fifth Special Forces of the US Army John J. McCarthy, who was also commanding officer of Project Cherry, a top-secret Cambodian operation. According to McCarthy, Thành was a "key figure" in his court-martial in 1968, where the captain stood accused of killing a member of the Khmer Serei who also served as an interpreter.[67]

According to the records of the trial, US military officers met several members of the Khmer Serei (possibly including Thành) in Saigon at a pagoda to pay a reported $25,000 indemnity for the death of their member. Court transcripts indicated that Project Cherry was created for the purpose of cross-border incursions into Cambodia, with members of the Khmer Serei often hired as interpreters and guides. McCarthy identified the group as "an organization which in effect plans the political overthrow of the Cambodian government." According to McCarthy, his attorneys requested Thành's appearance in Long Binh, South Vietnam, for the trial, but the army responded that foreign nationals could not be compelled to testify.[68]

As later reported by the *New York Times* in 1970, according to testimony at McCarthy's trial, "The United States used a Cambodian sect dedicated to the overthrow of the legitimate government of Cambodia on covert missions into that country in 1967." The "sect" in question was the Khmer Serei, members of which were predominantly used "as interpreters and guides for intelligence and operational groups operating against Communist forces in Cambodia." Khmer Serei agents were paid by the Special Forces and other American intelligence groups. According to the *New York Times*, "detachment B57 [also known as Project Gamma], Fifth Special Forces Group, used Khmer Serai [*sic*] during a project outside South Vietnam called Operation Cherry, and then got them employment with an unidentified American intelligence agency."[69]

Although all attempts were made to keep such activities as covert as possible, reports on an American–Khmer Serei connection soon leaked out. In the summer (June or July) of 1967, the professor George McT. Kahin traveled to several Southeast Asian countries, including Cambodia, and reported to the State Department on his findings. He returned from Phnom Penh impressed with the widespread belief both inside and outside of the Cambodian government that the American government was aiding the Khmer Serei in its dissident activities. UN representatives on the ground told him the same, and rumors that the Khmer Serei had received a recent "air lift" of supplies from South Vietnam swirled in the tropical air of the capital.[70]

The assistant secretary of state William Bundy denied that the US government was assisting the Khmer Serei in any way, and that it had been "to the extent of its ability . . . using its influence to prevent the South Vietnamese and Thai Governments from supporting the movement," although some small-scale support from Saigon remained possible. Bundy assured Kahin that consistent efforts were made to convince the Cambodian government of this, but that "they choose to remain unconvinced." Kahin acknowledged that this was the prudent course to take, and he "re-emphasized the unwiseness . . . of any such support, overt or covert."[71] It is unclear if Bundy's denials were simply an attempt to hide an unseemly truth from the public or if, once again, the State Department was unclear as to the exact nature of the relationship that the Special Forces had forged.

By 3 August 1967, the Cambodian army was estimated to consist of at most thirty-five thousand men, only half of which were actual combat troops. Of those, around half were stationed along the Thai border, ostensibly in an effort to thwart Thai incursions. On the Thai side, around eight hundred Khmer Serei were stationed.[72] According to J. F. Engers, the deputy to ambassador Herbert De Ribbing, the special representative of the UN, they received an air-lift there by the CIA.[73] In Battambang it was thought that the CIA was still actively involved with and supporting the Khmer Serei ("we think so" was one response).[74]

But why would they support the Khmer Serei? According to Engers, it was a reflection of the autonomous nature of American government agencies. "The CIA and the army feel it is a good thing to let Sihanouk know by these tangible measures that the United States does not appreciate his leaning to the left internationally, and that this is designed to keep him in place. They don't like Sihanouk."[75]

Tensions along the Thai border once again continued to increase. M. K. L. Bindra, the chairman of the ICC (International Control Commission), grew distressed that the number of people killed along that Thai border now far outpaced those along the border with South Vietnam. Battambang saw the heaviest casualty rate, oftentimes victims of plastic landmines planted five to ten kilometers inside the border. The main culprit was the Khmer Serei, which consistently carried out raids inside Cambodian territory. Bindra was "absolutely sure" that Saigon was involved, but not certain of CIA participation.[76]

Tensions on the Thai border were not, however, limited to Khmer Serei incursions. Following the election of a more conservative government in 1966, Sihanouk authorized the brutal repression of a peasant uprising in Samlaut, Battambang province, the following year. For the few prominent leftists that remained in the government, it was a signal that the years of tolerance Sihanouk had displayed for them were at an end. Sihanouk would, in fact, begin to play a less prominent role in the domestic political sphere for the remainder of the decade, instead turning his attention to film and jazz.[77]

In testimony during the Khmer Rouge Tribunal, Nuon Chea blamed the suppressive treatment by Lon Nol on local peasants during the Samlaut Rebellion as the impetus for the 17 January 1968 attack on a police station in the village of Bay Damren, located north of Battambang. Chea stated that a group of volunteers made up of the children of those who had been injured or killed by Lon Nol's forces and known as the Kang Chicapol "could not stand the situation anymore" and initiated the attack. This would later be celebrated as the catalyst for the growth of Khmer Rouge armed rebellion. According to Chea, "the movement was not the result of the peasants who became vicious and barbarous; it was the result of the mistreatment by the Lon Nol (clique), and Sirik Matak, and Son Ngoc Thanh."[78] David Chandler describes the three years following the Samlaut rebellion as a period "of the left's ascendancy, the urban elite's increasing restlessness, and Sihanouk's decline."[79] The northwest frontier had long been a hotbed for anti-Sihanouk activism of varying political persuasions. While the communists slowly cultivated their base of support, the Khmer Serei, with Thai support, remained a dominant factor in relations between Bangkok and Phnom Penh.

After years of covert support, Thai officials began to reassess their tacit support of the Khmer Serei. Provincial officials had raised concerns over the number of civilian casualties that resulted from Cambodian reprisals against Khmer Serei units based in Thailand. A lack of progress on the part of the Khmer Serei was also a headache for the Thai government. Controlling certain Khmer Serei elements and working cohesively with the South Vietnam government proved to be an ongoing difficulty as well. Thai animosity toward Sihanouk remained, however, which led American intelligence to conclude that, while it was "highly unlikely that Bangkok will completely forgo its Khmer Serei operations," a reduction in support would lessen a major obstacle between the two countries, perhaps paving the way for a détente of sorts.[80]

An astute observation, to say the least, but evidently it was a step that the Thais were not ready to make. That fall, the deputy prime minister and commander in chief of the Royal Thai Army Praphat Charusathien met with Westmoreland in Washington to discuss the communist insurgency in Thailand and the Khmer Serei. According to Praphat, now was the time to extend support to the Khmer Serei, whose forces were reported to number around ten thousand and who have been looting the Cambodian army's storage facilities for arms and ammunition. Westmoreland did not respond to his proposal but mentioned that Praphat had also broached the topic with the admiral John McCain.[81] Bangkok was poised to continue its support of the Khmer Serei through to the end. The ultimate goal of ousting Sihanouk, Thành's longstanding ambition, was the next step. Achieving success, however, would require more than just help from Sihanouk's neighboring enemies.

As is often the case when American intelligence services were allegedly involved in matters of a conspiratorial nature, the search for the true nature of American involvement in the coup that ousted Sihanouk on 18 March 1970 and brought Lon Nol to power leaves many unanswered questions. Dissecting the history of the overthrow of Sihanouk remains a difficult task. Historians such as David Chandler and Ben Kiernan and the reporters William Shawcross and T. D. Allman have all contributed mightily to this effort. What is clear is that, at a minimum, the United States was aware that a coup attempt was in the works and failed to inform Sihanouk, much as with the Dap Chhuon affair a decade prior. It is also clear that Lon Nol, Matak, and Thành were convinced that the United States supported their efforts, and the Thành-led Khmer

Serei played a significant role in not only the coup itself, but in securing the status of the new government in the months afterward. What follows is a reassessment of events and examination of the possible roles that the United States played in the overthrow of Norodom Sihanouk on 18 March 1970.

Many who have looked into the events that resulted in the expulsion of Sihanouk from power have concluded that it is likely that the United States, to some degree, was involved. That being said, hard, concrete evidence is hard to come by. According to Ben Kiernan, "There is in fact no evidence of CIA involvement in the 1970 events, but a good deal of evidence points to a role played by sections of the US military intelligence establishment and the Army Special Forces."[82] Milton Osborne largely agrees with Kiernan's assessment. While he dismisses any role for the CIA in the removal of Sihanouk, "the involvement of some American intelligence services is now beyond dispute."[83] Similarly, according to Shawcross, "no direct link between the United States government and Sihanouk's usurpers before the coup has been established." That being said, United States interests "coincided with and supported those who plotted against the Prince inside the country." Additionally, "there was ample American motive for Sihanouk's removal, and if the administration was . . . surprised by the coup, then its most senior members cannot have been reading their own intelligence reports."[84] Chandler mostly attributes the overthrow of Sihanouk to internal political considerations, although he does hint at a possible CIA connection with Matak.[85] Wilfred Deac declares that while the Americans did not plan the coup, the United States did have foreknowledge of the event and that there was some "unofficial encouragement by U.S. personnel."[86] Kenneth Conboy, who has written the most recent volume on American involvement in Cambodia, is largely skeptical. Conboy states that while it is likely American officials knew a coup was coming, "to say that the United States was pulling the strings was almost certainly not the case." With respect to the Khmer Serei, he claims that "there is no compelling evidence that the CIA, or any other part of the U.S. government, provided its own direct paramilitary assistance" to the group.[87]

At the time American officials denied any US involvement. Richard Nixon, in his memoirs, refers to Sihanouk's ouster as "an unexpected event . . . Lon Nol's coup came as a complete surprise. The CIA had received no indication that the opposition to Sihanouk had gone so far." Nixon claims he impatiently queried Bill Rogers, "What the hell do those clowns do out there in Langley?"[88]

Kissinger, in his memoirs, claims that the CIA, in fact, did not even have any agents stationed in the country following the resumption of diplomatic relations in 1969, "largely at Senator Mansfield's insistence." American intelligence was not focused on Cambodia, he claims, with attention being paid to China, Laos, and Vietnam instead. Sihanouk's precarious neutrality "was the best attainable situation" for America, and his ouster was a surprise.[89] However, in January 1977, two years before his memoirs were published, Kissinger told a group of European journalists that the United States was not involved with the coup, "at least not at the top level."[90]

William Bundy largely agrees with Kissinger's published denials, although he admits that "U.S. behavior had made Lon Nol and his associates confident that they would have U.S. support if they took power." A major factor in this was America's connection to Thành, who received "substantial CIA help" to train and organize Khmer Krom soldiers. According to Bundy, "There is no persuasive evidence that the CIA encouraged him to act against Sihanouk in 1970, but the fact that a tie persisted could hardly have failed to impress Lon Nol and political circles in Phnom Penh."[91]

Roger Morris, a senior staff member on the NSC, stated that "There is no conclusive evidence that the CIA or other U.S. intelligence agencies from the Pentagon instigated the coup," although "it was clear in the White House that the CIA station in Phnom Penh [a contradiction to Kissinger's claim that there was no CIA presence at the time] knew the plotters well, probably knew their plans, and did nothing to alert Sihanouk." They also "informed Washington well in advance of the coup, and joined the chorus from the U.S. military in Saigon and from the Pentagon urging immediate aid and political patronage for the new government."[92]

Aside from these official denials, there is a dearth of insider accounts from American sources related to coup plotting. One of the most complete came thanks to Kissinger, who wrote a scathing letter to the editor of *The Economist* to rebut several of William Shawcross's assertions in *Sideshow*. In this letter Kissinger stoutly denied any US involvement in overthrowing Sihanouk's government. Samuel R. Thornton, a naval intelligence yeoman who served in Vietnam from late 1968 to mid-1969, wrote a letter to the editor to *The Economist* in response to Kissinger. *The Economist* chose not to publish this important letter, which is possibly the only internal accounting of American involvement in the plot to take down Sihanouk. The following information comes from Thornton's letter.[93]

In late 1968 an American intelligence agent, a Khmer Krom who traveled frequently between Phnom Penh and Saigon, relayed a request from "a high official of the Sihanouk government" to his case officer, an undercover US intelligence officer. Thornton claims he was the first person to speak with the case officer after he debriefed the agent. The case officer stated that a request had been made from this powerful Cambodian official "for an indication of possible U. S. reaction to a call for military assistance by leaders of a coup against Prince Sihanouk in which General Lon Nol was to be the principal."[94]

After validating the request, "a special intelligence operations proposal was developed to support the coup," a plan that would eventually be codenamed "Sunshine Park."[95] Thornton was present at the discussions that followed, and helped draft the group's proposal. The initial plan was to insert an American-trained assassination squad, disguised as Vietcong insurgents, into the Cambodian capital to kill the prince "as a pretext for revolution and a request for use of Khmer Krom mercenaries . . . to infiltrate key Cambodian Army units stationed in Phnom Penh in order to support the first stages of the coup." After the assassination, Lon Nol was to declare a state of emergency and request US intervention "to preserve order in the country." This would include assaults on suspected communist sanctuaries inside Cambodia. Thornton personally delivered the portion of the proposal to use Khmer Krom mercenaries to the action officer of MACV intelligence. By late November or early December the proposal was submitted in full to the NSC, and by the following March "blanket approval to take any and all measure to implement the proposal was received" from the NSC, with "the highest level of government" expressing great interest. This was interpreted to mean that "the President or one of his top advisors had given personal approval to the plan."[96]

With authorization complete, the intelligence agent went to Phnom Penh to brief his contact and Lon Nol. Once Lon Nol was informed that the plan called for assassination, however, he voiced his objections. "He doubted that either he or the U. S. Army would be able to control the popular uprising he felt would develop from an attempt to assassinate the Prince, successful or otherwise, and denounced the idea in strong language."[97]

Lon Nol offered a counterproposal to lead a coup when Sihanouk was in France on one of his periodic rest cures. Lon Nol felt that "by confronting the Prince with a fait accompli when he was cut off from direct access to his resources they could discourage him from attempting to mount a counter-coup, to then a very real and frightening possibility." After the counterproposal was relayed to the NSC, "the response was surprisingly cool considering the original carte blanche authorization." Officially, Lon Nol was to be informed that "while the U. S. would support in principle the accession to power of a Phnom Penh regime more sympathetic to U. S. interests in the region, the U. S. would have to base a decision for commitment of U. S. forces in support of such a regime on the circumstances which obtained at the time the new regime came to power." Unofficially, word was sent that "although he could in fact expect the requested support, he must understand that the U. S. was sensitive to international criticism on this point, so that he must be prepared for a show of vacillation and great reluctance on our part to his initial, public requests for military assistance."[98]

Lon Nol was eager to move forward with the plan, and expressed a great interest in meeting with Thành to discuss the possibility of using Khmer Krom troops to infiltrate the army. Shortly thereafter the two met just inside the Cambodian border and reached an agreement to begin the infiltration process soon thereafter. Over the next several months this process was accomplished with little complication. In 1971, Thành confirmed that Lon Nol had requested, through him, American assurances that Khmer Krom soldiers would be sent to Cambodia to support an overthrow of Sihanouk. According to Thành, the CIA approved this measure.[99] In Thành's words, he had his men stationed "along the border before Sihanouk was overthrown. He knew he would fall. I had contact in advance with Lon Nol and [his] younger brother, Col. Lon Non." Thành's Khmer Serei forces crossed the border and engaged Vietnamese Communists almost immediately following Sihanouk's overthrow.[100]

Although Thornton was no longer in a position to have direct access to intelligence by the time the coup arose, after seeing how events unfolded and how closely they corresponded to the planning, he had no doubt about American involvement. While it is not possible to definitively substantiate Thornton's claims, much of his story can be corroborated.

As we have seen throughout this history, the removal of Sihanouk from power in Cambodia was consistently in play in various American governmental circles. This incarnation, which eventually succeeded, has roots as far back as the mid-1960s. Prom Thos, a senior minister in both Sihanouk's and Lon Nol's governments, claimed in an interview that Long Boret informed him that he was approached in 1965 by an unnamed CIA agent about overthrowing the prince. Long Boret then approached Lon Nol to request his aid in the operation. Lon Nol played coy, but told Long Boret to "maintain his contact with the agent."[101]

Perhaps with the prospect of overthrowing Sihanouk on his mind, Lon Nol himself was in touch with Indonesian army officers as early as 1967 and continued these contacts thereafter. Cambodians also frequented the Indonesian embassy, which led to speculation by the ambassador Boediardjo that Cambodian officers saw the Indonesian example of Sukarno's removal as one to possibly emulate.[102] It was later revealed at a US House of Representatives hearing that 360 Cambodians received training in Indonesia during this period.[103]

Allman asserts that Lon Nol began plotting to overthrow Sihanouk in early 1969. According to Allman, "what made the plotting all the more dangerous was that Lon Nol and his associates appreciated that they could achieve power only at the risk of plunging their country into full-scale war." Lon Nol in fact requested American arms and money in early 1969.[104] A senior minister (Prom Thos) for both Sihanouk and Lon Nol confirmed this, stating that the plans to overthrow Sihanouk began "a year before" the 18 March 1970 coup. At that time, Matak was insistent on assassination being the path forward, but Lon Nol was against it.[105]

Thành confirmed this timeline as well. According to Thành, his plans for an invasion of Cambodia began in 1969. He hoped to exploit the growing anti-Sihanouk fervor in the capital. "The plan was to penetrate the country from the South Vietnamese border and the Dangkrek mountains" along the Thai border in a two-pronged attack. "Our hope was that the Cambodian Army would rally to us. We would then negotiate with Sihanouk, to avoid bloodshed. He could either leave the country, or agree to become a constitutional monarch." The plan was "overtaken by events" and abandoned, but contacts with American intelligence continued throughout the end of the year and into 1970.[106]

During this period, the use of Khmer Serei mercenaries in Cambodia dramatically increased. Green Beret teams infiltrated Cambodia fewer than four hundred times in 1967 to 1968. In 1969 to 1970 that number ballooned to over one thousand. Khmer Serei were often involved in the most sensitive of these missions, despite the fact that this countered official US policy prohibiting the use of ethnic Khmer inside Cambodia.[107] Luke Thompson was a member of a mobile strike force that conducted search and destroy missions on the Cambodian border. According to Thompson, the Green Berets commanded three battalions of mercenary troops, the majority of whom were Cambodians.

"We were in and out of Cambodia all the time," Thompson recalled. The raids, which began on a small scale in 1967, grew in force and number over time.[108]

It was also around this time that Thành's foot soldiers began to infiltrate the government. On 5 January 1969, Sihanouk granted amnesty to any Khmer Serei soldier that rallied to the government. According to Thành, two hundred Khmer Serei solders crossed over the border from Thailand shortly thereafter to "surrender" to the Royal Army. On 12 June, several hundred more Khmer Serei did the same, and were quickly incorporated into the army. These men, natives of both Thailand and South Vietnam, ostensibly served as the conduit for CIA infiltration.[109] Osborne, Chandler, Turkoly-Joczik, Justin Corfield, and Shawcross have all given at least some credence to this "Trojan horse" theory of infiltration.[110]

The prominent Khmer Krom leader Kim Khet recounted his role in the infiltration of Phnom Penh to the anthropologist Gerald C. Hickey over Bloody Marys at Hotel Le Royal in the summer of 1970. As recalled by Hickey, Khet "hoodwinked Sihanouk into thinking he was a hopeless playboy by frequenting nightclubs . . . while he secretly was organizing the Khmer Krom."[111]

According to Thành there was a CIA agent attached to his staff whom he identified only as "Fred." By mid-1969 the US government, through this agent, indicated its support for anti-Sihanouk operations, including an invasion of Cambodia led by Thành-loyal units. The goal was to rally the Royal Khmer Armed Forces to their side, to which, according to "Fred," the United States would support such an operation with eight battalions. This specific plot, obviously, was never carried out.[112]

It should also be remembered that this period corresponds with the introduction of Operation Menu by the new Nixon administration. This extended series of covert bombings had the goal of destroying communist sanctuaries in Cambodia. The result, however, was to push the Vietcong deeper into Cambodia, where they came into frequent conflict with Cambodian troops.[113]

One of Kissinger's claims as proof that the CIA could not have been involved with the coup was the fact that a CIA station had not been reestablished in Phnom Penh following the resumption of diplomatic relations. While possibly true on its face, a Cambodian reports division was actually run out of the American embassy in the South Vietnamese capital. Frank Snepp, a strategic analyst for the CIA in Saigon, confirmed that CIA operations in Cambodia emanated from Saigon.[114]

Snepp claims that both the CIA and MACV supported replacing Sihanouk with Lon Nol. According to Snepp, the thought at the time was that Lon Nol "would welcome the United States with open arms and we would accomplish everything." There was also much "speculation amongst my colleagues that we were cultivating Son Ngoc Thanh as a possible replacement for Sihanouk. At the beginning of 1970 we were encouraging both him and Lon Nol."[115]

The Cambodian National Office of Mutual Aid was closed in January, which, according to Chandler, had long been "a conduit for Sihanouk's largesse." It was here that funds from casino profits, receipts from screenings of Sihanouk's films, and "voluntary" government employee contributions were turned around and distributed to victims of US bombing, gifted to monasteries, and other various handouts. Ostensibly closed due to a lack of funds, it was in actuality an attempt to lessen the influence of Sihanouk.[116]

As predicted, Sihanouk scheduled a respite in southern France for early 1970. Before his departure, Sihanouk briefly stayed at the Calmette Hospital in Phnom Penh. While there, machine guns and ammunition were reportedly found hidden in the hospital basement, ostensibly in support of an assassination or coup attempt.[117]

Later that month, Lon Nol traveled to France to meet with Sihanouk to discuss policies toward Vietnamese in Cambodia. Many in Phnom Penh were under the impression that the two had come to an agreement on the harsh anti-Vietnamese policy that began as soon as Lon Nol returned to Cambodia. His first move was to recall all five hundred riel notes. This was theoretically done to stamp out counterfeit bills, but in reality it denied National Liberation Front agents and North Vietnamese fighters the notes they used to purchase supplies in Cambodia.[118]

According to Thai intelligence officer Chana Samudavanija, Matak informed Thành on 26 or 27 January that there would be a coup against Sihanouk.[119] Chandler suggests Matak likely approached Thành with the approval of Sihanouk. According to this theory, Sihanouk's concerns about a widening war into Cambodia had him finally willing to stand up to communist infiltration of Cambodia's eastern border region, and he felt Thành's highly trained forces would serve as a deterrent to further encroachment. Because Lon Nol and Thành historically had a prickly relationship filled with suspicion for one another, Sihanouk did not think a collaboration of any sorts likely. In this, he was badly mistaken.[120] But after nearly twenty years of antagonism, could Sihanouk been so naïve as to believe that Thành would suddenly abandon his goals and ally himself with the man he had made his life goal to remove from power?

According to Thành, when Sihanouk left for France in January 1970, those close to Lon Nol and Matak considered ousting the prince, but remained wary of communist Vietnamese reprisal. In February, officials close to Lon Nol and Matak traveled to Thành's headquarters in South Vietnam to request support from Khmer Krom troops in case of a "Tet-style" communist attack on the Cambodian capital. Again, according to Thành, he gave assurances of support, but only after checking "with [his] American friends," who pledged to do "everything possible" in the event of such an attack. Thành relayed American assurances to Lon Nol in Phnom Penh. By the end of the month, Thành's headquarters was swarming with several American agents and upwards of a dozen Cambodian Army officers, all apparently working together and sharing information in preparation for a potential attack on Phnom Penh. It was also around this time that a meeting between Lon Nol and Thành was scheduled for somewhere along the South Vietnam–Cambodian border. Although the face-to-face meeting never took place (it is unclear why), the course was clearly set.[121] According to Thành, the process of incorporating approximately two thousand Khmer Serei into the capital police and the army was completed by this time.[122]

On 8 March, demonstrations against the presence of North Vietnamese troops on Cambodian soil broke out in several places near the Cambodian–South Vietnamese border. The demonstrations continued for two days. On 11 March, "the North Vietnamese and Provisional Revolutionary Government Embassies in Phnom Penh were sacked by a group of demonstrators." Like the protests of days earlier, the attacks against the embassies were reported to be "organized by those who [replaced Sihanouk as] head [of] the Cambodian Government."[123] There were also reports that the ten thousand demonstrators were led by solders in civilian dress, reportedly members of the Khmer Serei.[124] It is quite clear that Khmer Kampuchea Krom troops were instrumental in organizing the sacking of the Provisional Revolutionary Government and North Vietnamese embassies.[125] According to Prom Thos, Sihanouk had no involvement in orchestrating the anti-Vietnamese protests, but for them to proceed smoothly word was leaked out that the prince was, in fact, behind them.[126]

On 12 March, Lon Nol ordered all NLF and North Vietnamese troops off Cambodian soil by dawn, 15 March. It was an unrealistic demand, to say the least, and was intended as so. When the ultimatum period passed without a response, Lon Nol had the impetus to move forward.[127] When the deadline day arrived that Sunday, Cambodian forces moved against an NLF battalion in an attempt to push the NLF contingent over the border into South Vietnam. ARVN (Army of the Republic of Vietnam) artillery fire was called in to augment the attack. According to American officials, it was the first time that South Vietnam and Cambodia had openly worked together in such a manner.[128]

The *Bangkok Post* reported on 30 September 1971 that "Lon Nol, Sirik Matik [*sic*], and important members of the Cambodian high command and the Cambodian parliament" began the planning for Sihanouk's overthrow "by force of arms and assassinat[ion], if necessary" as early as six months before the eventual ouster of the prince. These same figures organized the supposed "spontaneous" 11 March demonstrations against the Vietcong. According to the *Post*, a second demonstration on 16 March failed to gain popular support and was broken up by Sihanouk loyalists, which delayed the coup by forty-eight hours.[129] Sihanouk, for his part, delayed his return to Phnom Penh, rerouting through Moscow and Beijing in an attempt to persuade the Soviet and Chinese governments to pressure Hanoi to stem its infiltration of Cambodian territory.

In an interview in 1973, Thành stated that the CIA fully endorsed and supported the overthrow of Sihanouk, although Thành added that "even if the CIA had not helped, the (national assembly) deputies would have overthrown Sihanouk anyway. . . . It would have materialized in another way."[130] According to Allman, "the CIA role appear[ed to be] not that of an organization stage-managing a coup, but of one assuring those who were already strongly in favor of a coup that U.S. aid would be available to save them from the consequences." If this is to be believed, the promise of American support may well have been the deciding factor in swaying Matak and Lon Nol to go ahead with their plan.[131]

While Lon Nol and those close to him never commented on the assumption of American support for the ouster of Sihanouk, what directly followed, as Allman astutely writes, was that "a total of ten Khmer Krom battalions, raised by Son Ngoc Thanh and equipped and paid by the U.S. government, were moved from South Vietnam to positions guarding Phnom Penh. In the darkest days of the war, these troops, camped in the Phnom Penh Olympic Stadium and encircling the capital, were the only viable forces protecting the Lon Nol regime from the North Vietnamese Army."[132]

According to E. W. Pfeiffer, these soldiers were paid in Cambodian currency even though their homes and families were in South Vietnam. US embassy officials noted that this caused some trouble. Nevertheless, these men, in addition to the Khmer Serei that "rallied" to the government earlier, served as a main line of defense for Lon Nol in the days following the coup.[133]

Additional corroboration of American involvement in the coup, or at minimum foreknowledge of it, comes from Forrest B. Lindley, a Green Beret captain in charge of a Special Forces team that often crossed the border into Cambodia. According to him, "In February of 1970 I was told that there would be a change of government in Cambodia. My radio operator, an enlisted man, actually told me. He got it from the Special Forces B team [a higher command]; they told him that Sihanouk was taking off for France. The radio operator also told me that the Khmer Serei would be going into Cambodia." Soon thereafter he was ordered to transfer two companies from under his command to replace Khmer Serei units that were sent to Cambodia. According to Lindley, "The policy was not to use Cambodians there because of the political ramifications of the United States supporting mercenary troops against their own government. This was a policy change."[134]

A few weeks after Lon Nol took over, the Green Beret officer Randolph Harrison was shown several photographs of mutilated and beheaded Cambodian communists. Standing and smiling next to their victims were Khmer Serei soldiers. "I knew those guys," Harrison recalled. "They'd been in my Special Forces Unit."[135] According to Thành, "We moved four battalions to Phnom Penh in April 1970, and a total of ten into Cambodia by the end of July."[136] By July 1970, Khmer CIDG were at the frontlines of battle, especially southeast of the capital.[137]

It was during this same period that Thành formally announced that the Khmer Serei, as it was known, would cease to exist. The old warrior pledged his allegiance to the new Lon Nol government.[138] Thus marked the dramatic end of the Sihanouk reign in Cambodia. The prince would not see Cambodia until 1975. When he did eventually return after five years under the Khmer Republic it would be a very different place.

As with much surrounding Thành's history, definitive conclusions are hard to come by. The case of the coup that unseated Sihanouk is no different. While much remains to be uncovered with respect to the coup in March 1970, what is abundantly clear is that Thành and the Khmer Serei were involved. He clearly had contacts with Lon Nol and other coup plotters beforehand. The period before Sihanouk's overthrow saw many of Thành's supporters defect ostensibly to rejoin the prince. There is much evidence that supports the theory that they were, in fact, planted in support of the eventual coup. Prom Thos, for one, has insisted that Thành had no involvement in the coup plotting and that he, in search of the spotlight that had for so long avoided him, simply took credit where none was due.[139] While Thành certainly had a thirst for a return to power and long festering hatred of Sihanouk, there is simply too much corroborating evidence to discount Thành's role in the coup outright.

The role of the Americans in the coup is even murkier. A great deal of circumstantial evidence supports an American role in the events that lead to Sihanouk's downfall. On 2 April, the *Far Eastern Economic Review* published a cartoon that captured the assumptions of many that not only was the CIA involved in Sihanouk's overthrow, but that it would be a boon to the communist war efforts.[140]

There is some evidence that points to a direct American involvement. American officials undoubtedly knew about coup plotting ahead of time and failed to alert Sihanouk. Thành, for one, said as much. The Thornton letter, as discussed earlier, while not completely ignored previously (Hersh, Allman, and Kahin all make fine use of it), certainly points to a deeper US involvement than most scholars have credited. This, along with the combination of essential materials from the Allman and Kahin archives with materials found in Cambodia and the National Archives have resulted in the most complete and current account of American involvement with the coup that unseated Sihanouk and augments much of the existing historiography on the subject. Whatever the level of US involvement, American officials welcomed the overthrow of Sihanouk and transfer of power to a more American-friendly government. As H. R. Haldeman put it in his diary, the coup was "all right with us."[141]

CHAPTER 6

Always an Outsider, 1970–1972

With the prince's ouster and Lon Nol's ascension to power in Phnom Penh, Sơn Ngọc Thành's years of clandestine subversion against Norodom Sihanouk came to an end. In the years that followed, Thành tepidly reentered the government he had been removed from a generation prior, where he had hoped to play a large role in the creation and maintenance of a republican government. But just as he has been overlooked for years by historians of modern Cambodia, so too was he overlooked by the new rulers of Cambodia. Thành would instead continue to recruit Khmer Krom into the Cambodian army, and Lon Nol attempted to placate him by appointing him an advisor the government. Due to his continued popularity among some segments of society, combined with a dearth of other willing candidates, Thành would later briefly find himself serving as the prime minister, although Lon Nol had successfully neutered that position. This chapter will analyze the fits and starts of a Cambodia without Sihanouk, the figurehead of the nation for the previous thirty years. These years are notable for the intensification of US intervention in Cambodia and for Thành's ambitious attempts to insert himself into the political process, a status he felt he deserved at minimum for his years of service against Sihanouk.

Thành's final stage of his career has not been examined in any depth. Justin Corfield has written the most extensive account of the Khmer Republic in *Khmers Stand Up!*, but even his account has Thành relegated to the periphery. To fully grasp the significance of the divergent political streams concurring in Phnom Penh during this time, the role of Thành and his loyal followers must be given full consideration. Although successfully marginalized by Lon Nol during this period, Thành remained an important political figure in Cambodia until his retirement in 1972.

The nonviolent overthrow of Sihanouk quickly led to a battle of the airwaves for the hearts and minds of the Cambodian populace. On 22 March 1970 Radio Phnom Penh announced that Lon Nol had barred the ousted prince from returning to Cambodia, as well as his wife and children. The following day Sihanouk announced from Peking the formation of a "national union government" and dissolution of the Lon Nol cabinet, Cheng Heng's National Assembly, and Ong Sim's Crown Council. He also announced plans to organize a "national liberation army." In Phnom Penh, word spread that Lon Nol's plan was to quickly declare the new government a republic to preemptively thwart any moves that Sihanouk might make to return to power.[1] Shortly thereafter, a radio station claiming to be the Voice of the National United Front of Kampuchea began broadcasting. This was the organization Sihanouk formed while in exile in Peking to rally opposition to Lon Nol's assentation to power. In actuality it was a CIA-operated station based out of southern Laos. On the surface, broadcasts appeared to support Sihanouk's Peking-based government in exile. In actuality, broadcasts fed listeners with information intended to hurt the communist effort.[2]

The journalist T. D. Allman reported in the *Far Eastern Economic Review* on the divergent voices of Cambodian opinion in the aftermath of Sihanouk's overthrow. According to Allman, "the common people continued to revere Sihanouk, but it was an unending insult for any Cambodian of education and ambition to have to kowtow constantly to the egotistical, but always brilliant leader Sihanouk had proved himself to be." Speaking to Allman, one worker stated, "Sihanouk is our hero. I cannot judge the new leaders because I do not know what is in their hearts." A young, educated, wealthy Cambodian had a different take: "We were bored with him and humiliated by him. His damn film shows and endless radio speeches in that sing-song voice. If he tries to come back I hope they shoot him at the airport." Opinions such as this were, according to Allman, a minority voice in Cambodia, but it was this very minority that toppled the modern-day god-king.[3]

In a telling, albeit simplistic, piece of prescience, Allman concluded with the following analysis:

> The irony of course is that it is Sihanouk's hold on the country-side and the peasants which have made insurrection in Cambodia impossible. The new rulers, as they busy themselves taking back in power and financial opportunities what Sihanouk took away from them, doubtlessly will have a much harder time retaining the loyalty of the countryside—where all real Asian revolutions begin and are won.
>
> By biting off the hand which fed them, the tiny group of aristocrats, army officers and businessmen which toppled Sihanouk may have insured its own doom.[4]

On 28 March, in an early test of the new Cambodian government, three thousand Vietcong troops crossed the border in the Prey Veng province. Cambodian troops were quickly dispatched to confront them.[5] South Vietnam's crusades over the border continued as well. Despite claims by the American administration that cross-border raids into Cambodian territory by the South Vietnamese army had been "discouraged" and were considered "inadvisable," such raids commenced within days of the coup. The secretary of state William P. Rogers said as much during an appearance before an executive session of the Foreign Relations Committee on 2 April. According to a staff report prepared for that same committee, such contentions were nothing but lip service. The report stated that it appeared "that the United States and South Vietnamese military regarded Sihanouk's fall as an 'opportunity' to strike at enemy sanctuaries along the border. In fact, many U.S. military officers in Vietnam used this exact word and said that had it not been for the sanctuaries the war would have been over long ago."[6]

A Saigon newspaper reported that the Khmer Serei were prepared to return to Phnom Penh, that Thành would assume the post of minister of state, and that his collaborators would occupy positions "in the heart of government." The Cambodian Department of Information responded that while it had issued a general appeal to invite all Khmer who had gone underground to return to Phnom Penh and support the new government, it had not had any contact with Thành or his collaborators, and it had no interest in their activities.[7] As much as Thành would have hoped for this to be true, this false statement was likely an effort on the part of the new Phnom Penh government to quell the persistent rumors of US involvement in the Sihanouk overthrow. In actuality, Thành's cohorts had already reestablished themselves in the capital. It is clear that both the American and Cambodian administrations considered the Khmer Serei units as essential in the nascent days of the government.

The first noted discovery of the Khmer Civilian Irregular Defense Group (CIDG) soldiers in Phnom Penh was "by a correspondent who had spent years in Vietnam. This correspondent noticed a Cambodian strolling through the center of the city wearing what appeared to be an American uniform. When asked, in English, if he was from Vietnam, the soldier replied, 'I am not authorized to speak to the press, sir.' With "little difficulty," the correspondent concluded that from the language used in his replies to questions that the soldier "had worked closely with American forces." A second correspondent reported speaking with a Khmer soldier who told him he had been in Phnom Penh since March.[8] It would not be long before the Khmer Serei would be a significant presence in Phnom Penh.

Back on 23 March 1970, the retired Australian army officer brigadier F. P. Serong, a specialist in the studies of insurgencies, wrote a memo detailing the situation in Cambodia along with recommendations for government of Vietnam assistance to the new Phnom Penh government. Among other suggestions was a recommendation to send three thousand Khmer Serei from the Vietnam delta to help secure the port at Sihanoukville. Henry Kissinger forwarded the memo to Richard Nixon on 9 April, to which Nixon responded, "These may be way out ideas. But they do show some imagination." He instructed the State Department, Department of Defense, and CIA to follow up with additional suggestions.[9]

Those recommendations would soon follow. On 18 April 1970, in a telegram to the chairman of the Joint Chiefs of Staff (JCS) Earle Wheeler, Creighton Abrams stated that there were currently 3,500 Khmer Serei serving in CIDG camps near the border. Abrams felt that most of them would respond if Cambodia made a specific request for assistance, although the government of South Vietnam might express opposition to losing such a highly trained group of soldiers.[10] On 20 April 1970, Lon Nol made just such a request, asking for the Khmer Krom to initiate cross-border attacks from Vietnam.[11] According to a staff report prepared for the Senate Foreign Relations Committee, the request came following consecutive days of the Army of the Republic of Vietnam (ARVN) penetrating into Cambodia. Lon Nol requested "in a personal letter to President Nixon, for U.S. arms and for the assistance of Khmer CIDG forces—ethnic Cambodians, native to South Vietnam, who had been serving in Civilian Irregular Defense Group teams with U.S. Special Forces in Vietnam."[12]

On 21 April 1970, the now chief of staff of the US army William Westmoreland wrote a memo to the secretary of defense Melvin Laird outlining a plan to utilize those Khmer Serei members of CIDG who were currently serving in camps adjacent to the Cambodian border. "My initial thought," Westmoreland wrote," is that they can best be utilized in raids across the border . . . which can be logistically supported by U.S. forces and, in which we can provide appropriate Vietnamese or U.S. Special Forces Advisors."[13] The following day, Nixon approved the transport of Khmer Serei in CIDG from South Vietnam to Phnom Penh "as soon as possible."[14]

Desperate for recruits, the Cambodian army welcomed these stealth recruits from Saigon. Some nights the Pochentong airport in Phnom Penh would suddenly close while troops were shipped in. One night in early May a few thousand trained Khmer Krom quietly made the short flight from Saigon. Formerly exiled Khmer Serei volunteers were also now returning to Phnom Penh. Anxious over the gloomy outlook with respect to the war against the Khmer Rouge, the government also obtained recruits through compulsory military training for all government employees and students. Men and women alike spent the mornings at work dressed in fatigues, with the rest of the day spent training. According to some sources, these young men were sometimes sent to the front lines after a mere two days of training.[15]

Despite the lack of training, there were some early successes. By 8 May, the new Cambodian government had received a reported six thousand captured AK-47s, 7,200 M-2 carbines, and ammunition. According to President Nguyễn Văn Thiệu, four thousand Khmer CIDG soldiers were sent from South Vietnam to Phnom Penh, "many, if not most, of whom had been serving as mercenaries under contract with U.S. Special Forces."[16] Thiệu spoke about the situation in Cambodia on 12 May 1970, stating "faced with the present situation, we must be clearsighted because we are in the process of gaining a friendly neighboring country to our side in order to move towards [the realization] of an anti-communist alliance."[17]

The New York Times reported on 27 May 1970 that American soldiers continued to recruit ethnic Cambodians living in the Mekong Delta for battle across the border in Cambodia. Colonel Richard W. Ellison, a senior advisor in the Vin Binh province in Vietnam, confirmed that

American Special Forces, along with "a head of the Khmer Serai [sic]" Thành, had recruited 230 Cambodians the previous week, who were soon thereafter "shipped out." Two hundred out of the 230 were members of the Khmer Serei. This was part of a larger effort, at the behest of the government in Phnom Penh, to recruit upwards of six hundred thousand ethnic Khmer in South Vietnam for service in the Cambodian military.[18]

The Cambodian information minister stated that while the initial goal was to increase the ranks of the army by ten thousand men, it had in fact absorbed some fifty thousand new recruits. This exacerbated economic issues for the government, but the need for experienced soldiers was paramount. While each new enlisted private, for instance, was to be paid a monthly salary of 1,750 riels, or about $32, elite Khmer Krom units, those imported from South Vietnam, demanded the same salary they previously had received from the Americans, about four thousand riels, or $73, for privates.[19]

Although elite, the Khmer Krom had a reputation for ruthlessness. One Khmer Krom mercenary stated, "You know, the KKK love to eat the flesh of the Vietnamese. Especially the liver. The liver, that's the best."[20] Bizarre as statements such as these were, the KKK's reputation was well earned. Robert L. Turkoly-Joczik, who commanded a battalion of thirteen camps in IV corps near the Cambodian border, heard of such gruesome tales from the Khmer members of the CIDG under his command.[21] Overnight on 6–7 June, rifle fire and mortars erupted in Phnom Penh. Khmer Krom soldiers, of which two battalions had been quietly smuggled into the city without the knowledge of local officials, hit up the local bars, and then proceeded to "hunt out Viet Cong whom they suspected were present in [the] city." Students and untrained troops in the city "opened fire on these strange and unknown troops" wandering the streets of Phnom Penh. Initial estimates of casualties were three dead and six wounded.[22]

On 8 June 1970 South Vietnam's foreign minister Charles Trần Văn Lắm relayed to American officials details of the recent South Vietnamese delegation, headed by Vice President Nguyễn Cao Kỳ, to Phnom Penh to discuss the current state of relations between the two nations following the ouster of Sihanouk. Kỳ and Lon Nol formed a quick, easy rapport, and the vice president's speech to the Cambodian National Assembly, which assured no expansionist aims on the part of the Saigon government, was reportedly well received. While such topics as economic agreements were addressed, the main focus of the talks was on the ongoing war. There was mutual agreement that Cambodian and Southern Vietnamese forces had reciprocal rights to conduct operations as far as sixteen kilometers inside existing borders, although such operations had to be "temporary" in nature.[23]

In the course of discussion, Lon Nol briefly mentioned that the Soviet Union had "offered to help," although he did not elaborate aside from stating his preference for Free World assistance and his suspicions of communist intentions. Lắm left with the impression that the new government had made great strides in political consolidation and that any dissent was insignificant.[24]

American officials inquired about Thành's status. Lắm reported that, with President Thiệu's consent, Thành continued his recruitment of Khmer Krom in Southern South Vietnam and had "several thousand" at his disposal. In due time Thành could return to Phnom Penh so long as it was done "discreetly."[25] By mid-June 1970 there were reports of seventy-five thousand Vietnamese living in refugee camps in Phnom Penh. Many were, in fact, the families of Khmer Krom troops that had been integrated into the Cambodian army.[26]

On 25 June 1970, Lon Nol's government declared a general mobilization where all Cambodians aged eighteen to sixty were subject to call "in this time of crisis" for a "corps for the defense of the country."[27] Additionally, several battalions of troops had already been trained in South Vietnam by the Americans and summarily shipped off to Cambodia. There were reportedly ten thousand Khmer Krom in Cambodia, four thousand of which were veterans of Mike Force. The remainders were drawn from the ranks of the South Vietnamese military. Convoys of US-donated trucks transported many of these soldiers over the border to Cambodia. US sources paid Khmer Krom recruits via South Vietnamese channels, and the soldiers were fully outfitted with American weapons. Two "mercenary officers" from Australia, also on the American payroll, accompanied them. American embassy officials in Phnom Penh claimed that they had "no knowledge" of payments emanating from Washington, but Khmer Krom officers stated that they were "being paid through U.S. aid."[28]

The shifting political tides in the capital made life miserable for the minority populations living there. About twenty-three thousand Vietnamese in Phnom Penh lived under a draconian curfew, allowing for freedom of movement for a mere three hours a day, from 8 to 11 AM. If seen in public outside of this short window, they were summarily sent to a detention camp.[29] In a not-so-moving gesture, Lon Nol gave tepid assurances of security to the large Chinese population, provided that they "keep quiet and respect laws."[30]

With so many divergent, clashing groups controlling different segments of the countryside, with the capital being divided by ethnicity, and with no respite from the violence on the horizon, there was little of Cambodia that resembled the mostly peaceful country of the previous two decades. Some pondered the question of whether at this point Cambodia existed in name only. According to one of Sihanouk's former confidants, "Cambodia? C'est fini [It is finished]."[31]

According to Charles Meyer, following Sihanouk's ouster "most politicians in the Cambodian capital were predicting a short term for Premier Lon Nol." They figured it was only a matter of time before he named Thành as his successor.[32] Lon Nol instead kept Thành at an arm's length, exploiting his influence among the Khmer Krom population to bolster recruits to the Cambodian armed forces and bring in highly trained soldiers. Over time it seemed that bringing Thành into the official fold would be a preferable move to make.

Thành undoubtedly felt he deserved much for his years of hard struggle against Sihanouk. Any position that he were to take had to be representative of his sacrifice. Thus, initially, Thành refused any role in the new government that was not a substantive one. He instead continued his recruitment of Khmer Krom into the Cambodian army and again published a newspaper in Phnom Penh.[33] In early August 1970, Thành made a week-long visit to Phnom Penh, where he stayed at the Government House. Thành met with Lon Nol to discuss a potential role in a future republican government. After some consideration, he finally accepted an offer to be vice president of the Council of Ministers, and he would concurrently serve as counselor of the state. Functionally, it was largely an honorary position, but it did bring Thành into the fold. For Lon Nol, this political accommodation meant that a popular Cambodian figure was associating himself with his government, and in a more important sense, validating his regime. For Thành, who retained aspirations for a larger role in government, potentially including becoming the first president of the republic, this was the first step in that process.[34]

The dynamics and power structure, however, was unlikely to change under the new banner of a republic. Structurally, the premier and president would be weak, almost ceremonial figures. According to one Western diplomat, "The republic will delight the students—for a while. There will not be genuine elections for a very long time. Nothing much will change. If Son Ngoc Thanh is desperate to become president, he might just get a figurehead post."[35]

Soon after, Thành spoke in Saigon on 28 August 1970 to the Agence France-Presse about his attempt to recruit Khmer volunteers to enlist in the Cambodian army. Thành declared that his ten battalions of Khmer Serei soldiers (approximately five thousand trained men) had already departed from Thailand and South Vietnam en route to Cambodia. In speaking about the relationship between the Khmer and Vietnamese, Thành noted that "cooperation between the two peoples is difficult, . . . but we have a common enemy, communism." He added that he hoped that the future would hold a "better comprehension and cooperation."[36] The next week, on 5 September, a Cambodian military tribunal "invalidated" the death sentence that Sihanouk had previously placed on Thành's head.[37]

On 8 February 1971 Lon Nol suffered a debilitating stroke. Rumors quickly spread about his health as he flew to Hawaii for treatment. At the time, the severity of the stroke was not clear, and two groups quickly formed in an attempt to fill any potential political void. The first, headed by Lon Nol's brother Lon Non, held sway with many sitting ministers of influence and had the support of the army. The second group consisted of "reformers who 'have been conspicuous in criticising corruption in government,'" and rallied around Thành. American support went to Lon Non. When the question arose of who might succeed Lon Nol in case he was unable to continue, the Americans never seriously considered Thành, the old warrior, although it is unclear exactly why.[38] The deputy prime minister Sirik Matak nominally took power while Lon Nol was debilitated.

For the next two months Lon Nol received treatment in Hawaii before returning on 12 April to Phnom Penh. Using a cane, yet still unsteady on his feet as he exited the aircraft, he had to be supported by assistants down the ramp to a wheelchair.[39] A week later, Lon Nol resigned. In a letter of resignation read to the cabinet by Matak, Lon Nol stated that he could not continue in his role of head of state due to health concerns. On 21 April, the president of the National Assembly In Tam and Senate leader Ung Sim urged Lon Nol to reconsider his resignation. Matak was seen by many as the main contender to take on the leadership of the new government if Lon Nol was unable to continue.[40] That same day, Chief of State Heng accepted Lon Nol's resignation, then immediately gave Lon Nol a renewed mandate to form a new government and the new rank of marshal for his "services to the nation."[41] The next day Lon Nol met with several advisors to discuss whether or not he should accept. A military aircraft was dispatched to fetch Thành in Saigon.

Thành returned to Phnom Penh from his home in Saigon on Thursday 22 April to address Lon Nol's health crisis. He was not permitted to speak with Lon Nol in person, as the latter's doctors feared that the general would use a courtesy visit such as this as an opportunity to raise political questions that would cause him too much strain.[42] The next day, however, Lon Nol named a new cabinet in which he retained the premiership and appointed three deputy prime ministers, Brigadier General In Tam, General Matak, and Thành.[43]

On 26 April Thành reported from the Palais du Gouvernement that Lon Nol was too sick to either make decisions or receive important news. Nonetheless, the situation was such that he had to continue to lead the Cambodian government. Thành stated in an interview that Lon Nol agreed to once again become premier, and that his announcement was expected shortly. Once that occurred, a new government would be formed. Three to four vice ministers were to represent several ministries and make the decisions that Lon Nol would otherwise make.

Thành also reported on the specifics of Lon Nol's health. Lon Nol's physician reported to Thành that the general could not be asked to make any decisions. The vice premiers were to take up this task and only inform Lon Nol after the fact. He was to only work one hour a day. But Lon Nol's physical presence and participation in Cambodia's government was deemed as too important to turn over power to any one of the deputies. Additionally, those with close ties to Lon Nol, especially his brother Lon Non, had much to lose if Lon Nol were to lose power.[44]

On 29 April, Lon Nol once again abruptly resigned. Chief of State Heng put Lon Nol's vice president, Matak, in charge of forming a new cabinet. In theory Matak was in a great position to become the next prime minister. It remained unclear whether or not Matak would make a move for the premiership, however, as he was not an overly popular figure, especially among students and certain members of the National Assembly. There were some who felt that if Matak was not capable of forming a new government that Thành would be next in line. Cambodia's youth, especially student groups, would likely be supportive of a Thành premiership, notwithstanding his rabid ambitions. Their voices rang loudest for a clearing of the top rungs of government. According to American intelligence, Thành also had "a powerful supporter in Lon Non, who probably views Thanh as a more congenial substitute for his brother than Matak."[45]

After reflection, and apparently before Matak had decided whether to accept the position, Heng nominated the National Assembly president In Tam for the prime ministership. But In Tam also hesitated. On 2 May 1971 Heng informed the press that In Tam had not yet decided whether he would accept the position or not, but that if he chose to, his cabinet would "consist of young technicians," and that Thành would be made his deputy—apparently because of his popularity. A "Central Intelligence Bulletin" from the next day cast doubt on whether an In Tam cabinet could even be formed, let alone survive. It opined, "If and when In Tam is eliminated, Cheng Heng is likely to turn to Thanh." In an attempt to demonstrate that he was searching for a candidate acceptable to all of the various political factions, Heng would have to run the gamut of aspirants. Thành apparently believed this process could only help him.[46] In Tam soon decided against accepting the post. Matak and Chuop Hell did as well. Heng realized that he had to turn back to Lon Nol. Matak was tapped to serve as his deputy, but held a considerable amount of power.[47]

Matak's proposed cabinet consisted mainly of members of the outgoing government and other important names in Phnom Penh. He planned to act as his own defense minister. Koun Wick remained in his role of minister of foreign affairs, and In Tam was to become first vice premier and minister of the interior. Although Thành was left out of Matak's proposed government, he had previously made claims that Sok Chhong, who was nominated as the second deputy prime minister in charge of economic affairs, and Hang Thun Hak, nominated as the third deputy prime minister and minister of community development, were members of "his group." Matak was in high spirits when, on 5 May 1971, he told official at the US embassy that he did not anticipate any difficulty in obtaining approval from the National Assembly for the new government.[48]

In an attempt to turn the tide of the military campaign, on 20 May Lon Nol launched a successful offensive to free several villages along Route 3 that had been controlled by Gouvernement Royal d'Union Nationale du Kampuchea (GRUNK, Sihanouk's government in exile) forces for the better part of a year. Journalists were brought along to witness the victory of "Akineth Moha Padevuth" (Operation Burning Eyes of the Great Revolution), and in the process Lon Nol gained a considerable amount of good publicity, both in Cambodia and abroad. To keep a hold on this newly acquired territory, psychological warfare teams were sent into action distributing food and treating medical ailments, among other actions.[49]

With this pacification program, In Tam sought to reorganize the national police force under his command as minister of interior. He maintained that an independent police force was necessary for government expansion into the countryside. In Tam claimed that control over police forces was a requirement of his entry into the cabinet. But this led to suspicions that he was attempting to build a "private army" for his own purposes.

Thành saw the pacification program as a potentially worthwhile endeavor as well. He proposed to Matak that a pacification campaign be organized to aid in the preparation of the elections that were to be held following the adoption of a new constitution. Thành's plan included several extensive tours of the countryside, with him acting as "missionary for the pacification effort." Such a tour would also provide the shrewd politician with an opportunity to boost his own political prospects in Phnom Penh.[50]

Bolstered by the success of the Akineth Moha Padevuth operation, and with concerns over Lon Nol's health having subsided, the Constitutional Drafting Committee was inaugurated on 16 June 1971 to resolve the lingering constitutional crisis. The hope was, in addition to the creation of a national constitution, that formal political parties would also be created. It was clear at the time that three political blocs existed in Cambodia, with adherents supporting Lon Nol, In Tam, and Thành, respectively, and it was believed that the United States supported the In Tam clique. A few months before that, on 8 March, in an effort to consolidate power, Ven Khieu Chum, the reliable Thànhist, was selected by Lon Nol to head the newly created Republican Committee, with Lon Non serving as the vice president. By combining political forces, the Republican Committee was able to dominate the Constitutional Committee and marginalize In Tam. Lon Nol's supporters, now known as the Dangkor faction, and newly aligned with Thành's Dangrek group of supporters, left Matak without a power base. Not wanting the Dangkor-Dangrek supergroup to dominate the Constitutional Committee, Matak scrapped it, and returned the task of drafting a constitution to the National Assembly. Lon Nol then put Thành in charge of economic affairs.[51]

On 28 July 1971, Lon Nol brought together several advisors and officials to discuss recent international developments and the outlook for various Southeast Asian nations. Among other directives, he ordered a strengthening of psychological warfare tactics in order to "safeguard independence, territorial integrity, and national unity." In addition, a central committee of economic warfare was established, which focused on fighting inflation and other destabilizing elements in the Cambodian economy.[52] Lon Nol announced that Thành would be placed in charge of the newly created "Central Committee for Economic Welfare." Lon Nol hoped to utilize Thành's reputation of being incorruptible to assuage critics of his government. A "Central Intelligence Bulletin" opined that, while possibly a shrewd move, "at the same time, Lon Nol has saddled a potential rival with one of the government's thorniest problems. This is the most important post Thanh has held; if the economy shows noticeable improvement under his aegis, Thanh may improve his over-all political position."[53]

On 23 September Lon Nol dismissed In Tam from his positions as the interior minister and first deputy prime minister. According to In Tam, Lon Nol gave no reason for his dismissal. "He just said I was not capable of performing my functions as minister." The following day Tim Nguon was appointed by the cabinet to replace In Tam as first deputy prime minister.[54] In Tam would, however, not leave the fractured Cambodian political scene for good.

As reported by Allman, "at the moment the government seems divided into innumerable factions, gravitating around Marshall Lon Nol, General (formerly Prince) Sirik Matak, Commandant Lon Non, Son Ngoc Thanh and various members of the National Assembly."[55] The divergent aspirations of the various groups all playing for power led to one of Lon Nol's more dramatic moves. On 16 October the government stripped the National Assembly of all lawmaking powers in what was claimed by the government to be a compromise between competing factions. One side favored the abolishment of a parliamentary system entirely; another wanted its lawmaking powers extended. The government then ordered the National Assembly to draft a new constitution. The next day a group of members of the assembly voted to defy government then orders to abolish the body and, in effect, submit lawmaking powers to the will of the cabinet. The legality of Heng's decree was also questioned.[56]

On 20 October Lon Nol announced over radio broadcast that he had formed what would actually resemble a de facto military dictatorship to halt the nation's drift toward anarchy. Because "certain groups, clans and associations" sought "to divide the nation by sowing confusion," Cambodia was headed "towards defeat." To "combat this anarchy," the nation had to end "this sterile game of democracy," which, according to Lon Nol, played into enemy hands. He defiantly declared, "My government has chosen the path to victory."[57] Rights of assembly, a free press, and habeas corpus were also significantly curtailed, and power was concentrated in the executive.

The next day, one thousand monks staged a demonstration against Lon Nol's speech. Such public pronouncements were uncommon for Cambodia's bonzes. The last significant demonstration was nearly thirty years prior, staged in protest of French rule. The fact that two of the organizers of the former were instrumental in organizing the latter showed, in some ways, how little had changed in Cambodia's political sphere. These monks maintained an alliance with Thành throughout this long period of time. Members of the former Democratic Party, themselves out of power for nearly two decades, yet still followers of Thành, continued to clash with Lon Nol's Republicans.[58]

Lon Nol continued to alienate important civilian leaders, notably In Tam and Thành. In Tam's abrupt shift from a leading government figure to leading opponent meant that one of Cambodia's most talented politicians was no longer contributing to its government. At this stage, he was also one of the few that could potentially organize a splintered opposition movement. Thành was in a similar position. He was one of the most well-known figures in the country, had extensive ties to both Buddhist and student leadership, and continued to retain his reputation as honest and sincere. He was also the only civilian in a position to field an army of loyal troops, the Khmer Krom. Thành was also a vocal critic of Heng's transformation of the two-house chambered National Assembly to a constituent assembly, at which point Lon Nol created a new government. Thành joined members of Buddhist leadership during their subsequent visit with Lon Nol. The marshal, however, knew Thành to be far too valuable a man to fully ostracize from government circles.[59]

On 8 November 1971, former deputy prime minister In Tam defeated Op Kim An, who was backed by the government, for the chairmanship of the new assembly. Thành actively promoted In Tam's candidacy. A CIA "Weekly Summary" stated that this was "more evidence that he is still playing an independent game despite protestations to the contrary."[60]

As dysfunction reigned supreme in the capital, the United States continued to shore up Cambodia's military situation. Despite a declaration from Washington that the only American personnel on the ground in Cambodia consisted of military equipment delivery teams, news broke that military intelligence teams were secretly sent into Cambodia. Assigned to military command in Saigon, these men then engaged in missions over the Cambodian border in cooperation with the Cambodian military. Their main tasks were to secure and evaluate intelligence obtained by the Cambodians.[61] Such operations were essential to the war effort, as the military tide was turning against the Cambodian government.

On 26 November 1971 communist forces shelled Pochentong airfield for the second straight day, although no damage or casualties were reported. The fact that communist forces were able to move into such proximity of an essential war-making element of the Khmer Republic underscored the failure of the government to defend the area surrounding Phnom Penh. To bolster defenses, nineteen government battalions were diverted from a major offensive against communist forces (Chenla II) to clear the area around the capital. Several elite Khmer Krom units were included in this operation.[62]

On 6 December 1971 a group of high-ranking officers in the Cambodian army met with Lon Nol to review various command problems that led to the disaster of Chenla II, where several thousand republican troops were massacred along Route 6 as they attempted to infiltrate communist territory. It was, according to Chandler, "the last major offensive mounted by the Khmer Republic." It was the first time that army leadership directly confronted Lon Nol's "interference" in the war. There was some feeling that an intransigent Lon Nol could alienate his support among the military and push them toward Matak. If Matak succeeded in consolidating such power, he could force Lon Nol's hand to delegate at least some authority. In Tam and Thành continued, however, to undermine Matak's position, and whispers continued that either could be a potential successor for Lon Nol or Matak.[63]

Lon Nol's direct involvement in the failure of Chenla II led to whispers of a coup in some government circles. That being said, a figure with broad-based political support simply did not exist to usurp power from him. Matak maintained a strong base of support among American officials, but he had limited popular appeal. In Tam was hard at work attempting to shore up a base of support but was currently ostracized from the government, making the task difficult. Thành maintained the backing of student and intellectual groups, both of which felt increasingly alienated by the Lon Nol regime. But none of the three, despite their ambitions, was in a position to command the popular support needed to successfully pull off a coup attempt. Any success was also predicated on, at a minimum, American tacit acceptance, if not outright support. That was not forthcoming at this point.[64]

Although things on the surface, politically, were calm, there remained an underlying current of discontent with Matak. According to a CIA memorandum, he had "incurred the enmity of many because of the often unwelcome decisiveness with which he administer[ed] the day-to-day affairs of the government and the lingering suspicion that Sirik Matak is seeking a return of the monarchy." A number of influential politicians, including In Tam, Yem Sambaur, and Thành, were convinced that Matak had lingering authoritarian tendencies and was a bad influence on Lon Nol. These dissenting voices did not form a bloc, however, as, according to the CIA, they remained motivated as much by personal ambition as by concern over the development of a republican form of government.[65]

Indicative of the chaotic political scene in Phnom Penh, on 17 December, the Agence Khmer de Presse (AKP), Cambodia's official news agency, announced that Heng had signed measures that banned all political meetings and gave law enforcement unlimited powers to investigate any elements in Cambodian society deemed subversive.[66] With Lon Nol once again ailing, potential successors made their moves. Matak seemed a logical choice as successor, but In Tam and Thành were seen as potential movers in the Cambodian political scene. Many young military officers supported Thành, as did influential Buddhist monks.[67]

The CIA Office of National Estimates felt that Thành would be a likely candidate to fill the power vacuum of opposition to Matak should Lon Nol be incapacitated or die. Thành was "widely respected" and commanded great support from the Khmer Krom population and leaders of the Mohannikay, the majority Buddhist sect. Despite the fact that the Khmer National Armed Forces (FANK) often sought recruits from the Khmer Krom, Thành's standing with the army was uncertain, and there were indications that the influence he had exerted on the Khmer Krom had begun to fade. In addition, Thành's years of collaboration with the government of South Vietnam left some in Cambodia uneasy.[68]

On 10 March Heng resigned, handing power over to Lon Nol, who became president of the republic. "Only Lon Nol has the capacity to lead the country" was Heng's departing remark. Said Thành, "This is the first step. It has taken us two years since the overthrow of Prince Norodom Sihanouk to reach the presidential system. Sure, we only have some of the pieces in place, but the marshall [sic] assured me this morning that this country is now irrevocably a republic with a president."[69] Matak became prime minister by default, but he faced massive student protests. One student leader stated, "Of course we are not protesting against Lon Nol. He is our leader. We are against Sirik Matak. We trust Marshal Lon Nol."[70]

Matak's tenure was short-lived, lasting a mere five days. He announced the dissolution of Cambodia's government and resigned on 12 March 1972. The next day, Lon Nol addressed the public as its new president. The new head of state claimed, "A project will soon materialize to form a new system of government."[71] This self-promotion also made him the president of the Council of Ministers and commander-in-chief of the armed forces. Matak's replacement as prime minister would, thus, wield little actual power. There were a number of potential replacements for Matak. Sim Var, serving as the ambassador to Japan at the time, cited the lack of a parliament or constitution when he refused the post. In Tam, Nguon, and Sambaur also declined. This left Thành as the only logical choice.[72]

With the outright refusal of various leading Cambodian politicians to accept the post, Lon Nol eventually named Thành as the new prime minister of the Cambodian government on 20 March. He concurrently served as minister of foreign affairs, and most of his days were spent in his office in the Foreign Ministry, which was located next to the Mekong Delta and overlooked a park. It was clear that Lon Nol intended to maintain his dominant role in Cambodian politics, and according to CIA estimates, "he probably does not intend to allow the new Prime Minister much freedom of action."[73]

On the second anniversary of the ouster of Sihanouk, the man that fought for two decades to overthrow him became prime minister of Cambodia for the second time. Described by The New York Times as "a short, wiry, intense man," on the night he was promoted to the position by Lon Nol, Thành defended the president's actions, and stated that they were both democratic and "in accord with the Cambodian Constitution of 1947." Agreeing that such dramatic changes were not necessarily in line with Western notions of democracy, Thành noted that "all these changes may be a little hard for Westerners to understand. The Khmer revolution is not like Western politics, it is not strictly logical, it is more like a complex piece of Angkor sculpture that unfolds slowly to the viewer." Reinforcing the power of Lon Nol, Thành also stated that the president retained the power to name the cabinet and members of the National Security Council.[74]

Some American officials located in Phnom Penh reportedly considered Thành a "dedicated patriot and democrat, but also as something of an eccentric and dreamer." Recently, Thành had even discussed leading his Khmer guerrillas against the North Vietnamese in the Cambodian jungle.[75] The CIA noted in the "President's Daily Brief" that

Thành's appointment could ease tensions and that his "anti-Sihanouk credentials and his reputation for honesty should mollify the restive students and others who have been agitating against royalist tendencies and corruption."[76]

In accepting his new position, Thành knew that Lon Nol would remain the dominant political figure in Cambodia, but Thành saw himself as a moderating voice and a potential check on Lon Nol's drift toward authoritarianism. Thành remained a crafty and skilled politician, and when he announced that it was Lon Nol alone who had selected the new cabinet, it was a move to maintain his independence. In many ways, Thành was one of the few assets the regime had. He had few enemies and strong anti-Sihanouk credentials. He had managed to preserve a reputation as an honest broker and had the respect of a number of popular politicians.[77]

Although Thành was the sixth choice to be offered the position of prime minister, his status was such that he was the only Cambodian figure who could rival In Tam in terms of popularity. This might explain why Lon Nol had him so low on the list of candidates. T. J. S. George of

Mr. SON NGOC THANH

FIGURE 6.1. Sơn Ngọc Thành shortly after being sworn in as prime minister, 1972. Courtesy of the Center for Khmer Studies, Siem Reap.

the *Far Eastern Economic Review* reported that a key factor in the selection of Thành as prime minister "may have been the Americans' anxiety to replace their friend, Sirik Matak, with an equally trustworthy ally."[78] *The New York Times* characterized him as "an ardent nationalist and an eccentric." Despite his relationship with American officials, the US embassy did not hold him in as high regard as it did Matak, although students favored Thành's appointment.[79] Speaking with reporters, Thành stated that he had "imposed no conditions, but only wanted to serve his country." His job would be to coordinate the Council of Ministers, which would be both composed of Lon Nol appointees and headed by him.[80]

Student groups, emboldened by their belief that their constant protestations had led to the removal of Matak, stood ready to continue agitation against the government.[81] Lon Nol hoped that appointing Thành would mollify such groups and other divergent voices protesting government corruption and "royalist tendencies." His gambit seemed to have worked, at least initially. Students' cries for "more new men" in government were somewhat muted with Thành's appointment, as student groups indicated they were content with his selection.[82] Thành's reputation as an honest man with strong anti-Sihanouk credentials filled a void in the government. He had few political enemies and had a deep respect from a number of former National Assemblymen and the elite Khmer Krom forces. That being said, Lon Nol intended to give Thành little leeway to forge his own path, something Thành appeared to accept. Many Cambodians, however, did not expect the new government to last long. The CIA estimated the same for the "energetic" Thành. He and Lon Nol were never close, and Thành "could soon become frustrated with the President's restraints and his constant interference in the government's day-to-day affairs."[83]

Judith Coburn reported in the *Far Eastern Economic Review* that despite Thành's support among students, intellectual circles, and government opponents, "he labours under the cloud of decades-long collaboration with the American CIA," and he was a main player in "at least one CIA-organized coup attempt from Thailand." Politically active monks, whose relationship with Thành dated back to his time at *Nagaravatta* and his organization of the "Revolution of the Umbrellas," played a key role in the campaign against Matak. They were also extremely active in organizing students to keep a steady pressure on the government. Thành was said to have earlier expressed a disappointment that he was not tapped for a high post in the government following Sihanouk's ouster. After his lengthy self-imposed exile and years of opposition, he felt he was owed more.[84]

Lon Nol's new cabinet reflected the heightened political role of the military. The ministers of defense, interior, education, and the head of the Commerce Ministry were all military men. The lieutenant colonel Thach Chea, who was named minister of education, was also Khmer Krom. His appointment could have been seen as a threat, of sorts, to student protestors.

Lon Nol apparently decided that he wanted to chair cabinet meetings and gave himself the additional title of prime minister. Thành's title was reduced to "first minister." In his new role, Thành coordinated but did not direct other ministers. He also ran the Foreign Ministry. As a "Central Intelligence Bulletin" opined, "This arrangement underscores the narrow limits of Thanh's authority."[85] He maintained, however, strong support from the student population. Thành's ties to the student and intellectual community, who remained suspicious and disdainful of the flaunted wealth of the new crop of nouveau riche politicians, were strengthened by his simple home, a small "tumble-down villa." The walls were adorned with photos from what looked to be the remnants of travel posters.[86]

When student leaders decided to end large-scale demonstrations, there was some hope that political tensions would end along with it. For the past week students had been flooding into Phnom Penh's independence monument, an Angkor-inspired stupa erected in the heart of the city in 1958 to celebrate Cambodia's independence from France five years earlier. When it became clear that the government was of no mind to grant concessions and that the students were vulnerable to countercharges of aiding the communists, leadership reconsidered the demonstrations. Student leadership's positions on the draft constitution would also have to be reconsidered.[87] According to American intelligence, the general population of Phnom Penh was showing some signs of sympathy for the demonstrators, as were Buddhists and members of the military. Students felt "betrayed" by Thành, who, according to student claims, had promised to quit if strong measures were taken against them but had not done so.[88]

While the draft constitution put no limits on the number of political parties that could enter and contest elections, Lon Nol was known to favor allowing only two, Democrats and Republicans. "I am in the middle. I am working with Marshal Lon Nol to help the country," Thành said. Thành also ruled out being either a candidate for president or for the

National Assembly. He hoped, however, to play a large role behind the scenes. He maintained strong support among the intellectual community, and his years of association with the CIA "have invested him with an aura of mystery that he does nothing to dispel." Despite his claims of admiration and allegiance for Lon Nol, many remained convinced that a face-off between the two was almost inevitable.[89] Despite potential tensions, the draft constitution was overwhelmingly approved at the 30 April 1972 polls.[90] The interior minister Thappana Nginn reported that 97.45 percent of Cambodians voted in approval of the new Constitution in the 30 April referendum. Lon Nol subsequently announced that the new constitution would go into effect on 12 May.[91] The election, which was marked with excessive fraud, intimidation, and violence, was held soon after on 4 June. Lon Nol captured victory, purportedly receiving 57 percent of the vote. He was followed by In Tam with 24 percent and Keo An with 18 percent. Over eight hundred thousand people cast votes.[92]

On 6 June 1972, Thành defended the transparency and accuracy of the election when he told the nation it was held "in freedom and order without compulsion." Results were delayed, however, when In Tam lodged a complaint with the Constitutional Court over the electoral process. In a 13 June press release, Thành stated, "Any candidates or newspapers wishing to make public any facts which they know are incorrect are therefore asked to do so plainly to avoid inciting the people to rebellion, and groundlessly defaming" the current regime.[93] The next day, Thành made good on his threat. He accused the newspapers *Khmer Angkor* and *Sangruos Cheat* of attempting to discredit the electoral results and Lon Nol's presidency. The papers, which were founded to support In Tam's campaign five weeks prior, were ordered to cease production for publicizing "false news."[94] In Tam himself owned the *Khmer Angkor*, while Duoc Rasy owned *Sangkruos Cheat*. The government also forced the closure of the *Damnoeung Pil Puth* newspaper for "insulting the Government and writing articles designed to destroy the people's confidence in the Government." A fourth paper, the *Independent Khmer*, owned by Sim Var, was also shuttered.[95]

There was speculation as to who would be selected as Lon Nol's vice president. With Lon Nol's health remaining a concern, whoever held that office would hold a strong claim to take power in the event he suffered a debilitating stroke. Matak had turned down the position prior to the past election, which left the situation muddled, with no clear consensus that would be agreeable to all political and military segments of the government. For Thành, his close association with South

Vietnam was seen as a detriment to potential leadership. American intelligence also estimated that it was "doubtful that he has the adroitness and forcefulness to whip his opponents into line."[96]

Meanwhile, government forces faced another setback in the Parrot's Beak, east of Angtassom, in an attempt to clear the eastern portion of Highway 1. Two battalions of Khmer Krom troops fell into a familiar trap as guerrilla forces encircled them as they advanced along the highway, and they found themselves unable to break out. Cambodian newspapers reported that some six hundred Khmer Krom soldiers were killed or captured, decimating the ranks of the most elite fighting force in the republic. Some reports had soldiers resorting to suicide in lieu of capture. In their final communications, battalion officers pleaded for their position to be shelled. Better to die by the bomb than face their would-be captors. In a hallmark of similarly failed campaigns, the battalions had run out of ammunition, and when the airstrikes were called in, they never came.[97]

According to reporter Boris Baczynskyi of the *Far Easter Economic Review*, "the defeat's most serious effect on the situation in Cambodia might be its contribution to the breaking of the spirit of the Khmer Krom troops." In a 10 July interview, Thành denied reports that a sense of dissatisfaction and frustration had permeated Khmer Krom units. A young soldier in the first minister's office, however, disagreed. He disparaged the government for placing troops in unwinnable situations and not supplying them with sufficient ammunition and supplies.[98] Earlier Thành spoke of his government's concern over the expanding war in South Vietnam and the recent communist offensive, which he deemed more political than military in nature. "It is a risk—perhaps not of World War III—but of a possible glimmering of a third world war.[99] Defeat was beginning to look inevitable to many, and Lon Nol faced the brunt of public pressure to make changes.

The cracks in Lon Nol's popularity seemed to be turning into deep fissures. Matak saw this as an opening and made a political break with his old friend. On 15 June, Matak and several other political veterans established the new Republican Party, with Matak serving as the secretary-general. This was, in effect, Matak's bid to succeed Lon Nol as the leader of the Khmer Republic.[100] Matak was staking a claim to succeed Lon Nol, although Lon Non and Thành remained as potential foes.[101] By the end of June, the only political organization with overt associations with Lon Nol was the Socio-Republican Party. With legislative elections coming in September, however, new parties were expected to soon surface. The Socio-Nationalist Party, comprised mainly of teachers, and a Khmer Krom party were likely candidates to join Lon Nol. These were two groups that traditionally supported Thành, but because he remained in the good graces of the marshal, he helped to siphon off support for such rival parties.[102] Matak and In Tam would boycott the elections.[103]

Throughout such political and military tensions, Thành's public face remained optimistic, confident even. In a July interview, he stated unequivocally that his government was "determined to push out the enemy.... At the same time we will strengthen the regime we have built up." Such bold statements were overshadowed by outlandish claims, however. "We are now establishing a true Khmer of Cambodian republic.... Now there are no more quarrels. The people can decide whom they want to lead them." Delusions are beset by reality.[104]

One of the responsibilities Thành was tasked with, and one that he possessed the greatest ability of accomplishing, was generating a better relationship with the South Vietnamese government. The previous year the Cambodian information minister Long Boret issued the not-so-subtle backhanded compliment, "We can have no real friendship with any of the Vietnamese, but we have chosen the least dangerous Vietnamese for our allies."[105] Thành worked to relax any lingering tensions, although he would soon face great tensions himself.

On 21 August, as Thành rode in a motorcade to the Foreign Ministry, a mine detonated, wounding several guards in the jeep following Thành's car. The bomb was hidden inside of an old French automobile and triggered by a wire strung across the road between the former Royal Palace and the National Museum. The debris was scattered over a fifty-yard radius. Three of Thành's bodyguards were wounded, as was a monk riding in a jeep near Thành's Mercedes. The damage would have been far more severe, but only one of two mines successfully detonated. Two assailants were captured, and Thành was unharmed, but tensions only grew in the Cambodian capital.[106]

On 29 August 1972, Thành traveled to Saigon to meet with the Republic of Vietnam's prime minister Trần Thiện Khiêm. This was a continuation of a previous meeting held in Phnom Penh in May 1971. After being greeted by a nineteen-gun salute and the national anthems of both the Khmer Republic and Republic of Vietnam, Thành released a statement to the press detailing the renewed cooperation between the two nations, in which he affirmed that "we have managed together a common struggle for our defense and for the reestablishment of the countries in

Indochina." He noted that the government of the Republic of Vietnam had declared that any ceasefire must encompass all three of the Indochinese nations, and that the government of the Khmer Republic was prepared to support it in this stance.[107] Following his statement, according to *Le Républicain*, Thành, "standing to the right of the Vietnamese Prime Minister in a jeep decorated in the colors of the two countries . . . reviewed the honor guard." He next traveled to the National Assembly and Senate, where the presidents of each respective chamber greeted him. In the upper chamber, he met with his brother, Sơn Thái Nguyên, who represented more than one million Kampuchea Krom in the Vietnamese Senate.

The following day, South Vietnamese president Nguyễn Văn Thiệu and vice president Trần Văn Hương welcomed Thành for a meeting. The ninety-minute meeting focused on the military and political situation in Indochina as well as the negotiations for a potential joint cease fire among Cambodia, Laos, and Vietnam. Noted as two "strong personalities," the two then shared lunch at the Palais Dec Lap (Independence Palace). Thiệu assured Thành that the war was coming to a close.[108]

Shortly after the national elections, Nixon wrote a letter to Lon Nol, urging him to include opposition members in his government and to nominate a vice president. Within Cambodian political circles, there were seen to be four potential suitors for the position: Thành, In Tam,

FIGURE 6.2.   Sơn Ngọc Thành greets Thomas Enders, the US chargé in Phnom Penh, 1972. Courtesy of the Center for Khmer Studies, Siem Reap.

Matak, and Au Chhloe. Thành had the apparent backing of republicans and intellectuals in Phnom Penh, who were so extremely anti-Sihanouk that they preferred a negotiated settlement with the Khmer Rouge rather than to see Sihanouk back at the head of government. They were bolstered by Soviet promises to push for a Vietnamese withdrawal if an agreement could be reached to end the war. The United States was concerned that a very sick Lon Nol had no immediate successor. It was also concerned with the perception that Matak and In Tam's boycott of the elections had in the world community.[109]

With Lon Nol attempting to promote his government as neutralist, Thành's rightist credentials and reputation were no longer seen in a positive light. Just before the election for National Assembly on 3 September, Lon Nol designated his information minister, Long Boret, as the replacement for Thành as head of the Foreign Ministry. He also urged some of his main civilian critics to take up various key roles in the new government. In Tam, the leader of the Democratic Party, was offered the position of "special adviser to the President." The vice presidency was reserved for the Republican Party leader Matak. Both men faced pressure from their respective party members to refuse.[110]

Thành's cabinet resigned on 14 October as the Cambodian government transitioned to install a new constitutional government.[111] The date of 15 October marked Thành's departure. Officially he resigned. According to Article 33 of the Khmer Constitution (which was adopted by national referendum on 30 April 1972), Lon Nol was to choose a successor. He selected Hang Thun Hak.[112]

Despite Nixon's plea, the new government included no representatives from opposition parties. There were hopes that representatives from the Republicans and Democrats would be included as a show of national unity. Instead, the list of new ministers presented to Lon Nol by Hak, the first minister-designate, were predominantly holdovers from the Thành cabinet, as well as a scattered few minor faces from within the Socio-Republican Party.[113]

Following his resignation, Thành reminisced on what he considered to be his greatest achievement during his seven months in office. According to Thành, it was "the setting up of republican institutions according to the Constitution." Thành had long resented the lack of power and authority granted to him in office. He was at this point, however, resigned to his fate. After his resignation, in acknowledgement that his political career was at an end, Thành stated, "I'm old. I would like to go back to South Vietnam."[114]

Conclusion
An Unglamorous Ending

Sơn Ngọc Thành's second departure from
the position of prime minister was drastically different than his first
nearly thirty years prior. Instead of leaving Cambodia as a political
martyr in chains as he did following his arrest by returning French
forces in 1945, Thành left on his own accord in late 1972 to return to
Saigon.

Thành's popularity, while still strong in some circles, had dissipated
greatly over the years. His reputation had long been based on the nationalist, anticolonial ideals expressed under the French protectorate
and on the antimonarchal stance he took during the 1950s and 1960s.
Both of those enemies had since been vanquished. Unable to flex his
political muscle under the leadership of Lon Nol, there was no place for
Thành in Phnom Penh. Now nearly sixty-three years old, Thành retired
to South Vietnam. He remained, however, a semiactive player with the
former Khmer Serei, and he continued to recruit for the Cambodian
army. The next phase of Cambodian history was dominated by the civil
war and the murderous rule of the Khmer Rouge. Thành is a mere foot-
note to events during this period, and both his life during this time and
his death are shrouded in mystery.

After leaving office, Thành returned to Saigon a humbled and sick
man. With the war against the insurgent Khmer Rouge continuing to

FIGURE C.1.   Sơn Ngọc Thành plays with his grandchildren in the surf in this undated photo. Courtesy of Vann Ung.

turn sour, Cambodian officials sought a way to end the war in a manner that would allow them to retain power. In a shift to a conciliatory approach, at least in terms of presentation, on 3 November 1972 the government created a National Committee of Action for Peace and Concord. Its promise was to work with the Khmer Rouge within the existing republic. In an interview, Hang Thun Hak stated that "If there is a rally by the Khmer Rouge, they can have a political party, participate in elections, work for any changes they want in a legal way. . . . If an international détente keeps them from being rearmed, they'll see after a while that it is a good thing to enter into the life of the republic." In a show of unity, Sirik Matak and Thành endorsed the committee. The following day, Lon Nol proclaimed that "circumstances are favorable for a union of hearts and spirits in the republic," a statement far removed from the truth, both politically and militarily, as the Khmer Rouge had no interests in negotiations.[1]

On 25 April 1973, the US ambassador to Vietnam Ellsworth Bunker received word from the Phnom Penh embassy that Thành, then in Saigon after recovering from dorsal pleurisy, was expected to return to the Cambodian capital shortly.[2] On 30 April 1973, the State Department circulated a press summary that indicated the Supreme Council in Cambodia was weighing options on a new premier. Those under consideration included Hak, Op Kim Ang, Sok Chhong, and Thành.[3] In reality, Thành was a spent force. He would not return to the government as the country slowly crumbled. His Khmer Krom, however, would continue the fight.

On 11 August 1973, the US embassy at Phnom Penh relayed to Saigon that Lon Nol had developed a new plan for Khmer Krom recruitment from South Vietnam to serve in the Khmer National Armed Forces (FANK). A recruiting team of twenty would work in the Mekong Delta region of South Vietnam with an initial recruitment goal of one thousand. Thành was in charge of the recruitment team. The Khmer Republic would supply one million riels for initial expenditures. The plan was for the United States to provide an airlift for recruits via a C-130 aircraft from South Vietnam to Ream Airfield in Cambodia. They would then undergo four weeks of "secret" training at the Ream training center. Panh Laun was designated to work out the details with the government of Vietnam "work[ing] through Son Ngoc Thanh." Ambassador Emory Swank was skeptical that the plan was viable, even referring to it as a "scheme" in his telegram to Saigon. Despite his doubts, he nonetheless requested authority for the use of a C-130 to transport any potential recruits.[4]

Around this same time, Thành visited Tinh Bien district and Chau Doc City on the Cambodian border, where he visited relatives and Khmer refugees. Rumors abounded that he was also recruiting soldiers to fight in Cambodia, although the Chau Doc Civil Consul claimed that "there has been nothing to indicate he did any recruiting."[5] In a press summary distributed by the Department of State to various key embassies, it was noted that Thành's brother, Sơn Thái Nguyên, had claimed that he had cabled Senator Mike Mansfield with a request to "intervene to prolong bombing."[6]

Those Khmer Krom who made the journey to Phnom Penh to join in the fight against the Khmer Rouge faced much hardship outside of battle. As recounted by the journalist James Fenton:

> the reception they got from the Cambodians there was lukewarm at best. They were thought to be more Vietnamese than Khmer. Their superior attitude, their military sophistication and their ruthlessness were resented. They were used as cannon fodder in a

series of disastrous campaigns. Eventually they were almost wiped out. You could still find a few of them in Phnom Penh [before it fell on 17 April 1975]. They were the gung-ho officers with the perfect command of GI slang. But the experience of returning to the mother country had not been a success. They had found out, although they would not admit this, that they were not Cambodians after all. And if they were not Cambodians, and not Vietnamese, what the hell were they?[7]

To the Khmer Rouge, they were certainly enemies of the state they wished to create. The insurgents' covert radio station indicted Lon Nol and six other prominent Cambodian politicians in a 3 March 1975 broadcast. It proclaimed, "Our Cambodian people . . . cannot forgive these traitors. We must eliminate them." Three days later, Sihanouk, now allied (at least on the surface) with the Khmer Rouge, verified what most suspected, that six out of the seven enemies of the revolution would "probably be executed." Somewhat mysteriously, Thành was not included.[8] Hidden in Saigon, Thành was reportedly too old and sick to even engage in politics at this point.[9]

Soon thereafter, on 17 April 1975 Phnom Penh fell to the Khmer Rouge. Two weeks later, North Vietnamese troops captured Saigon; the war had finally come to an end. Word of Khmer Rouge brutality had already begun to filter back to Vietnam by this point, to which a North Vietnamese officer could only say that the Khmer communists did not revere the laws of Ho Chi Minh. Many Khmer Krom that had been close to Thành feared reprisals and sought asylum in Vietnam. Several officers living with their families in Saigon were told to meet Thành and the head of the monastery at a local pagoda. The four who did go never returned, undoubtedly taken prisoner (or killed) by victorious North Vietnamese forces.[10]

One officer befriended Fenton and stayed with him in his hotel room. The two discussed Sihanouk's memoirs, and the officer confirmed much of the information, including the fact that he had worked with the CIA. Fenton asked why Thành had decided to stay in Saigon. Surely, due to his close connections with the Americans, he could have found asylum elsewhere. The officer replied, according to Fenton, "that Ho Chi Minh and Son Ngoc Thanh, both being nationalist leaders, had a respect for each other, and that there was a stipulation in Ho's will that Son Ngoc Thanh must not be harmed in any way. He had nothing to fear from the PRG." Unfortunately for Thành's followers, Ho Chi

Minh's last will and testament said no such thing. It is unclear why this officer believed this, and he disappeared soon after.[11]

Even with his organization crushed, and the two governments he was allied with defeated, the specter of a resurgent Thành remained. On 1 October 1975 the US ambassador to France Kenneth Rush informed Henry Kissinger of a phone call received at the embassy from a representative of the "Khmer Libre Movement." The caller stated that Thành was the leader of the organization, and that an organizational meeting was being held that day in Paris. He inquired as to whether the United States was interested in sending a representative to the meeting. The embassy declined.[12] It is unlikely that Thành was in such a position to command such a movement at this time, and he was surely not in Paris.

As refugees flowed over the "bamboo curtain" into Thailand (as the border was sometimes referred to in the Thai press), numerous stories about what was happening inside of the new Democratic Kampuchea leaked out. While many were reportedly simply based on hearsay, some stories told of resistance movements against the communist government. Refugees "frequently described this activity as Khmer Serei and cited the name of General Norodom Chantarangsey as one of the resistance leaders" (although in fact Chantarangsey was only involved with the earlier Issarak movement). While the embassy in Bangkok was skeptical of the reports, it noted that "this conclusion does not detract from the premise that there is some dissidence occurring."[13]

Activity among resistance groups was reported in both the southwest and northwest. In the southwest, a group of possibly two thousand men (some estimates were as high as an implausible twenty thousand) held together in the Cardamom mountains, from which the group attacked convoys on Route 4 between Kompong Som and Kompong Speu in early July 1975. In the northwest, former Khmer Serei leader Bun Sang reportedly formed a new group called "Cobra." Bun Sang, who rallied to the Sihanouk government in 1969 with 640 of his followers (for which he was named captain in the Royal Khmer Armed Forces), supposedly formed this group in Kompong Chhnang prior to the fall of the Khmer Republic.[14]

Many refugees used the term "Khmer Serei" loosely to refer to resistance groups sprouting up at the time. The Bangkok embassy noted that "Cambodians generally agree thaa [sic] the leader of the old Khmer Serei, Son Ngoc Tha h [sic], succeeded in making his way from South Viet-nam after its fall to Paris." His deputy, Lek Sam Oeun, fled to Surin as a refugee, where he hoped to gain entry to the United States.[15]

On 23 February 1976, Charles Whitehouse, the US ambassador to Thailand, sent notice to Kissinger on the status of certain category three refugees in Thailand. The goal was to provide the Department of State a "better picture of remaining CAT III caseload and for possible use with congress in discussions extended parole program." One of the noted refugees was Son Le, a thirty-two-year-old former lieutenant in the Khmer army. Previously, he was a special forces company commander in the third Mike Force Company in Tay Ninh, Vietnam. What makes his case notable is that Son Le was Thành's nephew, who is noted in the cable as being the "prior director of all Mike Force operations in Vietnam."[16]

The Khmer Serei, or at least those claiming to be affiliated with the group, would maintain a presence on the Thai border throughout the refugee crisis that resulted from the demonic Khmer Rouge rule. Later, after the Khmer Rouge fell from power in 1979, these groups coalesced with various Khmer Rouge and pro-Sihanouk groups to fight against the new People's Republic of Kampuchea. This was more a coalition of convenience than anything else, and provided little more than an annoyance to the new government. The Khmer Serei was leaderless, and according to Robert L. Turkoly-Joczik, "they bear little resemblance" to Thành's old group. In fact, "many Khmer Serei groups are little more than black marketers or bands of extortionists who prey on the defenseless in the border refugee camps." According to William Shawcross, while some groups "had links with the intelligence or special-operations branches of the army, . . . none was impressive; for the most part they smuggled teak, gems, small amounts of gold and occasional statues out of Kampuchea." They were reportedly also quick to take vengeance against rival Khmer Serei, "a practice that could not have survived under the charismatic and forceful leadership of Son Ngoc Thanh."[17]

Thành himself was likely taken prisoner by the victorious communist Vietnamese forces shortly after the fall of Saigon on 30 April 1975. He then languished for the next two years in Chi Hoa Prison, where he died on 8 August 1977. As recalled by a relative who had served in the South Vietnamese military and was also imprisoned, Thành refused to cooperate or work with his communist captors. Already suffering from diabetes, he went on a hunger strike, likely the ultimate cause of his death.[18] Such was the unglamorous end to one of the fathers of Cambodian nationalism. Thành died in the same place he was born, South Vietnam. It was a place that he also spent many of the intervening years.

For a man that saw himself as truly Cambodian, he was most often outside of that country's borders. Despite his absence in body, he was never absent in spirit. He constantly influenced the trajectory of the country.

Thành was undoubtedly prominent among Cambodian nationalists in the years leading up to World War II. Such was his position that the Japanese sought to protect him from French authorities, and Thành became the prime minister of a briefly independent Cambodia in the waning days of the war. French authorities were well aware of the danger he posed to their return to power and expelled him to France, which allowed the seemingly more compliant Sihanouk to become the face of the country. His compliance only went so far as internal political pressure would allow it, however. Once Thành returned from France in the early 1950s and relaunched his crusade against the protectorate, Sihanouk redoubled his efforts for political concessions from France, which ultimately resulted in independence by the end of 1953. Afterward, Sihanouk spent much energy burying Thành's importance in the struggle for independence, and many historians have complied accordingly. Sihanouk does deserve much credit for this accomplishment, but Thành's role in these developments merits additional consideration. The path to Cambodian independence cannot be fully understood or explained without granting Thành his place among those most responsible for acquiring it.

Thành's Khmer Serei, formed with the intent of overthrowing Sihanouk's government, in reality was more of a consistent nuisance than threat to take power. What the group did do was exacerbate tensions between Cambodia and its Thai and South Vietnamese neighbors. The regional protector of the so-called Free World alliance, the United States, became involved with Thành's machinations as it expanded its war in Vietnam. The result was a Cambodia diplomatically severed from its neighbors and in search of aid from the communist bloc, especially China. Internally, political tensions built until 1970, when Sihanouk was ousted. Thành is central to these developments. As this book has shown, he is a key piece in the tense relationship Cambodia had with its neighbors, in the drift toward involvement in the Vietnam War, and in the global Cold War conflict.

The dismissal of the prince did not end the struggle for the country, however. Cambodia saw itself ensconced in a civil war. Thành funneled Khmer Krom mercenaries from the Mekong Delta into Phnom Penh to buttress the fledgling army of the Khmer Republic. Thành maintained his reputation as an ardent nationalist among some segments of the population, and he was elevated to the position of prime minister under Lon Nol in 1972. Finally victorious in his decades-long battle to unseat Sihanouk, his political rebirth was short-lived, and he was soon pushed out of the government to semiretirement back in South Vietnam. No matter the limited formal role he had in the Khmer Republic government, it is clear that Lon Nol relied on Thành and his recruits for the former to ascend to and maintain power. This factor has not been previously explored to the depths that it deserves.

All of this speaks to Thành as an underrepresented figure in modern Cambodian history. His life is also an important historical tool that can be used to study the great transformations that Cambodia faced during this period. Thành was an essential figure in the fight for independence from French and Japanese occupation during the Second World War, and this book casts Thành as a central figure in this fight, where he belongs. One also cannot understand Cambodia's tense relationship with its neighbors without studying Thành's impact. He was an important figure in American involvement in Cambodia, especially during the Vietnam War. Although Thành's relationship with US intelligence and military agencies remains murky, this work explores the connections in considerably more depth than has been attempted before.

Thành was also involved in the overthrow of Sihanouk, the calamitous event that put Cambodia on the path to destruction. The updated, thorough examination of the coup, and Thành's role in it, greatly expands our understanding of the event that sent Cambodia spiraling out of control. Thành's brief return to politics in the dysfunctional Khmer Republic was a shallow victory to his long war, but his important role in the Republic has not previously received much serious attention.

In sum, Thành's significance in modern Cambodian history has been undervalued. He was, in fact, one of the era's most important figures. Knowing Thành's roles helps us better understand modern Cambodia's transformation.

NOTES

Abbreviations

AAD   Access to Archival Databases, National Archives II

CREST CIA Records Search Tool, Central Intelligence Agency, National Archives II

DC   Documentation Center of Cambodia, Phnom Penh

JIC   Joint Intelligence Committee

NAC   National Archives of Cambodia, Phnom Penh

NAII   National Archives II, College Park, MD

OSS   Office of Strategic Services

RG   record group

Introduction

1. Some important works focused on the Khmer Rouge include David Chandler, *A History of Cambodia* (Boulder, CO: Westview Press, 2007); David Chandler, *The Tragedy of Cambodian History: Politics, War, and Revolution since 1945* (New Haven, CT: Yale University Press, 1991); Ben Kiernan, *How Pol Pot Came to Power: A History of Communism in Kampuchea, 1930–1975* (New Haven, CT: Yale University Press, 2004); Elizabeth Becker, *When the War was Over: The Voices of Cambodia's Revolution and Its People* (New York: Simon & Schuster, 1986); Craig Etcheson, *The Rise and Demise of Democratic Kampuchea* (Boulder, CO: Westview, 1984); Michael Vickery, *Cambodia, 1975–1982* (Boston: South End Press, 1984); Ben Kiernan, *The Pol Pot Regime: Race, Power, and Genocide in Cambodia under the Khmer Rouge, 1975–1979* (New Haven, CT: Yale University Press, 2008); Philip Short, *Pol Pot: Anatomy of a Nightmare* (New York: Henry Holt, 2005).

2. Sihanouk is a key player in many of the titles noted above. See also Milton Osborne, *Sihanouk: Prince of Light, Prince of Darkness* (Honolulu: University of Hawaii Press, 1994); Kenton J. Clymer, *The United States and Cambodia, 1870–1969: From Curiosity to Confrontation* (New York: Routledge, 2004); *The United States and Cambodia, 1969–2000: A Troubled Relationship* (New York: Routledge, 2004); William J. Rust, *Eisenhower in Cambodia: Diplomacy, Covert Action, and the Origins of the Second Indochinese War* (Lexington: University Press of Kentucky, 2016).

3. Sơn Ngọc Thành receives some attention in David Chandler's excellent work, *The Tragedy of Cambodian History*, and Kenton Clymer's two-volume study of the US-Cambodian relationship. Kiernan, *How Pol Pot Came to Power*; Kiernan, *The Pol Pot Regime*; Penny Edwards, *Cambodge: The Cultivation*

of a Nation, 1860–1945 (Honolulu: University of Hawaii Press, 2007); and Osborne, *Sihanouk*, also discuss Thành, but overall he largely remains a peripheral figure.

1. The First Independence, 1908–1945

1. David Chandler, *The Tragedy of Cambodian History: Politics, War, and Revolution since 1945* (New Haven, CT: Yale University Press, 1991), 18; National Intelligence Survey, Cambodia: Subversion, NIS 43A, section 57, January 1965, National Intelligence Survey Reports: Cambodia (3 of 3), RG 472, box 57, NAII, 24; David P. Chandler, "The Kingdom of Kampuchea, March–October 1945: Japanese-Sponsored Independence in Cambodian in World War II," *Journal of Southeast Asian Studies* 17, no. 1 (March 1986): 83; Son Ngoc Thanh letter, 3 April 1955, Son Ngoc Thanh Papers, Monash University.

2. V. M. Reddi, *A History of the Cambodian Independence Movement, 1863–1955* (Tirupati, India: Sri Venkateswara University Press, 1970), 29–33.

3. Kenton Clymer, *Troubled Relations: The United States and Cambodia since 1870* (Dekalb: Northern Illinois University Press, 2007), 5; "Minister King to the Secretary of State," 30 March 1905, *Papers Relating to the Foreign Relations of the United States, with the Annual Message of the President Transmitted to Congress December 5, 1905* (Washington, DC: Government Printing Office, 1906), https://history.state.gov/historicaldocuments/frus1905/d927.

4. John Tully, *France on the Mekong: A History of the Protectorate in Cambodia, 1863–1953* (Lanham, MD: University Press of America, 2002), 83–84. During the Vietnamese occupation in the 1980s many streets in Phnom Penh were renamed in honor of leaders of the rebellion.

5. Reddi, *History of the Cambodian Independence Movement*, 43–46.

6. Penny Edwards, *Cambodge: The Cultivation of a Nation, 1860–1945* (Honolulu: University of Hawaii Press, 2007), 95, 183.

7. Also known as Khmer Krom (Krom meaning "lower" in the Khmer language), they reside in the Mekong Delta of modern-day southern Vietnam. This area was once part of the great Khmer Empire that ended in 1431. Due to Cambodia's weakened state, between the seventeenth and eighteenth centuries this area was absorbed and eventually annexed by the Vietnamese, although the Khmer population remained. The archaeologist and writer Louis Malleret contends that only French acquisition of Cochinchina saved them from extinction or assimilation. See John Tully, *A Short History of Cambodia: From Empire to Survival* (Crows Nest, NSW, Australia: Allen & Unwin, 2005), 69.

8. Edwards, *Cambodge*, 185, 187–88.

9. Son Ngoc Thanh letter, 3 April 1955.

10. Chandler, "Kingdom of Kampuchea," 83; National Intelligence Survey, Cambodia: Subversion, NIS 43A, section 57, January 1965, National Intelligence Survey Reports: Cambodia (3 of 3), 24; Ben Kiernan and Chanthou Boua, *Peasants and Politics in Kampuchea, 1942–1981* (New York: M. E. Sharpe, 1982), 117–18; Henri Locard, "*Achar* Hem Chieu (1898-1943), the 'Umbrella Demonstration' of 20th July 1942 and the Vichy Regime," *Siksacakr*, no. 8-9 (2006-2007): 72;

Elizabeth Becker, *When the War Was Over: Cambodia and the Khmer Rouge Revolution* (New York: PublicAffairs, 1998), 40.

11. National Intelligence Survey, Cambodia, section 53: Political Dynamics, October 1955, National Intelligence Survey Reports: Cambodia (2 of 3), RG 472, box 57, NAII, 53-3; Edwards, *Cambodge*, 207.

12. Ian Harris, *Cambodian Buddhism: History and Practice* (Honolulu: University of Hawaii Press, 2005), 137–38.

13. Edwards, *Cambodge*, 207-8.

14. Edwards, *Cambodge*, 216, 222, 225.

15. Edwards, *Cambodge*, 215.

16. Le Résident Supérieure, "Titre de Permission," 5 November 1938, file no. 15374, NAC; Le Secrétaire Général de L'Institut à Monsieur Le Chef de Cabinet, Résidence Supérieure à Phnom Penh, 3 October 1938, file no. 15374, Records of the Résidence Supérieure du Cambodge (French Colonial Administration), NAC; "Lon Nol Aide Will Accept High Post," *Eugene Register-Guard*, 19 March 1972, 5A.

17. Son Ngoc Thanh letter, 3 April 1955; Vasinh Son, email to author, 6 January 2022.

18. Mark R. Peattie, *"Nanshin*: The 'Southward Advance,' 1931–1941, as a Prelude to the Japanese Occupation of Southeast Asia," in *The Japanese Wartime Empire, 1931–1945*, ed. Peter Duus, Ramon Myers, and Mark Peattie (Princeton, NJ: Princeton University Press, 1996), 189, 191.

19. Peattie, *"Nanshin*," 194-97, 202, 204-5.

20. Peattie, *"Nanshin*," 211-12, 229, 233, 237, 238.

21. OSS contribution to the JIC, "Japanese Seizure of French Indochina," 29 March 1945, folder Indochina—political relations: Japan 1940-1945 13.109, RG 59, General Records of the Department of State, Records of the Philippine and Southeast Asia Division, Country Files, 1929-53, box 9, NAII, 3.

22. OSS contribution to JIC, "Japanese Seizure of French Indochina," 1.

23. "The Minister in Thailand (Grant) to the Secretary of State," *Foreign Relations of the United States Diplomatic Papers, 1940*, vol. 4, *The Far East* (Washington, DC: Government Publishing Office, 1955), https://history.state.gov/historicaldocuments/frus1940v04/d226.

24. "MAGIC Summary," War Department, Office of Assistant Chief of Staff, reel 2, SRS 673, 4 August 1942, *The MAGIC Documents: Summaries and Transcripts of the Top Secret Diplomatic Communications of Japan, 1938–1945* (Washington, DC: University Publications of America, 1980), 9-10.

25. Ralph B. Smith, "The Japanese in Indochina and the Coup of March 1945," *Journal of Southeast Asian Studies* 9, no. 2 (September 1978): 268; Michael Leifer, "The Cambodian Opposition," *Asian Survey* 2, no. 2 (April, 1962): 11; National Intelligence Survey, Cambodia: Subversion, NIS 43A, Section 57, January 1965, National Intelligence Survey Reports: Cambodia (3 of 3), 25; Chandler, "Kingdom of Kampuchea," 83; Ben Kiernan, *How Pol Pot Came to Power: Colonialism, Nationalism, and Communism in Cambodia, 1930–1975* (New Haven, CT: Yale University Press, 2004), 41–42; Chandler, *Tragedy of Cambodian History*, 19; Locard, *"Achar* Hem Chieu."

26. Harris, *Cambodian Buddhism*, 140.

27. Bunchan Mul, "The Umbrella War of 1942," in *Peasants and Politics in Kampuchea, 1942–1981*, ed. Ben Kiernan and Chanthou Boua (Armonk, New York: M. E. Sharpe, 1982), 118–22.

28. Son Ngoc Thanh letter, 3 April 1955. Thanh claims he was arrested in 1941, although he does not state why. See George McT. Kahin, interview with Son Ngoc Thanh, 25 August 1971, folder: Son Ngoc Thanh 1971–72, box 67, Papers of George McT. Kahin, Division of Rare and Manuscript Collections, Cornell University, 4.

29. Chandler, "Kingdom of Kampuchea," 83–84.

30. Kiernan, *How Pol Pot Came to Power*, 45.

31. "MAGIC Summary," reel 3, SRS 818, 26 December 1942, *The MAGIC Documents*, 6–8.

32. "MAGIC Summary," reel 3, SRS 818, 26 December 1942, *The MAGIC Documents*, 6–8.

33. "MAGIC Summary," reel 4, SRS 834, 11 January 1943, *The MAGIC Documents*, 8–9.

34. "MAGIC Summary No. 321," reel 4, War Department, Office of Assistant Chief of Staff, SRS 872, 10 February 1943, *MAGIC Documents*, 12.

35. Ken'ichi Goto, *Tensions of Empire: Japan and Southeast Asia in the Colonial and Postcolonial World* (Athens: Ohio University Press, 2003), 152.

36. James L. McClain, *Japan: A Modern History* (New York: W. W. Norton, 2002), 494–95.

37. Goto, *Tensions of Empire*, 79–80, 102.

38. Kiernan, *How Pol Pot Came to Power*, 45–46; Chandler, "Kingdom of Kampuchea," 83–84; "Our Far-Flung Correspondents: Back and Forth in Phnom Penh," *New Yorker*, 18 April 1964, folder: Cambodia, H–N General, box no. RM4, The Personal Papers of Bernard Fall, John F. Kennedy Library, 157.

39. "MAGIC Summary," reel 5, SRS 982, 31 May 1943, *MAGIC Documents*, 7–9.

40. MAGIC Summary, reel 4, SRS 916, 26 March 1943, *MAGIC Documents*, 4.

41. Edwards, *Cambodge*, 236.

42. Edwards, *Cambodge*, 233.

43. Justin Corfield, *Khmers Stand Up! A History of the Cambodian Government 1970–1975* (Clayton, Victoria, Australia: Centre of Southeast Asian Studies, Monash University, 1994), 7.

44. Arthur J. Dommen, *The Indochinese Experience of the French and the Americans: Nationalism and Communism in Cambodia, Laos, and Vietnam* (Bloomington: Indiana University Press, 2001), 83.

45. Central Intelligence Agency, "Communism and Cambodia," 1 February 1972, General CIA Records, CREST, NAII, 1, https://www.cia.gov/reading room/docs/CIA-RDP74B00415R000100050037-2.pdf.

46. Memorandum for the President, "Indochina," 13 January 1945, folder: U.S. Policy re Indochina and China, RG 59, General Records of the Department of State, Records of the Philippine and Southeast Asia Division, Country Files, 1929–53, box 7, NAII, 1–2.

47. Clymer, *Troubled Relations*, 15.

48. Robert J. McMahon, "Toward a Post-Colonial Order: Truman Administration Policies Toward South and Southeast Asia," in *The Truman Presidency*, ed. Michael J. Lacey (New York: Woodrow Wilson International Center for Scholars, 1989), 340–42; Robert Dallek, *Franklin D. Roosevelt and American Foreign Policy, 1932–1945* (New York: Oxford University Press, 1995), 513.

49. "For The Weekly," 8 February 1945, folder: Indochina—political relations: Japan 1940–1945 13.109, RG 59, General Records of the Department of State, Records of the Philippine and Southeast Asia Division, Country Files, 1929–53, box 9, NAII.

50. Chandler, "Kingdom of Kampuchea," 81.

51. OSS contribution to JIC, "Japanese Seizure of French Indochina," 6.

52. Smith, "Japanese in Indochina," 286.

53. Corfield, *Khmers Stand Up!*, 8.

54. "Indo-China French in Firmer Stands," *New York Times*, 14 March 1945, 12.

55. Edwards, *Cambodge*, 240; Smith, "Japanese in Indochina," 286; Chandler, "Kingdom of Kampuchea," 80.

56. "Kubota, 1944–1945 (9 March 1946 Interrogation by Magistrate d'Instruction)," enclosure to letter from Leonard Overton to David P. Chandler, 23 May 1989 (drawn from Overton's research conducted in Paris in 1959), courtesy of David Chandler.

57. OSS contribution to JIC, "Japanese Seizure of French Indochina," 1.

58. Caffery to Secretary to State, 13 March 1945, folder: Indochina—political relations: Japan 1940–1945 13.109, RG 59, General Records of the Department of State, Records of the Philippine and Southeast Asia Division, Country Files, 1929–53, box 9, NAII, 1–2.

59. William D. Leahy, "Memorandum for the Secretary of State," 17 March 1945, folder: Indochina—political relations: Japan 1940–1945 13.109, RG 59, General Records of the Department of State, Records of the Philippine and Southeast Asia Division, Country Files, 1929–53, box 9, NAII.

60. Dallek, *Franklin D. Roosevelt and American Foreign Policy*, 512–13.

61. "Kubota, 1944–1945 (9 March 1946 Interrogation by Magistrate d'Instruction)," Smith, "Japanese in Indochina," 285.

62. OSS contribution to JIC, "Japanese Seizure of French Indochina," 8.

63. "Kubota, 1944–1945 (9 March 1946 Interrogation by Magistrate d'Instruction)."

64. "Acte d'Accusation against Son Ngoc Thanh (Tribinal Militaire Permanent de Saigon)," 24 August 1946, enclosure to letter from Leonard Overton to David P. Chandler, 23 May 1989 (drawn from Overton's research conducted in Paris in 1959), courtesy of David Chandler. It seems these issues of *Nagaravatta* have not survived.

65. Chandler, "Kingdom of Kampuchea," 85.

66. "Kubota, 1944–1945 (9 March 1946 Interrogation by Magistrate d'Instruction)."

67. "Acte d'Accusation against Son Ngoc Thanh (Tribinal Militaire Permanent de Saigon)," 24 August 1946; "Kubota, 1944–1945 (9 March 1946 Interrogation by Magistrate d'Instruction)."

68. "Ordonnons," Kram No. 53-NS, 31 May 1945, folder #23487, NAC.

69. Reddi, *History of the Cambodian Independence Movement*, 94–95.

70. "Cambodian–Vietnamese Relations Period June-Oct 1945 (From Sûreté, SNT 17 + 18 Oct 1945), enclosure to letter from Leonard Overton to David P. Chandler, 23 May 1989 (drawn from Overton's research conducted in Paris in 1959), courtesy of David Chandler.

71. "Policy Paper Prepared in the Department of State, Washington, 22 June 1945," *Foreign Relations of the United States: Diplomatic Papers, 1945*, vol. 6, *The Far East* (Washington, DC: Government Publishing Office, 1969), https://history.state.gov/historicaldocuments/frus1945v06/d386.

72. Ben Kiernan, "Origins of Khmer Communism," *Southeast Asian Affairs 1981* (1982), 163.

73. Chandler, "Kingdom of Kampuchea," 87.

74. "Acte d'Accusation against Son Ngoc Thanh (Tribinal Militaire Permanent de Saigon)."

75. "Thanh Defends Self: Declaration, 1947; In Reply to Act of Accusation: 25 February 1947," enclosure to letter from Leonard Overton to David P. Chandler, 23 May 1989 (drawn from Overton's research conducted in Paris in 1959), courtesy of David Chandler.

76. "Kubota, 1944–1945 (9 March 1946 Interrogation by Magistrate d'Instruction)."

77. "Acte d'Accusation against Son Ngoc Thanh (Tribinal Militaire Permanent de Saigon)."

78. "Le Ministre des Affaires Etrangères à Son Excellence le Consul Général du Japon, Conseiller Suprême auprès du Royaue de Cambodge," 13 August 1945, folder #23707, Relations Diplomatique, NAC.

79. "MAGIC Summary," reel 14, SRS 1768, 23 August 1945, *MAGIC Documents*, 7.

80. Chandler, "Kingdom of Kampuchea," 88.

81. Chandler, "Kingdom of Kampuchea," 86; "Acte d'Accusation against Son Ngoc Thanh (Tribinal Militaire Permanent de Saigon)."

82. Chandler, "Kingdom of Kampuchea," 88.

83. "MAGIC Summary," reel 14, SRS 1779, 3 September 1945, *MAGIC Documents*, 10.

84. McMahon, "Toward a Post-Colonial Order," 342.

85. Lloyd C. Gardner, *Approaching Vietnam: From World War II through Dienbienphu, 1941–1954* (New York: W. W. Norton, 1988), 52.

86. SEA: Draft (1) ALM 8/20/45, folder: Indochina—political policy 13.105, RG 59, General Records of the Department of State, Records of the Philippine and Southeast Asia Division, Country Files, 1929–53, box 7, NAII, 1.

87. SEA: Draft (1) ALM 8/20/45, 4.

88. SEA: Draft (1) ALM 8/20/45, 5.

89. SEA: Draft (1) ALM 8/20/45, 1–3.

90. SEA: Draft (1) ALM 8/20/45, 5.

91. "Proces-Verbal de la Commission Permanente du Conseil des Ministres, Réunie le 20 Août 1945, Sous la Présidence de S. E. le Premier Ministre Son Ngoc Thanh," 20 August 1945, folder #34190, Relations Diplomatique, NAC.

92. Chandler, "Kingdom of Kampuchea," 89.

93. "MAGIC Summary," reel 14, SRS 1779, 3 September 1945, *MAGIC Documents*, 9.

94. Michael Leifer, *Cambodia: The Search for Security* (New York: Frederick A. Praeger, 1967), 27.

95. "Kubota, 1944–1945 (9 March 1946 Interrogation by Magistrate d'Instruction)."

96. Chandler, *Tragedy*, 23; Michael Vickery, "Cambodia (Kampuchea): History, Tragedy and an Uncertain Future," *Bulletin of Concerned Asian Scholars* 21, 2–4 (1989), 40.

97. There is some discrepancy on the date of the plebiscite, with some sources citing the date as 14 August 1945. See Dieter Nohlen, Florian Grotz, and Christof Hartmann, eds., *Elections in Asia and the Pacific: A Data Handbook*, vol. 2, *Southeast Asia, East Asia, and the South Pacific* (Oxford: Oxford University Press, 2001), 45–68; Phouk Chhay, "Le Pouvoir Politique au Cambodge, Essaye d'Analyse Sociologique 1945–1965," *Monash Collections Online*, accessed 1 September 2022, https://repository.monash.edu/items/show/1316, 139; Chandler, "Kingdom of Kampuchea," 89.

98. "Review of Indochina's Political Position," *Far Eastern Economic Review* 2, no. 12 (19 March 1947): 150–51.

99. Chandler, "Kingdom of Kampuchea," 89.

100. Chandler, "Kingdom of Kampuchea," 90; Dommen, *Indochinese Experience*, 137.

101. Chandler, "Kingdom of Kampuchea," 90.

102. Kim Tit, "Un Episode de L'Histoire Conteporaine du Cambodge," *Réalités Cambodgiennes*, no. 553, 16 June 1967, box 678, Charles Meyer Collection, NAC, 15.

103. Kim Tit, "Un Episode," 15.

104. "MAGIC Summary," reel 14, SRS 1736, 22 July 1945, *MAGIC Documents*, B5.

105. "Extract from the Report to the Combined Chiefs of Staff by the Supreme Allied Commander, Southeast Asia 30th June, 1947," *Documents Relating to British Involvement in the Indochina Conflict 1945–1965*, cmnd. 2834 (London: Her Majesty's Stationery Office, 1965), 51–52.

106. Chandler, "Kingdom of Kampuchea," 90.

107. "Brazzaville in French at 7:00 A.M. to Indo-China 10/11 mcn," folder: Indochina—Reports misc. 1944–53 13.121, RG 59, General Records of the Department of State, Records of the Philippine and Southeast Asia Division, Country Files, 1929–53, box 10, NAII, 1–2.

108. "Acte d'Accusation against Son Ngoc Thanh (Tribinal Militaire Permanent de Saigon)."

109. Chandler, *Tragedy of Cambodian History*, 26.

110. Chandler, "Kingdom of Kampuchea," 90.

111. "Extract from the Report to the Combined Chiefs of Staff by the Supreme Allied Commander, Southeast Asia 30th June, 1947," 52.

112. "French In New Positions: Stubborn Opposition," *Times* (UK), 15 October 1945, 4

113. "Arrest of Thanh, 1945 (18 April 1946; Interrogation by Magistrate d'Instruction), enclosure to letter from Leonard Overton to David P. Chandler, 23 May 1989 (drawn from Overton's research conducted in Paris in 1959), courtesy of David Chandler.

114. Chandler, *Tragedy*, 26.

115. "Prime Minister Ousted in Cambodia," *Times* (UK), 23 October 1945, 4.

116. "Indo-China Official Removed By British," *New York Times*, 22 October 1945, 2.

117. "Running Food to Saigon: Convoys on Canals," *Times* (UK), 29 October 1945, 4.

118. Chandler, "Kingdom of Kampuchea," 90.

119. "Acte d'Accusation against Son Ngoc Thanh (Tribinal Militaire Permanent de Saigon)."

120. "Thanh Defends Self: Declaration, 1947; In Reply to Act of Accusation: 25 February 1947."

121. "From handwritten note in pencil (13 sheets = 25 pages) inserted," enclosure to letter from Leonard Overton to David P. Chandler, 23 May 1989 (drawn from Overton's research conducted in Paris in 1959), courtesy of David Chandler.

122. National Intelligence Survey, Cambodia, section 53: Political Dynamics, October 1955. National Intelligence Survey Reports: Cambodia (2 of 3), RG 472, box 57, NAII, 53-3.

123. Chandler, "Kingdom of Kampuchea," 91.

124. "The Assistant Chief of the Division of Southeast Asian Affairs (Landon) to the Secretary of State," *Foreign Relations of the United States, 1946*, vol. 8, *The Far East* (Washington, DC: Government Publishing Office, 1971), https://history.state.gov/historicaldocuments/frus1946v08/d18.

2. Return to Exile, 1946–1955

1. Martin Florian Herz, *A Short History of Cambodia: From the Days of Angkor to the Present* (New York: F. A. Praeger, 1958), 78. Herz, a career Foreign Service officer, was stationed in Cambodia for a period of time. Sihanouk was quite critical of both Herz and his book upon its publication.

2. "Policy and Information Statement of French Indochina," 28 February 1946, folder: Indochina—political 13.105 policy, RG 59, General Records of the Department of State, Records of the Philippine and Southeast Asia Division, Country Files, 1929-53, box 7, NAII.

3. Dean Acheson, 9 March 1946, folder: O.F. 203—(1945-1949), Official File, 201 A Endorsements—203 (February, 1951), box #769, Papers of Harry S. Truman, Harry S. Truman Library.

4. David Chandler, *The Tragedy of Cambodian History: Politics, War, and Revolution Since 1945* (New Haven, CT: Yale University Press, 1991), 29, 38.

5. Tillman Durdin, "Flight Puts Focus on Cambodia Scene," *New York Times*, 21 April 1952, 4; Philip Short, *Pol Pot: Anatomy of a Nightmare* (New York: Henry Holt, 2005), 35, 42.

6. The Consul at Saigon (Reed) to the Secretary of State, 14 June 1947, *Foreign Relations of the United States, 1947*, vol. 6, *The Far East* (Washington, DC: Government Publishing Office, 1972), 103–5, https://history.state.gov/historicaldocuments/frus1947v06/d121.

7. "Do all Patriots Know Son Ngoc Thanh?" nd, Document #9273, Records of the Résidence Supérieure du Cambodge (French Colonial Administration), NAC; see also Penny Edwards, *Cambodge: The Cultivation of a Nation, 1860–1945* (Honolulu: University of Hawaii Press, 2007), 241.

8. Ellen J. Hammer, *The Struggle for Indochina, 1940–1955* (Sanford, CA: Stanford University Press, 1966), 254.

9. Arthur J. Dommen, "Letters to the Editor," *Far Eastern Economic Review*, 9 July 1970, 77.

10. Chantaraingsey to Austin, Free Cambodian Committee, Bangkok branch No 1 Opposite Boromnivad Pagoda, Bangkok, Siam, 14 January 1947, folder: Indochina Cambodia, General 1947, RG 59, General Records of the Department of State, Records of the Philippine and Southeast Asia Division, Country Files, 1929–53, box 10, NAII, 1–5.

11. Austin to Secretary of State, No. 1881, 3 February 1947; Draft reply to letter to Senator Austin from the Free Cambodian Committee, 18 February 1947, folder: Indochina Cambodia, General 1947, RG 59, General Records of the Department of State, Records of the Philippine and Southeast Asia Division, Country Files, 1929–53, box 10, NAII.

12. Southeast Asia Regional Conference, June 21-June 26, 1948, Bangkok, Siam, Section VI, "Regional Repercussions of Continued Hostility in Indochina," folder: Southeast Asia File, Southeast Asia Regional Conference, Bangkok, Siam, folder 2 Melby, Southeast Asia File, General, 1950–1952, Joint MDAP Survey, Southeast Asia Regional Conference, Miscellaneous File, box #9, Papers of John F. Melby, Harry S. Truman Library, 1–2.

13. "The Situation in Indochina," *Far Eastern Economic Review*, 25 May 1949: 641.

14. "Prince Sihanouk and the Khmer People," *Far Eastern Economic Review*, 6 September 1956, 310.

15. There is a long tradition of the use of fetal amulets, or *koan kroach*, in Cambodian history. According to the historian Trude Jacobsen, "the father of the child might trick his wife into saying the words 'this is your child, do with it what you will'; he would then take her to a remote part of the forest and remove the fetus, killing the mother in the process. He would then dehydrate the fetus... over a ritual fire and wear it around his neck in a small bag, from where it would advise him of potential danger." During the Cambodian civil war (1970–1975), many of Lon Nol's soldiers relied on such amulets for protection. Khmer Rouge cadre were known to forcibly remove fetuses from women as well. The practice, while significantly diminished, exists to this day. See Trudy Jacobsen, *Lost Goddesses: The Denial of Female Power in Cambodian History* (Copenhagen, Denmark: NIAS Press, 2008), 97, 228.

16. Norman Lewis, *A Dragon Apparent: Travels in Indo-China* (Oxford: The Book Society, 1951), 205.

17. George M. Abbott, memorandum, "Remarks on Agenda for Bangkok Regional Conference as Pertaining to Indochina," folder: Southeast Asia File, Southeast Asia Regional Conference, Bangkok, Siam, folder 1 Melby, Southeast Asia File, General, 1950-1952, Joint MDAP Survey, Southeast Asia Regional Conference, Miscellaneous File, box #9, Papers of John F. Melby, Harry S. Truman Library, 3.

18. John P. Armstrong, *Sihanouk Speaks: Cambodia's Chief of State Explains His Controversial Policies* (New York: Walker and Company, 1964), 58.

19. "Problem Paper Prepared by a Working Group in the Department of State," 1 February 1950, *Foreign Relations of the United States, 1950*, vol. 6, *The Far East* (Washington, DC: Government Printing Office, 1976), 714-15, https://history.state.gov/historicaldocuments/frus1950v06/d457; Dean Acheson, *Cross Reference Sheet*, 2 February 1950, folder: O. F. (1950-Feb. 1951), Official File, 201 A Endorsements—203 (February, 1951), box #769, Papers of Harry S. Truman, Harry S. Truman Library.

20. Dean Acheson, Memorandum for the President, "Subject: U.S. Recognition of Vietnam, Laos and Cambodia," 2 February 1950, folder: O.F. 203 F (Cambodia—Laos/Vietnam), Official File, 203 Misc. (1951)—204 Misc. (October 1945), box #771, Papers of Harry S. Truman, Harry S. Truman Library.

21. Truman to Sihanouk, 4 February 1950, folder: O.F. 203 F (Cambodia—Laos/Vietnam), Official File, 203 Misc. (1951)—204 Misc. (October 1945), box #771, Papers of Harry S. Truman, Harry S. Truman Library.

22. Chandler, *Tragedy of Cambodian History*, 57-58, 326 n22.

23. Charles Meyer, "Behind Phnom Penh's Musical," *National Guardian*, 2 June 1971, General CIA Records, CREST, NAII, https://www.cia.gov/reading room/docs/CIA-RDP80-01601R000800200001-4.pdf; Michael Leifer, *Cambodia: The Search for Security* (New York: Frederick A. Praeger, 1967), 40. According to David Chandler, twenty issues of *Khmer Krauk!* were issued between January and late March 1952. The paper emphasized Thành's push for independence through editorials, poems, and articles. See Chandler, *Tragedy of Cambodian History*, 326 n27.

24. Herz, *Short History of Cambodia*, 84.

25. Leifer, *Cambodia*, 40; Son Ngoc Thanh letter, 3 April 1955, Son Ngoc Thanh Papers, Monash University; Phouk Chhay, "Le Pouvoir Politique au Cambodge, Essaye d'Analyse Sociologi-que 1945-1965," *Monash Collections Online*, 165, accessed September 1, 2022, https://repository.monash.edu/items/show/1316.

26. "Interview with General Chana Samuda-vanija," 1981, David Chandler Cambodia Collection, Monash University, 1, http://arrow.monash.edu.au/hdl/1959.1/483755.

27. "Interview with General Chana Samuda-vanija," 2.

28. Herz, *Short History of Cambodia*, 84.

29. David J. Steinberg, *Cambodia: Its People, Its Society, Its Culture* (New Haven, CT: Hraf Press, 1959), 102.

30. William J. Rust, *Eisenhower & Cambodia: Diplomacy, Covert Action, and the Origins of the Second Indochinese War* (Lexington: University Press of Kentucky, 2016), 11-12.

31. Durdin, "Flight Puts Focus on Cambodia Scene," 2.

32. Robert Shaplen, "Our Far-Flung Correspondents: Back and Forth in Phnom Penh," *New Yorker*, 18 April 1964, folder: Cambodia, H–N General, box no. RM4, The Personal Papers of Bernard Fall, John F. Kennedy Library, 158.

33. "Interview with General Chana Samuda-vanija," 2.

34. "Interview with General Chana Samuda-vanija," 1–3.

35. Khmer Surin refers to ethnic Khmer living in the former Cambodian province of Surin, which was annexed by Thailand in the eighteenth century.

36. "Interview with General Chana Samuda-vanija," 3–4.

37. Central Intelligence Agency, "Current Intelligence Digest, Central Intelligence Agency, OCI no. 3894, 17 March 1952," General CIA Records, CREST, NAII, 5, https://www.cia.gov/readingroom/docs/CIA-RDP79T0114 6A000800220001-0.pdf.

38. Quoted in Rust, *Eisenhower & Cambodia*, 12. So'n Ngọc Minh, like Thành, was born in Tra Vinh in southern Vietnam. Also known as Achar Mean, Minh took his nomme de guerre in an attempt to capitalize on the popularity of both Ho Chi Minh and Thành. He was the leader of the leftist Issarak groups and one of the most important figures representing the Vietnamese communist influence in Cambodia. For more on Minh, see Ben Kiernan, *How Pol Pot Came to Power: A History of Communism in Kampuchea, 1930–1975* (London: Verso, 1986).

39. Michael Leifer, "The Cambodian Opposition," *Asian Survey* 2, no. 2 (April, 1962): 12.

40. Durdin, "Flight Puts Focus on Cambodia Scene," 4.

41. "The Counselor of Embassy in France (Bonsal) to the Director of the Office of Philippine and Southeast Asian Affairs (Lacy)," 31 March 1952, *Foreign Relations of the United States, 1952–1954*, vol. 13, part 1, *Indochina* (Washington, DC: Government Publishing Office, 1982), 96–97, https://history.state.gov/historicaldocuments/frus1952-54v13p1/d48.

42. Rust, *Eisenhower & Cambodia*, 12–13.

43. Ben Kiernan and Chanthou Boua, eds., *Peasants and Politics in Kampuchea, 1942–1981* (New York: M. E. Sharpe, 1982), 128.

44. Kenton Clymer, *The United States and Cambodia, 1870–1969: From Curiosity to Confrontation* (London: RoutledgeCurzon, 2004), 28–29.

45. Durdin, "Flight Puts Focus on Cambodia Scene," 5.

46. "Cambodian Band Dispersed," *New York Times*, 21 October, 1952, 3.

47. Milton Osborne, *Sihanouk: Prince of Light, Prince of Darkness* (Honolulu: University of Hawaii Press, 1994), 68.

48. Clymer, *The United States and Cambodia, 1870–1969*, 29.

49. Nguon Hong, "Who is the Thief?" Committee of Khmer Issarak, Building the Nation, 20 August 1952, document #9273, Records of the Résidence Supérieure du Cambodge (French Colonial Administration), NAC.

50. "The Chargé at Phnom Penh (Corcoran) to the Department of State," 17 June 1952, *Foreign Relations of the United States, 1952–1954*, vol. 13, part 1, *Indochina* (Washington, DC: Government Publishing Office, 1982) 196, https://history.state.gov/historicaldocuments/frus1952-54v13p1/d81.

51. Chandler, *Tragedy of Cambodian History*, 63–64.

52. Central Intelligence Agency, "Current Intelligence Digest, Central Intelligence Agency, OCI no. 6416, 10 June 1952," General CIA Records, CREST, NAII, 8, https://www.cia.gov/readingroom/docs/CIA-RDP79T01146 A001000200001-9.pdf.

53. Shaplen, "Our Far-Flung Correspondents," 158.

54. Quoted in Herz, *Short History of Cambodia*, 86.

55. "The Chargé at Saigon (Gullion) to the Department of State," 30 June 1952, *Foreign Relations of the United States, 1952–1954*, vol. 13, part 1, *Indochina* (Washington, DC: Government Publishing Office, 1982), 215–19, https:// history.state.gov/historicaldocuments/frus1952-54v13p1/d91.

56. Central Intelligence Agency, "NIE-35/2: Probable Developments in Indochina through Mid-1953, 23 August 1952," General CIA Records, CREST, NAII, 7, https://www.cia.gov/readingroom/docs/CIA-RDP79R01012 A001000040014-0.pdf.

57. Central Intelligence Agency, "NIE-35/2: Probable Developments in Indochina Through Mid-1953," 6,

58. Central Intelligence Agency, "NIE-35/2: Probable Developments in Indochina Through Mid-1953," 6.

59. "The Secretary of State to Certain Diplomatic and Consular Offices," 1 October 1952, *Foreign Relations of the United States, 1952–1954*, vol. 13, part 1, *Indochina* (Washington, DC: Government Publishing Office, 1982), 263, https:// history.state.gov/historicaldocuments/frus1952-54v13p1/d118.

60. Chandler, *Tragedy of Cambodian History*, 65.

61. "The Ambassador at Saigon (Heath) to the Department of State," 12 January 1953, *Foreign Relations of the United States, 1952–1954*, vol. 13, part 1, *Indochina* (Washington, DC: Government Publishing Office, 1982), 347, https:// history.state.gov/historicaldocuments/frus1952-54v13p1/d164.

62. Rust, *Eisenhower & Cambodia*, 14.

63. Chandler, *Tragedy of Cambodian History*, 71–72.

64. Central Intelligence Agency, "Location and Disposition of Son Ngoc Thanh's Forces in Cambodia, 31 December 1952," General CIA Records, CREST, NAII, 1–2, https://www.cia.gov/readingroom/docs/CIA-RDP82-0045 7R015700360003-0.pdf.

65. "Memorandum by Ambassador Donald R. Heath to the Assistant Secretary of State for Far Eastern Affairs (Robertson)," 20 April 1953, *Foreign Relations of the United States, 1952–1954*, vol. 13, part 1, *Indochina* (Washington, DC: Government Publishing Office, 1982), 475–77, https://history.state.gov/ historicaldocuments/frus1952-54v13p1/d226.

66. Herz, *Short History of Cambodia*, 89.

67. Quoted in Rust, *Eisenhower & Cambodia*, 17.

68. Cynthia Frederick, "Cambodia: 'Operation Total Victory No. 43,'" *Bulletin of Concerned Asian Scholars* 2, no. 3 (April–July 1970): 7.

69. Norman Lewis, *Dragon Apparent*, 208.

70. Shaplen, "Our Far-Flung Correspondents," 158–59. For a summary of Sihanouk's visit to the United States, see "Memorandum of Discussion at the 143d Meeting of the National Security Council, Wednesday, May 6, 1953," *Foreign Relations of the United States, 1952–1954*, vol. 2, part 2, *National Security Affairs*

(Washington, DC: Government Publishing Office, 1984), 546–50, https://his tory.state.gov/historicaldocuments/frus1952-54v02p2/d87.

71. Herz, *Short History of Cambodia*, 90.

72. "Memorandum by Ambassador Donald R. Heath to the Assistant Secretary of State for Far Eastern Affairs (Robertson)," 475–77.

73. "Memorandum by Ambassador Donald R. Heath to the Secretary of State," 28 April 1953, *Foreign Relations of the United States, 1952–1954*, vol. 13, part 1, *Indochina* (Washington, DC: Government Publishing Office, 1982), 525, https:// history.state.gov/historicaldocuments/frus1952-54v13p1/d250; Michael James, "King, Here, Warns Cambodia May Rise," *New York Times*, 19 April 1953, 1.

74. "The Chargé at Phnom Penh (Montllor) to the Department of State," 15 June 1953, *Foreign Relations of the United States, 1952–1954*, vol. 13, part 1, *Indochina* (Washington, DC: Government Publishing Office, 1982), 609, https:// history.state.gov/historicaldocuments/frus1952-54v13p1/d305.

75. Shaplen, "Our Far-Flung Correspondents," 158–59.

76. Clymer, *United States and Cambodia*, 31.

77. Phouk Chhay, "Le Pouvoir Politique au Cambodge, Essaye d'Analyse Sociologi-que 1945-1965," *Monash Collections Online*, 179, accessed September 1, 2022, https://repository.monash.edu/items/show/1316. There is some interesting newsreel footage that captured Sihanouk as he ventured into the jungle northwest of Siem Reap. Alongside Commander Dap Chhuon, in this semi-staged footage Sihanouk is shown leading an expedition through the jungle, at times through water past his knees, although he is also seen riding a horse through deep waters. Also shown are doctors aiding the sick, Sihanouk meeting with monks and local villagers, and the planning of military strategy. See "The Cooperation with Cambodian King," ECPAD Collection (Establissement de communication et de production audiovisuelle de la défense), PAD_V1_001215 (Archive Reference), 1952, Bophana Center.

78. FE—Mr. Johnson, PSA—Mr. Day, "Background on Cambodian Crisis," 30 June 1953, folder: Indochina 1, RG 59 General Records, Bureau of Far Eastern Affairs, 1953, Miscellaneous Subject Files for the year 1953, Far East—General—1—Japan—July thru December [1953]—1, box 5, NAII, 1.

79. FE—Mr. Johnson, PSA—Mr. Day, "Background on Cambodian Crisis," 2.

80. "The Chargé at Phnom Penh (Montllor) to the Department of State," 17 September 1953, *Foreign Relations of the United States, 1952–1954*, vol. 13, part 1, *Indochina* (Washington, DC: Government Publishing Office, 1982), 808, https:// history.state.gov/historicaldocuments/frus1952-54v13p1/d408.

81. "The Ambassador at Saigon (Heath) to the Department of State," 12 September 1953, *Foreign Relations of the United States, 1952–1954*, vol. 13, part 1, *Indochina* (Washington, DC: Government Publishing Office, 1982), 798–800, https://history.state.gov/historicaldocuments/frus1952-54v13p1/d402.

82. Clymer, *United States and Cambodia*, 32.

83. Craig Etcheson, "The Khmer Way of Exile: Lessons from Three Indochinese Wars," *Journal of Political Science* 18, no. 1 (November 1990): 99.

84. Chandler, *Tragedy of Cambodian History*, 70–71; Shaplen, "Our Far-Flung Correspondents," 158–59.

85. "Concern over Indo-China," *Times* (UK), 8 February 1954, 6.

86. Clymer, *United States and Cambodia*, 32–33.

87. Central Intelligence Agency, "Special National Intelligence Estimate: The Effects of Certain Possible Developments on the Military Security and Political Stability of Laos and Cambodia Through 1954," 9 June 1954, General CIA Records, CREST, NAII, 3, https://www.cia.gov/readingroom/docs/CIA-RDP79R01012A004400060001-8.pdf.

88. Central Intelligence Agency, "Central Intelligence Bulletin," 25 April 1954, CIA General Records, CREST, NAII, https://www.cia.gov/reading room/docs/CIA-RDP79T00975A001500380001-3.pdf.

89. Clymer, *United States and Cambodia*, 34; Herz, *Short History of Cambodia*, 94.

90. "Final Declaration of the Geneva Conference, 12 July, 1954," *Documents Relating to British Involvement in the Indochina Conflict 1945–1965*, cmnd. 2834 (London: Her Majesty's Stationery Office, 1965), 83–84.

91. James Waite, *The End of the First Indochina War: A Global History* (New York: Routledge, 2012), 1–2.

92. Leifer, "Cambodian Opposition," 12.

93. Herz, *Short History of Cambodia*, 94–95; Central Intelligence Agency, "Communism and Cambodia," 1 February 1972, General CIA Records, CREST, NAII, 23, https://www.cia.gov/readingroom/docs/CIA-RDP74B00 415R000100050037-2.pdf.

94. C. L. Sulzberger, "The Man Who Would Not Be King," *New York Times*, 7 March 1955, 26.

95. National Intelligence Estimate, "Post-Geneva Outlook in Indochina," 3 August 1954, *Foreign Relations of the United States, 1952–1954*, vol. 13, part 2, *Indochina* (Washington, DC: Government Publishing Office, 1982), 1907, https://history.state.gov/historicaldocuments/frus1952-54v13p2/d1105.

96. Central Intelligence Agency, "FDD Exploitation of Southeast Asia Language Materials, 5 August 1954," CIA General Records, CREST, NAII, 6, https://www.cia.gov/readingroom/docs/CIA-RDP78-03130A000100020027-4.pdf; the report stated that "any information on Son Ngoc Thanh, whether of a background or current nature, would be useful."

97. National Intelligence Survey, Cambodia: Subversion, NIS 43A, section 57, January 1965, National Intelligence Survey Reports: Cambodia (3 of 3), RG 472, box 57, NAII, 1.

98. Central Intelligence Agency, "Probable Developments in South Vietnam, Laos, and Cambodia Through July 1956," 23 November 1954, General CIA Records, CREST, NAII, 11, https://www.cia.gov/readingroom/docs/CIA-RDP79R01012A004500040001-9.pdf.

99. Chandler, *Tragedy of Cambodian History*, 75.

100. Reuters, "Cambodian King Abdicates Throne in Favor of Father," *New York Times*, 3 March 1955, 2.

101. Armstrong, *Sihanouk Speaks*, 75.

3. Lost in the Wilderness, 1955–1959

1. Central Intelligence Agency, "Central Intelligence Bulletin," 25 January 1955, General CIA Records, CREST, NAII, 6, https://www.cia.gov/reading room/docs/CIA-RDP79T00975A001900610001-3.pdf.

2. "Cambodia Vote Tests Power of Jazz-Loving, Young King," *News and Courier* (Charleston, SC), 8 February 1955, 3A.

3. David Chandler, *The Tragedy of Cambodian History: Politics, War, and Revolution since 1945* (New Haven, CT: Yale University Press, 1991), 77.

4. Central Intelligence Agency, "Central Intelligence Bulletin," 25 January 1955, 6; Central Intelligence Agency, "Current Intelligence Weekly Summary," 17 February 1955, General CIA Records, CREST, NAII, 8, https://www.cia.gov/readingroom/docs/CIA-RDP79-00927A000400190001-9.pdf.

5. Chandler, *Tragedy of Cambodian History*, 75.

6. Central Intelligence Agency, "Current Intelligence Weekly Summary," 17 February 1955, 8.

7. Central Intelligence Agency, "Current Intelligence Weekly Summary," 3 March 1955, General CIA Records, CREST, NAII, 7, https://www.cia.gov/readingroom/docs/CIA-RDP79-00927A000400210001-6.pdf.

8. "King of Cambodia Quits in Favor of His Father," *Gettysburg Times*, 2 March 1955, 1.

9. Chandler, *Tragedy of Cambodian History*, 78–79.

10. David J. Steinberg, *Cambodia: Its People, Its Society, Its Culture* (New Haven, CT: Hraf Press, 1959), 20.

11. "New Ruler Enthroned: Cambodian King Abdicates in Row Over Election Laws," *Reading Eagle* (Reading, PA), 3 March 1955, 10.

12. "New Ruler Enthroned," 10.

13. "King Quits His Throne in Cambodia," *Bend Bulletin*, 2 March 1955, 1.

14. "Deputy Assistant Secretary of State for Far Eastern Affairs (Sebald) to Secretary of State," 4 March 1955, *Foreign Relations of the United States, 1955–1957*, vol. 21, *East Asian Security; Cambodia; Laos* (Washington, DC: Government Printing Office, 1990), 436, https://history.state.gov/historicaldocuments/frus1955-57v21/d194.

15. See Chandler, *Tragedy of Cambodian History*, 81–84, for more on the election.

16. Memorandum of Conversation, "Canadian Attitude Toward Indian Involvement in Cambodia," 19 July 1955, 50A, folder 513.1 Cambodia 1955, Records Relating to South Asia 1947–59, RG 59, box 6, NAII, 1.

17. "Telegram from the Department of State to the Embassy in the United Kingdom," 2 July 1955, *Foreign Relations of the United States, 1955–1957*, vol. 21, *East Asian Security; Cambodia; Laos* (Washington, DC: Government Printing Office, 1990), 464, https://history.state.gov/historicaldocuments/frus1955-57v21/d210.

18. Norodom Sihanouk. *Shadow over Angkor*, Vol. 1, *Memoirs of His Majesty King Norodom Sihanouk of Cambodia*, ed. Julio A. Jeldres (Phnom Penh, Cambodia: Monument Books, 2005), 58.

19. Central Intelligence Agency, "Address by Mr. Robert Amory before the Army War College, Carlisle Barracks, Pennsylvania: The Current World Situation," 29 March 1955, General CIA Records, CREST, NAII, 21–22, https://www.cia.gov/readingroom/docs/CIA-RDP79-01048A000100030006-9.pdf.

20. Walter LaFeber, *America, Russia, and the Cold War, 1945–2006* (New York: McGraw-Hill, 2008), 147. For an in-depth analysis of Eisenhower's policies with respect to Vietnam, see David L. Anderson, *Trapped by Success: The Eisenhower*

Administration and Vietnam, 1953–1961 (New York: Columbia University Press, 1991).

21. "Memorandum of a Conversation, Department of State, Washington, 12 August 1955," *Foreign Relations of the United States, 1955–1957*, vol. 22, *Southeast Asia* (Washington, DC: Government Printing Office, 1989), 832–33, https://history.state.gov/historicaldocuments/frus1955-57v22/d478.

22. "National Intelligence Estimate," 16 August 1955, *Foreign Relations of the United States, 1955–1957*, vol. 21, *East Asian Security; Cambodia; Laos* (Washington, DC: Government Printing Office, 1990), 478, https://history.state.gov/historicaldocuments/frus1955-57v21/d217.

23. National Intelligence Survey, Cambodia, section 53: Political Dynamics, October 1955, National Intelligence Survey Reports: Cambodia (2 of 3), RG 472, box 57, NAII, 53-1.

24. "Prince Sihanouk and the Khmer People," *Far Eastern Economic Review*, 6 September 1956, 312.

25. "Memorandum of a Conversation, Department of State, Washington, September 25, 1956," *Foreign Relations of the United States, 1955–1957*, vol. 1, *Vietnam* (Washington, DC: Government Printing Office, 1985), 741, https://history.state.gov/historicaldocuments/frus1955-57v01/d347.

26. Office of the Assistant Chief of Staff, G-2, Intelligence, "Viet Minh and Issarak Capabilities in Cambodia," Department of the Army, Cambodia–U.S. Plans and Policy–Relations, RG 472, box 58, NAII.

27. George McT. Kahin, *Southeast Asia: A Testament* (New York: Routledge-Curzon, 2003), 260–61.

28. Kahin, *Southeast Asia*, 258–59.

29. "Memorandum From the Deputy Director of the Office of Southeast Asian Affairs (Jenkins) to the Assistant Secretary of State for Far Eastern Affairs (Robertson)," 21 August 1958, *Foreign Relations of the United States, 1958–1960*, vol. 16, *East Asia–Pacific Region; Cambodia; Laos* (Washington, DC: Government Printing Office, 1992), 247, https://history.state.gov/historicaldocuments/frus1958-60v16/d79.

30. William J. Rust, *Eisenhower & Cambodia: Diplomacy, Covert Action, and the Origins of the Second Indochina War* (Lexington, KY: University of Kentucky Press, 2016). See also Chandler, *Tragedy of Cambodian History* and Clymer, *The United States and Cambodia, 1870-1969: From Curiosity to Confrontation* (London: RoutledgeCurzon, 2004) for more on the Dap Chhuon Affair.

31. Chandler, *Tragedy of Cambodian History*, 99–100.

32. Sihanouk, *My War with the CIA*, 104–5.

33. Chandler, *Tragedy of Cambodian History*, 99–100.

34. "L'Histoire Edifiante d'un Rallié," *Réalités Cambodgiennes*, no. 557, 14 July 1967, box 678, Charles Meyer Collection, NAC, 12.

35. Norodom Sihanouk, *My War with the CIA: The Memoirs of Prince Norodom Sihanouk* (New York: Pantheon, 1972), 107.

36. Oral History Interview with William C. Trimble by Dennis J. O'Brien, 12 August 1969, folder 9, Trimble Oral History, box 38, SPX, SEA, Kenton Clymer, folders 1–10, Misc. Files, Kenton Clymer Collection, Rare Books and Special

Collections, Northern Illinois University, 4; Chandler, *Tragedy of Cambodian History*, 101.

37. FE–Mr. Robertson, SEA–Keneth T. Young Jr. "Ninth Sangkum Cabinet," 30 July 1957, folder Cambodia 1957, RG 59, Records of the Bureau of Far Eastern Affairs, 1957, Country File–1957, Far East–General to Name File–1957, Irwin, John N II, box 1, NAII.

38. Oral History Interview with William C. Trimble, 4; Chandler, *Tragedy of Cambodian History*, 101.

39. "Une Nouvelle Production de Samdech Chef de l'Etat: "Ombre sur Angkor," *Réalités Cambodgiennes*, no. 570, 20 October 1967, box 678, Charles Meyer Collection, NAC, 8.

40. Central Intelligence Agency, "Cambodia," 4 April 1956, General CIA Records, CREST, NAII, 2, https://www.cia.gov/readingroom/docs/CIA-RDP79R00890A000700040006-0.pdf.

41. Oral History Interview with William C. Trimble, 4; Chandler, *Tragedy of Cambodian History*, 101-2; Nicholas Tarling, *Britain and Sihanouk's Cambodia* (Singapore: National University of Singapore Press, 2014), 29.

42. "Une Nouvelle Production de Samdech Chef de l'Etat," 8. See also Rust, *Eisenhower & Cambodia*, 169-89.

43. "Memorandum from Cumming to Herter, 25 June 1958, Intelligence Note: Cambodian Government claims South Vietnam troops invade northeast Cambodia," *Foreign Relations of the United States, 1958–1960*, vols. 15/16, part 1, microfiche supplement, *Burma; Malaya-Singapore; East Asia Region; Cambodia* (Washington, DC: Government Printing Office, 1993), document 340.

44. "Telegram From the Embassy in Cambodia to the Department of State," 7 July 1958, *Foreign Relations of the United States, 1958–1960*, vol. 16, *East Asia–Pacific Region; Cambodia; Laos* (Washington, DC: Government Printing Office, 1992), 233-35, https://history.state.gov/historicaldocuments/frus1958-60v16/d73.

45. "Telegram From the Embassy in Vietnam to the Department of State," 9 July 1958, *Foreign Relations of the United States, 1958–1960*, vol. 16, *East Asia–Pacific Region; Cambodia; Laos* (Washington, DC: Government Printing Office, 1992), 235-36, https://history.state.gov/historicaldocuments/frus1958-60v16/d74.

46. "Telegram From the Embassy in Cambodia to the Department of State," 25 July 1958, *Foreign Relations of the United States, 1958–1960*, vol. 16, *East Asia–Pacific Region; Cambodia; Laos* (Washington, DC: Government Printing Office, 1992), 240, https://history.state.gov/historicaldocuments/frus1958-60v16/d77.

47. "Telegram 56 from Phnom Penh, 10 July 1958," *Foreign Relations of the United States, 1958–1960*, vols. 15/16, part 1, microfiche supplement, *Burma; Malaya-Singapore; East Asia Region; Cambodia* (Washington, DC: Government Printing Office, 1993), document 343.

48. "Telegram 118 from Saigon, 18 July 1958," *Foreign Relations of the United States, 1958–1960*, vols. 15/16, part 1, microfiche supplement, *Burma; Malaya-Singapore; East Asia Region; Cambodia* (Washington, DC: Government Printing Office, 1993), document 346.

49. "Telegram 118 from Saigon, 18 July 1958."

50. "Telegram 589 to Bangok, 23 September 1958," *Foreign Relations of the United States, 1958–1960,* vols. 15/16, part 1, microfiche supplement, *Burma; Malaya-Singapore; East Asia Region; Cambodia* (Washington, DC: Government Printing Office, 1993), document 355.

51. Tarling, *Britain and Sihanouk's Cambodia,* 30.

52. "Memorandum of Conversation," participants Trinh Hoanh and Edmund H. Kellogg, 30 September 1958; folder 1.7 Key Personalities in Cambodia, 1958–1959, RG 59 General Records of the Department of State, Bureau of Far Eastern Affairs, Office of Southeast Asian Affairs, Cambodia Files 1958–1963, 1958–1960, 1.1 The King and Royal Family to 1-C.1 Official Informal Letters, box 4, NAII.

53. "Dispatch 120 from Phnom Penh, 6 October 1958," *Foreign Relations of the United States, 1958–1960,* vols. 15/16, part 1, microfiche supplement, *Burma; Malaya-Singapore; East Asia Region; Cambodia* (Washington, DC: Government Printing Office, 1993), document 358.

54. "Letter from Strom to Robertson, 20 October 1958. Sihanouk visit to U.S. and Cambodian-Vietnamese relations" *Foreign Relations of the United States, 1958–1960,* vols. 15/16, part 1, microfiche supplement, *Burma; Malaya-Singapore; East Asia Region; Cambodia* (Washington, DC: Government Printing Office, 1993), document 359.

55. "Telegram 594 from Phnom Penh, 21 November 1958," *Foreign Relations of the United States, 1958–1960,* vols. 15/16, part 1, microfiche supplement, *Burma; Malaya-Singapore; East Asia Region; Cambodia* (Washington, DC: Government Printing Office, 1993), document 361.

56. Kahin, *Southeast Asia,* 265.

57. Milton Osborne, *Sihanouk: Prince of Light, Prince of Darkness* (Honolulu: University of Hawaii Press, 1994), 110–11.

58. "Telegram from the Embassy in Cambodia to the Department of State," 16 February 1959, *Foreign Relations of the United States, 1958–1960,* vol. 16, *East Asia–Pacific Region; Cambodia; Laos* (Washington, DC: Government Printing Office, 1992), 276–77, https://history.state.gov/historicaldocuments/frus1958-60v16/d95.

59. "Un Autre Traitre Démasqué: Chhuon Mchulpich," *La Dépêche du Cambodge,* no. 464, 24 February 1959, newspaper box 39, Cambodge (Le) 06/01/1948-30/06/1950, Dépêche du Cambodge (La) 13/03/1959-18/01/1966, NAC.

60. "Telegram from the Embassy in Cambodia to the Department of State," 3 March 1959, *Foreign Relations of the United States, 1958–1960,* vol. 16, *East Asia–Pacific Region; Cambodia; Laos* (Washington, DC: Government Printing Office, 1992), 295–97, https://history.state.gov/historicaldocuments/frus1958-60v16/d106.

61. William Colby and Peter Forbath, *Honorable Men: My Life in the CIA* (New York: Simon and Schuster, 1978), 149–50; R.L. Turkoly-Joczik, "The Military Role of Asian Ethnic Minorities in the Second Indochina War, 1959–1975" (PhD diss., University of Wales, 1986), 306; John Prados, *Lost Crusader: The Secret Wars of CIA Director William Colby* (New York: Oxford University Press, 2003), 68.

62. "Telegram from the Embassy in Cambodia to the Department of State," 16 February 1959, 276–77.

63. Kenton Clymer, *Troubled Relations: The United States and Cambodia since 1870* (Dekalb: Northern Illinois University Press, 2007), 40.

64. Sihanouk, *My War with the CIA*, 104.

65. Prados, *Lost Crusader*, 67.

66. Edward Geary Lansdale, *In the Midst of Wars: An American's Mission to Southeast Asia* (New York: Fordham University Press, 1991), 183.

67. For more on the inspiration for *Shadows over Angkor*, see Sihanouk, *My War with the CIA*, 111.

68. Sihanouk, *My War with the CIA*, 107–8; for clarification purposes, note that Felt was the commander in chief of the Pacific Command and Hopwood was the commander in chief of the Pacific Fleet.

69. Cecil B. Currey, *Edward Lansdale: The Unquiet American* (Boston: Houghton Mifflin Company, 1988), 200.

70. Currey, *Edward Lansdale*, 203–4.

71. Currey, *Edward Lansdale*, 214.

72. "Memorandum From the Deputy Director of the Office of Southeast Asian Affairs (Jenkins) to the Assistant Secretary of State for Far Eastern Affairs (Robertson)," 21 August 1958, 246.

73. Prados, *Lost Crusader*, 67–68; "Telegram from the Embassy in Cambodia to the Department of State," 12 January 1959, *Foreign Relations of the United States, 1958–1960*, vol. 16, *East Asia–Pacific Region; Cambodia; Laos* (Washington, DC: Government Printing Office, 1992), 272n, https://history.state.gov/his toricaldocuments/frus1958-60v16/d93; "Synopsis of Intelligence and State Material Reported to the President," 2 January 1959, folder: Dap Chhuon 1958–1970, box 67, Papers of George McT. Kahin, Division of Rare and Manuscript Collections, Cornell University.

74. Oral History Interview with William C. Trimble, 4.

75. Sihanouk, *My War with the CIA*, 105–6.

76. "Telegram 589 to Bangkok, 23 September 1958," *Foreign Relations of the United States, 1958–1960*, vols. 15/16, part 1, microfiche supplement, *Burma; Malaya-Singapore; East Asia Region; Cambodia* (Washington, DC: Government Printing Office, 1993), document 355.

77. Walter S. Robertson to the Acting Secretary, "Discussion of Southeast Asia with Secretary General Hammarskjold," 22 April 1959; folder 1.6 Prince Sihanouk, Jan 1958–Jan 1959, RG 59 General Records of the Department of State, Bureau of Far Eastern Affairs, Office of Southeast Asian Affairs, Cambodia Files 1958–1963, 1958–1960, 1.1 The King and Royal Family to 1-C.1 Official Informal Letters, box 4, NAII; "Memorandum of a Conversation, Department of State, Washington, 3 March 1959," *Foreign Relations of the United States, 1958–1960*, vol. 16, *East Asia–Pacific Region; Cambodia; Laos* (Washington, DC: Government Printing Office, 1992), 294. https://history.state.gov/historicaldocuments/frus1958-60v16/d105.

78. Oral History Interview with William C. Trimble, 5.

79. "Telegram from the Embassy in Cambodia to the Department of State," 28 February 1959, *Foreign Relations of the United States, 1958–1960*, vol. 16,

East Asia–Pacific Region; Cambodia; Laos (Washington, DC: Government Printing Office, 1992), 291–92. https://history.state.gov/historicaldocuments/frus1958-60v16/d104.

80. FE–Walter S. Robertson, SEA–Eric Kocher, "Talk with UN Secretary General, June 11, 1959," Tab B–Paper on Cambodia, 10 June 1959; folder 1-A.1 Background Papers, 1957–1960, RG 59 General Records of the Department of State, Bureau of Far Eastern Affairs, Office of Southeast Asian Affairs, Cambodia Files 1958–1963, 1958–1960, 1.1 The King and Royal Family to 1-C.1 Official Informal Letters, box 4, NAII.

81. Kahin, *Southeast Asia*, 265.

82. "Secret, Cambodia, Material for Mr. Parsons' Talk with Prince Sieanouk," n. d., folder 1-A.2 Briefing Papers, 1959–1960, RG 59 General Records of the Department of State, Bureau of Far Eastern Affairs, Office of Southeast Asian Affairs, Cambodia Files 1958–1963, 1958–1960, 1.1 The King and Royal Family to 1-C.1 Official Informal Letters, box 4, NAII.

83. Oral History Interview with William C. Trimble, 4.

84. T. D. Allman, untitled draft, July 1971, folder: Allman file, box 67, Papers of George McT. Kahin, Division of Rare and Manuscript Collections, Cornell University, 3.

85. Osborne, *Sihanouk*, 110.

86. "Secret, Cambodia," n. d., folder 1-A.2 Briefing Papers, 1959–1960, RG 59 General Records of the Department of State, Bureau of Far Eastern Affairs, Office of Southeast Asian Affairs, Cambodia Files 1958–1963, 1958–1960, 1.1 The King and Royal Family to 1-C.1 Official Informal Letters, box 4, NAII.

87. John F. Kennedy Presidential Recordings, Kennedy Dictabelt Conversation 34, https://www.jfklibrary.org/asset-viewer/archives/JFKPOF/TPH/JFK-POF-TPH-34/JFKPOF-TPH-34. See also "Memorandum of Conversation with the President—11/20/63–11:12 a.m.," folder 2, Countries, Cambodia–India, Sino-Indian Border Clash, 1962, Implications Analysis, Reference Box, box 1, Papers of Roger Hilsman, Cambodia—Conversation with President, 11/20/63, John F. Kennedy Library.

88. Such disagreements were certainly not limited to Cambodia during this period. According to the historian William J. Rust, "The Eisenhower administration's efforts to thwart communism in Laos were complicated by the divided views of State Department, Pentagon, and CIA officials, many of whom were prisoners of the parochial views of their agencies. Though united in their aim of preventing a communist takeover, diplomats, military officers, and intelligence operatives often proposed and pursued contradictory actions in the field." William J. Rust, *Before the Quagmire: American Intervention in Laos, 1954–1961* (Lexington: University Press of Kentucky, 2012), 5.

89. Central Intelligence Agency, "Central Intelligence Bulletin," 16 May 1959, General CIA Records, CREST, NAII, 10, https://www.cia.gov/readingroom/docs/CENTRAL%20INTELLIGENCE%20BULL%5B15787488%5D.pdf.

90. FE–Mr. Parsons, SEA–Daniel V. Anderson, "Implications of the Diem-Sihanouk Talks," 13 August 1959; folder 1-A.1 Background Papers, 1957–1960, RG 59 General Records of the Department of State, Bureau of Far Eastern Affairs, Office of Southeast Asian Affairs, Cambodia Files 1958–1963,

1958-1960, 1.1 The King and Royal Family to 1-C.1 Official Informal Letters, box 4, NAII.

91. Chandler, *Tragedy of Cambodian History*, 106-7.

92. From our Correspondent, "Friends of Former Envoy Questioned," *Times* (UK), 3 September 1959, 8.

93. Memorandum of Conversation, "Arrest of Phan Vinh Tong," 16 September 1959, folder 1.11, Bomb Plot (8/31/59), RG 59 General Records of the Department of State, Bureau of Far Eastern Affairs, Office of Southeast Asian Affairs, Cambodia Files 1958-1963, 1958-1960, 1.1 The King and Royal Family to 1-C.1 Official Informal Letters, box 4, NAII.

94. Hugh S. Cumming Jr. to The Acting Secretary, "Intelligence Note: Attempted Assassination of the Queen of Cambodia," 2 September 1959; folder 1.11, Bomb Plot (8/31/59), RG 59 General Records of the Department of State, Bureau of Far Eastern Affairs, Office of Southeast Asian Affairs, Cambodia Files 1958-1963, 1958-1960, 1.1 The King and Royal Family to 1-C.1 Official Informal Letters, box 4, NAII.

95. Central Intelligence Agency, "Status Report on Covert Actions in Vietnam (Keyed to 28 November Report)," 18 April 1962, FOIA Collection, CREST, NAII, 4, https://www.cia.gov/readingroom/docs/DOC_0000530446.pdf.

96. "Telegram from the Embassy in Vietnam to the Department of State," 7 October 1959, *Foreign Relations of the United States, 1958-1960*, vol. 16, *East Asia–Pacific Region; Cambodia; Laos* (Washington, DC: Government Printing Office, 1992), 343n, https://history.state.gov/historicaldocuments/frus1958-60v16/d125.

97. Richard E. Usher to Mr. Steeves, "Year-End Assessment of US-Cambodian Relations," 11 March 1960; folder 1-A.2 Briefing Papers, 1959-1960, RG 59 General Records of the Department of State, Bureau of Far Eastern Affairs, Office of Southeast Asian Affairs, Cambodia Files 1958-1963, 1958-1960, 1.1 The King and Royal Family to 1-C.1 Official Informal Letters, box 4, NAII.

98. "16 Sentenced to Death," *Times* (UK), 3 October 1959, 6.

99. Quoted in Central Intelligence Agency, "Central Intelligence Bulletin," 8 October 1959, General CIA Records, CREST, NAII, 1, https://www.cia.gov/readingroom/docs/CIA-RDP79T00975A004700330001-3.pdf.

100. "Telegram From the Embassy in Vietnam to the Department of State," 22 September 1959, *Foreign Relations of the United States, 1958-1960*, vol. 16, *East Asia–Pacific Region; Cambodia; Laos* (Washington, DC: Government Printing Office, 1992), 335-37, https://history.state.gov/historicaldocuments/frus1958-60v16/d122.

101. Daniel V. Anderson to Parsons, "Your Talk with Cambodian Minister Son Sann," 25 September 1959, folder 1-General, Administration and Organization, Cambodia, RG 59, General Records of the Department of State, Bureau of Far Eastern Affairs, Office of Southeast Asia Affairs, Cambodia Files 1958-1963, 1959, 1. Administration and Organization, General to 19.3 GATT, box 2, NAII.

102. "Background visit—Saccio Visit," Cambodia, U/MSC, 25 November 1959 in folder 1.1, Briefing Papers and Materials, Cambodia, RG 59, General Records of the Department of State, Bureau of Far Eastern Affairs, Office

of Southeast Asia Affairs, Cambodia Files 1958–1963, 1959, 1. Administration and Organization, General to 19.3 GATT, box 2, NAII.

103. Australian Embassy, Bangkok, Department of External Affairs, Inward Savingram, 28 November 1959, Intra Regional Relations—Cambodia Relations with Thailand 1959–1959, A1838, 3006/3/3 Part 3, Australian National Archives, 2, https://recordsearch.naa.gov.au/SearchNRetrieve/Interface/ViewImage.aspx?B=1500689. This newspaper was owned by Thai prime minister Sarit Thanarat, who himself rose to power via a coupe d'etat just two years prior.

104. Department of External Affairs, Inward Cablegram, Australian Embassy, Washington, Department of External Affairs, 27 November 1959, Intra Regional Relations—Cambodia Relations with Thailand 1959–1959, A1838, 3006/3/3 Part 3, Australian National Archives, 10, https://recordsearch.naa.gov.au/SearchNRetrieve/Interface/ViewImage.aspx?B=1500689.

105. Richard E. Usher to Mr. Steeves, "Year-End Assessment of US-Cambodian Relations," 11 March 1960; folder 1-A.2 Briefing Papers, 1959–1960, RG 59 General Records of the Department of State, Bureau of Far Eastern Affairs, Office of Southeast Asian Affairs, Cambodia Files 1958–1963, 1958–1960, 1.1 The King and Royal Family to 1-C.1 Official Informal Letters, box 4, NAII.

106. E. W. Pfeiffer, "Remember Cambodia?" *The Nation*, 27 November 1972, General CIA Records, CREST, NAII, 52–54, https://www.cia.gov/readingroom/docs/CIA-RDP77-00432R000100020001-4.pdf.

107. T. D. Allman, "Camp with No Cash," *Far Eastern Economic Review*, 6 August 1970, 13.

4. The Breaking Point, 1960–1964

1. Kenton Clymer, *The United States and Cambodia, 1969–2000: A Troubled Relationship* (London: RoutledgeCurzon, 2004), 85.

2. William C. Trimble, "Memorandum of Conversation: Cambodia's Foreign Relations," 12 January 1960, folder 1.4 Neutral Policy of Government of Cambodia, 1958–1960, RG 59 General Records of the Department of State, Bureau of Far Eastern Affairs, Office of Southeast Asian Affairs, Cambodia Files 1958–1963, 1958–1960, 1.1 The King and Royal Family to Official Informal Letters, box 4, NAII.

3. "Sihanouk Sorry He Accused U.S.: Cambodian Had Charged 2 Ex-Aides of Embassy with Links to His Exiled Foe," *New York Times*, 7 February 1960, 22; Kenton Clymer, *Troubled Relations: The United States and Cambodia since 1870.* (DeKalb: Northern Illinois University Press, 2007), 43.

4. FE—Mr. Parsons, SEA—Daniel V. Anderson, "Your Conversation with Cambodian Ambassador," 5 February 1960, folder 1-A.2 Briefing Papers, 1959–1960, RG 59 General Records of the Department of State, Bureau of Far Eastern Affairs, Office of Southeast Asian Affairs, Cambodia Files 1958–1963, 1958–1960, 1.1 The King and Royal Family to 1-C.1 Official Informal Letters, box 4, NAII.

5. FE—Mr. Parsons, SEA—Daniel V. Anderson, "Your Conversation with Cambodian Ambassador," 5 February 1960; "Sihanouk Sorry He Accused U.S.," 22.

6. "Sihanouk Sorry He Accused U.S.," 22.

7. Charles N. Spinks to Hugh S. Cumming Jr., Memorandum, "The *Blitz* Incident and Prince Sihanouk's Views of the US," 16 February 1960, folder 1.5 Key Personnel; Biographic Data, 1958-1960, RG 59 General Records of the Department of State, Bureau of Far Eastern Affairs, Office of Southeast Asian Affairs, Cambodia Files 1958-1963, 1958-1960, 1.1 The King and Royal Family to Official Informal Letters, box 4, NAII.

8. "Adequacy of U.S. Policy in Mainland Southeast Asia," in "Official- Informal, Secret," letter to William C. Trimble, 18 March 1960, folder 1—Gen, Administration and Organization, RG 59, General Records of the Department of State, Bureau of Far Eastern Affairs, Office of Southeast Asian Affairs, Cambodia Files 1958-1963, 1960, 1 Administration and Organization, General to 18.5 Shipping, box 3, NAII.

9. John P. Armstrong, *Sihanouk Speaks: Cambodia's Chief of State Explains his Controversial Policies* (New York: Walker and Company, 1964), 48.

10. David Chandler, *The Tragedy of Cambodian History: Politics, War, and Revolution since 1945* (New Haven, CT: Yale University Press, 1991), 115-16.

11. Memorandum of Conversation, "Demonstration at Battambang," 18 May 1960, folder 1.1 The King and Royal Family, 1958-1960, RG 59 General Records of the Department of State, Bureau of Far Eastern Affairs, Office of Southeast Asian Affairs, Cambodia Files 1958-1963, 1958-1960, 1.1 The King and Royal Family to Official Informal Letters, box 4, NAII.

12. Chandler, *Tragedy of Cambodian History*, 116.

13. Chandler, *Tragedy of Cambodian History*, 117.

14. "(S)econd Manifeste Du Mouvement Khmer-Serei Au Sujet D'un Nouveau Referendum Propose Par Le Prince Machiavelique Norodom Sihanouk," 26 May 1960, B: 691, ID: 6232, Records of Post-Colonial Governments of Cambodia, NAC, 1.

15. "(S)econd Manifeste Du Mouvement Khmer-Serei," 2-3.

16. "(S)econd Manifeste Du Mouvement Khmer-Serei," 3.

17. Quoted in Chandler, *Tragedy of Cambodian History*, 117.

18. Laurin B. Askew to Mr. Anderson, "Meeting with UK, French and Australian Representatives, 11:30 a.m., June 30," 29 June 1960, folder 1-A.2 Briefing Papers, 1959-1960, RG 59 General Records of the Department of State, Bureau of Far Eastern Affairs, Office of Southeast Asian Affairs, Cambodia Files 1958-1963, 1958-1960, 1.1 The King and Royal Family to 1-C.1 Official Informal Letters, box 4, NAII.

19. Laurin B. Askew to Mr. Anderson, "Meeting with UK, French and Australian Representatives, 11:30 a.m., June 30," 29 June 1960.

20. A. E. Thomas, "Far Eastern Roundup," *Far Eastern Economic Review*, 18 August 1960, 370.

21. A. E. Thomas, "Far Eastern Roundup," *Far Eastern Economic Review*, 22 December 1960, 622.

22. Wilfred Deac, *Road to the Killing Fields: The Cambodian War of 1970–1975* (College Station: Texas A&M University Press, 1997), 38-39; Shane Strate, "A Pile of Stones? Preah Vihear as a Thai Symbol of National Humiliation," *South East Asia Research* 21, no. 1 (March 2013), 66. See also John Burgess, *Temple in the Clouds: Faith and Conflict at Preah Vihar* (Bangkok: River Books, 2015).

23. "Telegram From the Embassy in Vietnam to the Department of State," 15 June 1961, *Foreign Relations of the United States, 1961–1963*, vol. 23, *Southeast Asia* (Washington, DC: Government Printing Office, 1994), 156, https://history.state.gov/historicaldocuments/frus1961-63v23/d71.

24. A. E. Thomas, "Far Eastern Roundup," *Far Eastern Economic Review*, 5 October 1961, 3.

25. Department of State Telegram, 26 September 1961, folder: National Security Files, Countries, Cambodia/General 9/26/61–10/23/61, Papers of President Kennedy, National Security Files, Countries, Reference Copy, box 16, John F. Kennedy Library.

26. Memorandum of Conversation, 25 September 1961, folder: National Security Files, Countries, Cambodia/General 9/26/61–10/23/61, Papers of President Kennedy, National Security Files, Countries, Reference Copy, box 16, John F. Kennedy Library.

27. Department of State, Incoming Telegram, 13 October 1961, folder: National Security Files, Countries, Cambodia/General 9/26/61–10/23/61, Papers of President Kennedy, National Security Files, Countries, Reference Copy, box 16, John F. Kennedy Library.

28. Trimble to Rusk Telegram, 23 October 1961, folder: National Security Files, Countries, Cambodia/General 9/26/61–10/23/61, Papers of President Kennedy, National Security Files, Countries, Reference Copy, box 16, John F. Kennedy Library.

29. Trimble to Rusk Telegram, 31 October 1961, folder: National Security Files, Countries, Cambodia/General 10/29/61–10/31/61, Papers of President Kennedy, National Security Files, Countries, Reference Copy, box 16, John F. Kennedy Library.

30. Trimble to Rusk Telegram, 31 October 1961.

31. Trimble to Rusk Telegram, 27 October 1961, folder: National Security Files, Countries, Cambodia/General 10/24/61–10/28/61, Papers of President Kennedy, National Security Files, Countries, Reference Copy, box 16, John F. Kennedy Library.

32. Bangkok to Secretary of State, 31 October 1961, folder: National Security Files, Countries, Cambodia/General 10/29/61–10/31/61, Papers of President Kennedy, National Security Files, Countries, Reference Copy, box 16, John F. Kennedy Library.

33. Robert H. Johnson, "Memorandum for Mr. Bundy," 2 November 1961, folder: National Security Files, Countries, Cambodia/General 11/1/61–11/9/61, Papers of President Kennedy, National Security Files, Countries, Reference Copy, box 16, John F. Kennedy Library.

34. Trimble to Rusk, Telegram, 25 January 1962, folder: National Security Files, Countries, Cambodia, General 1/18/62–3/28/62; Papers of President Kennedy, National Security Files, Countries, Reference Copy, box 16A, John F. Kennedy Library.

35. Herbert D. Spivack, "Khmer Serei Activities—Cambodian Reports and Reactions," 19 October 1962, folder: National Security Files, Countries, Cambodia, General 10/12/62–10/22/62, Papers of President Kennedy, National Security Files, Countries, Reference Copy, box 17, John F. Kennedy Library. In

early 1962, reports of a new movement emanating from South Vietnam began to surface. This "new" group, the Sangkum Khmer Thmey, or Union of Free Khmer, was reportedly a new manifestation of the Khmer Serei, whose name had supposedly been sufficiently tarnished in Cambodia to the point that a new name was required. According to the Saigon paper *Tieng Chuong*, the goal of the new group was use paramilitary units to create a free, anticommunist, republican government in Cambodia. Its leadership consisted of Thành and Sary. As far as can be traced, this name change was short lived, as the Cambodian press and the Khmer Serei themselves quickly reverted back to the original name. See Spivack, "Khmer Serei Activities—Cambodian Reports and Reactions," 19 October 1962; "Cambodian Press Comment on Khmer Serei," folder: National Security Files, Countries, Cambodia, General 10/12/62–10/22/62, Papers of President Kennedy, National Security Files, Countries, Reference Copy, box 17, John F. Kennedy Library, 2.

36. Rusk to Bangkok, Phnom Penh, Saigon Embassies, 1 June 1962, folder: National Security Files, Countries, Cambodia, General 5/22/62–6/16/62, Papers of President Kennedy, National Security Files, Countries, Reference Copy, box 16A, John F. Kennedy Library.

37. Trimble to Rusk, 4 June 1962, folder: National Security Files, Countries, Cambodia, General 5/22/62–6/16/62, Papers of President Kennedy, National Security Files, Countries, Reference Copy, box 16A, John F. Kennedy Library.

38. Trimble to Rusk, 5 June 1962, folder: National Security Files, Countries, Cambodia, General 5/22/62–6/16/62, Papers of President Kennedy, National Security Files, Countries, Reference Copy, box 16A, John F. Kennedy Library.

39. "Cambodian Press Comment on Khmer Serei," 1.

40. "Cambodian Press Comment on Khmer Serei," 3; Clymer, *United States and Cambodia, 1870–1969*, 92.

41. "Cambodian Press Comment on Khmer Serei," 4.

42. "Cambodian Press Comment on Khmer Serei," 5.

43. "Cambodian Press Comment on Khmer Serei," 5.

44. Trimble to Rusk, 7 June 1962, folder: National Security Files, Countries, Cambodia, General 5/22/62–6/16/62, Papers of President Kennedy, National Security Files, Countries, Reference Copy, box 16A, John F. Kennedy Library.

45. Spivack, "Khmer Serei Activities—Cambodian Reports and Reactions," 19 October 1962.

46. Central Intelligence Agency, Information Report, "Plan to Overthrow Sihanouk Government," 13 June 1962, folder: National Security Files, Countries, Cambodia, General 5/22/62–6/16/62, Papers of President Kennedy, National Security Files, Countries, Reference Copy, box 16A, John F. Kennedy Library.

47. Richard M. Gibson and Wenhua Chen, *The Secret Army: Chiang Kaishek and the Drug Warlords of the Golden Triangle* (Singapore: John Wiley & Sons, 2011), 1–2.

48. Central Intelligence Agency, Information Report, "Plan to Overthrow Sihanouk Government," 13 June 1962.

49. Spivack, "Khmer Serei Activities—Cambodian Reports and Reactions," 19 October 1962.

50. State Department to Bangkok, Phnom Penh, Saigon, Taipei Embassies, 13 August 1962, folder: National Security Files, Countries, Cambodia, General 8/7/62–8/15/62, Papers of President Kennedy, National Security Files, Countries, Reference Copy, box 16A, John F. Kennedy Library.

51. Sprouse to Rusk, 17 August 1962, folder: National Security Files, Countries, Cambodia, General 8/16/62–8/19/62, Papers of President Kennedy, National Security Files, Countries, Reference Copy, box 16A, John F. Kennedy Library.

52. Moore to Rusk, 6 August 1962, folder: National Security Files, Countries, Cambodia, General 7/16/62–8/7/62, Papers of President Kennedy, National Security Files, Countries, Reference Copy, box 16A, John F. Kennedy Library.

53. Sprouse to Rusk, 21 August 1962, folder: National Security Files, Countries, Cambodia, General 8/20/62–8/24/62, Papers of President Kennedy, National Security Files, Countries, Reference Copy, box 16A, John F. Kennedy Library.

54. Sprouse to Rusk, 25 August 1962, folder: National Security Files, Countries, Cambodia, General 8/25/62–8/27/62, Papers of President Kennedy, National Security Files, Countries, Reference Copy, box 16A, John F. Kennedy Library.

55. Oral History Interview with William C. Trimble by Dennis J. O'Brien, 12 August 1969, folder 9, Trimble Oral History, box 38, SPX, SEA, Kenton Clymer, folders 1–10, Misc. Files, Kenton Clymer Collection, Rare Books and Special Collections, Northern Illinois University, 17.

56. Department of State, Outgoing Telegram, 31 August 1962, folder: National Security Files, Countries, Cambodia, General 8/30/62–8/31/62, Papers of President Kennedy, National Security Files, Countries, Reference Copy, box 16A, John F. Kennedy Library.

57. Spivack, "Khmer Serei Activities—Cambodian Reports and Reactions," 19 October 1962.

58. Chandler, *Tragedy of Cambodian History*, 125.

59. Chandler, *Tragedy of Cambodian History*, 125–26.

60. Sprouse to Rusk, Telegram, 1 March 1963, folder: National Security Files, Countries, Cambodia, General 2/16/63–3/3/63, Papers of President Kennedy, National Security Files, Countries, Reference Copy, box 17, John F. Kennedy Library; A. E. Thomas, "Far Eastern Round-Up," *Far Eastern Economic Review*, 7 March 1963, 488.

61. K. E. Chantarit, "Sea of Troubles," *Far Eastern Economic Review*, 21 March 1963, 601.

62. Sprouse to Rusk, Telegram, 3 March 1963, folder: National Security Files, Countries, Cambodia, General 2/16/63–3/3/63, Papers of President Kennedy, National Security Files, Countries, Reference Copy, box 17, John F. Kennedy Library.

63. Sprouse to Rusk, Telegram, 31 July 1963, folder: National Security Files, Countries, Cambodia, General 4/24/63–8/4/63, Papers of President Kennedy, National Security Files, Countries, Reference Copy, box 17, John F. Kennedy Library.

64. "Far Eastern Round-Up," *Far Eastern Economic Review*, 1 August 1963, 272.

65. "Far Eastern Round-Up," *Far Eastern Economic Review*, 8 August 1963, 320.

66. "Far Eastern Round-Up," *Far Eastern Economic Review*, 29 August 1963, 568.

67. Sprouse to Rusk, Telegram, 12 October 1963, folder: National Security Files, Countries, Cambodia, General 9/12/63–11/7/63, Papers of President Kennedy, National Security Files, Countries, Reference Copy, box 17, John F. Kennedy Library.

68. Sprouse to Rusk, Telegram, 12 October 1963.

69. Robert Shaplen, "Our Far-Flung Correspondents: Back and Forth in Phnom Penh," *New Yorker*, 18 April 1964, folder: Cambodia, H–N General, box no. RM4, The Personal Papers of Bernard Fall, John F. Kennedy Library, 176–77.

70. Spivack to Rusk, Telegram, 25 October 1963, folder: National Security Files, Countries, Cambodia, General 9/12/63–11/7/63, Papers of President Kennedy, National Security Files, Countries, Reference Copy, box 17, John F. Kennedy Library.

71. Spivack to Rusk, Telegram, 28 October 1963, folder: National Security Files, Countries, Cambodia, General 9/12/63–11/7/63, Papers of President Kennedy, National Security Files, Countries, Reference Copy, box 17, John F. Kennedy Library.

72. Benjamin H. Read, "Memorandum for Mr. McGeorge Bundy, The White House," 25 October 1963, folder: National Security Files, Countries, Cambodia, General 9/12/63–11/7/63, Papers of President Kennedy, National Security Files, Countries, Reference Copy, box 17, John F. Kennedy Library.

73. Spivack to Rusk, Telegram, 4 November 1963, folder: National Security Files, Countries, Cambodia, General 9/12/63–11/7/63, Papers of President Kennedy, National Security Files, Countries, Reference Copy, box 17, John F. Kennedy Library.

74. Sprouse to Rusk, 20 November 1963, folder: National Security Files, Countries, Cambodia, General 11/20/63–11/22/63, Papers of President Kennedy, National Security Files, Countries, Reference Copy, box 17A, John F. Kennedy Library.

75. Spivack to Rusk, Telegram, 7 November 1963, folder: National Security Files, Countries, Cambodia, General 9/12/63–11/7/63, Papers of President Kennedy, National Security Files, Countries, Reference Copy, box 17, John F. Kennedy Library.

76. Benjamin H. Read, "Memorandum for Mr. McGeorge Bundy, The White House," 25 October 1963; Clymer, *Troubled Relations*, 58.

77. Sprouse to Rusk, Telegram, 13 November 1963, folder: National Security Files, Countries, Cambodia, General 11/8/63–11/16/63, Papers of President Kennedy, National Security Files, Countries, Reference Copy, box 17, John F. Kennedy Library.

78. Sprouse to Rusk, Telegram, 13 November 1963.

79. Dean Rusk, "Outgoing Telegram," 13 November 1963, folder: National Security Files, Countries, Cambodia, General 11/8/63–11/16/63, Papers of President Kennedy, National Security Files, Countries, Reference Copy, box 17, John F. Kennedy Library.

80. Martin to Rusk, Telegram, 14 November 1963, folder: National Security Files, Countries, Cambodia, General 11/8/63–11/16/63, Papers of President Kennedy, National Security Files, Countries, Reference Copy, box 17, John F. Kennedy Library.

81. Sprouse to Rusk, Telegram, 15 November 1963, folder: National Security Files, Countries, Cambodia, General 11/8/63–11/16/63, Papers of President Kennedy, National Security Files, Countries, Reference Copy, box 17, John F. Kennedy Library.

82. Sprouse to Rusk, Telegram, 16 November 1963, folder: National Security Files, Countries, Cambodia, General 11/8/63–11/16/63, Papers of President Kennedy, National Security Files, Countries, Reference Copy, box 17, John F. Kennedy Library.

83. Sprouse to Rusk, 18 November 1963, folder: National Security Files, Countries, Cambodia, General 11/17/63–11/19/63, Papers of President Kennedy, National Security Files, Countries, Reference Copy, box 17A, John F. Kennedy Library.

84. Rusk to American Embassy Saigon, "Relations with Cambodia," 16 November 1963, folder: National Security Files, Countries, Cambodia, General 11/8/63–11/16/63, Papers of President Kennedy, National Security Files, Countries, Reference Copy, box 17, John F. Kennedy Library.

85. Rusk to American Embassy Phnom Penh, "Re Sihanouk's Threats and Khmer Serei Problem," 16 November 1963, folder: National Security Files, Countries, Cambodia, General 11/8/63–11/16/63, Papers of President Kennedy, National Security Files, Countries, Reference Copy, box 17, John F. Kennedy Library.

86. Central Intelligence Agency, "Central Intelligence Bulletin," 20 November 1963, General CIA Records, CREST, NAII, 4, https://www.cia.gov/reading room/docs/CIA-RDP79T00975A007300440001-2.pdf.

87. Sprouse to Rusk, 17 November 1963, folder: National Security Files, Countries, Cambodia, General 11/17/63–11/19/63, Papers of President Kennedy, National Security Files, Countries, Reference Copy, box 17A, John F. Kennedy Library.

88. Sprouse to Rusk, 18 November 1963, folder: National Security Files, Countries, Cambodia, General 11/17/63–11/19/63, Papers of President Kennedy, National Security Files, Countries, Reference Copy, box 17A, John F. Kennedy Library.

89. Sprouse to State Department, 18 November 1963, folder: National Security Files, Countries, Cambodia, General 11/17/63–11/19/63, Papers of President Kennedy, National Security Files, Countries, Reference Copy, box 17A, John F. Kennedy Library.

90. Rusk to Embassy Phnom Penh, Bangkok, 18 November 1963, folder: National Security Files, Countries, Cambodia, General 11/17/63–11/19/63, Papers of President Kennedy, National Security Files, Countries, Reference Copy, box 17A, John F. Kennedy Library.

91. Sihanouk to Kennedy, 17 November 1963, folder: National Security Files, Countries, Cambodia, General 11/17/63–11/19/63, Papers of President

Kennedy, National Security Files, Countries, Reference Copy, box 17A, John F. Kennedy Library.

92. Quoted in William J. Rust, *Eisenhower & Cambodia: Diplomacy, Covert Action, and the Origins of the Second Indochinese War* (Lexington: University Press of Kentucky, 2016), 276.

93. K. E. Chantarit, "The Khmer Serei," *Far Eastern Economic Review*, 5 December 1963, 495–98.

94. Benjamin H. Read to McGeorge Bundy, 19 November 1963, folder: National Security Files, Countries, Cambodia, General 11/17/63–11/19/63, Papers of President Kennedy, National Security Files, Countries, Reference Copy, box 17A, John F. Kennedy Library.

95. John F. Kennedy, "Proposed Message," n.d., folder: National Security Files, Countries, Cambodia, General 11/17/63–11/19/63, Papers of President Kennedy, National Security Files, Countries, Reference Copy, box 17A, John F. Kennedy Library. It was around this time that Thành reportedly attempted to meet with representatives from the American embassy in Saigon, although he was unsuccessful.

96. Rusk to American Embassy Saigon, "Re Sihanouk's threats and Khmer Serei," 19 November 1963, folder: National Security Files, Countries, Cambodia, General 11/17/63–11/19/63, Papers of President Kennedy, National Security Files, Countries, Reference Copy, box 17A, John F. Kennedy Library.

97. Sprouse to Rusk, 21 November 1963, folder: National Security Files, Countries, Cambodia, General 11/20/63–11/22/63, Papers of President Kennedy, National Security Files, Countries, Reference Copy, box 17A, John F. Kennedy Library.

98. Central Intelligence Agency, "Central Intelligence Bulletin," 4; Text of a speech given by Sihanouk, 20 November 1963, folder: National Security Files, Countries, Cambodia, General 11/20/63–11/22/63, Papers of President Kennedy, National Security Files, Countries, Reference Copy, box 17A, John F. Kennedy Library

99. Foreign Broadcast Information Services, "CPR Statement on Cambodia," 21 November 1963, folder: National Security Files, Countries, Cambodia, General 11/20/63–11/22/63, Papers of President Kennedy, National Security Files, Countries, Reference Copy, box 17A, John F. Kennedy Library; Sprouse to Rusk, 20 November 1963; folder: National Security Files, Countries, Cambodia, General 11/20/63–11/22/63, Papers of President Kennedy, National Security Files, Countries, Reference Copy, box 17A, John F. Kennedy Library.

100. Sprouse to Rusk, 20 November 1963; folder: National Security Files, Countries, Cambodia, General 11/20/63–11/22/63, Papers of President Kennedy, National Security Files, Countries, Reference Copy, box 17A, John F. Kennedy Library.

101. Text of a speech given by Sihanouk, 20 November 1963.

102. Sprouse to Department of State, 20 November 1963; folder: National Security Files, Countries, Cambodia, General 11/20/63–11/22/63; Papers of President Kennedy, National Security Files, Countries, Reference Copy, box 17A, John F. Kennedy Library.

103. Department of State to Phnom Penh Embassy, 20 November 1963, folder: National Security Files, Countries, Cambodia, General 11/20/63–11/22/63, Papers of President Kennedy, National Security Files, Countries, Reference Copy, box 17A, John F. Kennedy Library.

104. Melvin L. Manfull to Rusk, 21 November 1963, folder: National Security Files, Countries, Cambodia, General 11/20/63–11/22/63, Papers of President Kennedy, National Security Files, Countries, Reference Copy, box 17A, John F. Kennedy Library.

105. Foreign Broadcast Information Services, "CPR Statement on Cambodia," 21 November 1963.

106. Roger Hilsman, *To Move a Nation: The Politics of Foreign Policy in the Administration of John F. Kennedy* (Garden City, NY: Doubleday, 1967) 361.

107. "Memorandum of Conversation with the President—11/20/63–11:12 a.m.," folder 2, Countries, Cambodia-India, Sino-Indian Border Clash, 1962, Implications Analysis, reference box, box 1, Papers of Roger Hilsman, Cambodia—Conversation with President, 11/20/63, John F. Kennedy Library.

108. "Memorandum of Conversation with the president, 3:40 p.m., 11/20/63," folder 2, Countries, Cambodia-India, Sino-Indian Border Clash, 1962, Implications Analysis, reference box, box 1, Papers of Roger Hilsman, Cambodia—Conversation with President, 11/20/63, John F. Kennedy Library.

109. Roger Hilsman to Mr. Hughes, 4 December 1963, folder 1, Countries, Cambodia-India, Sino-Indian Border Clash, 1962, Implications Analysis, reference box, box 1, Papers of Roger Hilsman, Cambodia 1963, John F. Kennedy Library.

110. Quoted in Robert Shaplen, "Our Far-Flung Correspondents," 181.

111. Shaplen, "Our Far-Flung Correspondents," 182.

112. T. D. Allman, untitled draft, July 1971, folder Allman file, box 67, Papers of George McT. Kahin, Division of Rare and Manuscript Collections, Cornell University, 3.

113. George McT. Kahin, interview with Donald Lancaster, 4 August 1967, folder 23, 1967 Interviews—Cambodia, box 67, Papers of George McT. Kahin, Division of Rare and Manuscript Collections, Cornell University.

114. Shaplen, "Our Far-Flung Correspondents," 175–76.

5. Path to Power, 1965–1970

1. Gerald C. Hickey, *Accommodation and Coalition in South Vietnam* (Santa Monica, CA: RAND Corporation, 1970), 31–32, https://www.rand.org/content/dam/rand/pubs/papers/2008/P4213.pdf.

2. Robert Louis Turkoly-Joczik, "Military Role of Asian Ethnic Minorities in the Second Indochina War, 1959-1975" (PhD diss., University of Wales, 1986), 291.

3. Joann L. Schrock et al. *Minority Groups in the Republic of Vietnam* (Washington, DC: Department of the Army, 1966), 1103; Turkoly-Joczik, "Military Role of Asian Ethnic Minorities," 293.

4. Charles M. Simpson III, *Inside the Green Berets: The First Thirty Years—A History of the U.S. Army Special Forces* (Novato, CA: Presidio Press, 1983), 96–100.

5. Simpson III, *Inside the Green Berets*, 112–13.

6. Turkoly-Joczik, "Military Role of Asian Ethnic Minorities," 299–300, 308.

7. Robert L. Turkoly-Joczik, "The Khmer Serei Movement," *Asian Affairs* 15, no. 1 (Spring 1988), 53.

8. Turkoly-Joczik, "Military Role of Asian Ethnic Minorities," 299; Allan E. Goodman, *Government and the Countryside: Political Accommodation and South Vietnam's Communal Groups* (Santa Monica, CA: RAND Corporation, 1968), 25, https://www.rand.org/content/dam/rand/pubs/papers/2008/P3924.pdf.

9. Turkoly-Joczik, "Military Role of Asian Ethnic Minorities," 308–9.

10. Schrock, Joann et al., *Minority Groups in the Republic of Vietnam* (Arlington, VA: Headquarters, Department of the Army, 1966), 1051.

11. Turkoly-Joczik, "Military Role of Asian Ethnic Minorities," 309, n117.

12. Francis J. Kelley, *The Green Berets in Vietnam, 1961–1971* (Washington, DC: Brassey's Inc., 1991), 36.

13. Kelley, *The Green Berets in Vietnam*, 46.

14. Simpson III, *Inside the Green Berets*, 113; Turkoly-Joczik, "Khmer Serei Movement," 53.

15. Turkoly-Joczik, "Khmer Serei Movement," 53.

16. Simpson III, *Inside the Green Berets*, 113.

17. Simpson III, *Inside the Green Berets*, 114.

18. Quoted in Seymour M. Hersh, *The Price of Power: Kissinger in the White House* (New York: Summit Books, 1983), 177–78.

19. Turkoly-Joczik, "Khmer Serei Movement," 59.

20. National Intelligence Survey, Cambodia, Subversion, January 1965, folder National Intelligence Survey Reports—Cambodia (3 of 3), Office of the Deputy Chief, Cambodian Background File, RG 472, box 57, NAII, 21.

21. "Note From the Assistant Secretary of State for Far Eastern Affairs (Bundy) to the Director of the Office of Southeast Asian Affairs (Trueheart)," 30 June 1964, *Foreign Relations of the United States, 1964–1968*, vol. 27, *Mainland Southeast Asia; Regional Affairs* (Washington, DC: Government Printing Office, 2000), 316, https://history.state.gov/historicaldocuments/frus1964-68v27/d138.

22. Robert Shaplen, "Our Far-Flung Correspondents: Back and Forth in Phnom Penh," *New Yorker*, 18 April 1964, folder: Cambodia, H–N General, box no. RM4, The Personal Papers of Bernard Fall, John F. Kennedy Library, 176–77.

23. Central Intelligence Agency, "Central Intelligence Bulletin," 14 July 1964, General CIA Records, CREST, NAII, 3, https://www.cia.gov/reading room/docs/CIA-RDP79T00975A007800070001-8.pdf.

24. Quoted in Shaplen, "Our Far-Flung Correspondents," 179.

25. Quoted in Keith Buchanan, "Cambodian Between Peking and Paris," *Monthly Review: An Independent Socialist Magazine*, December 1964, 480.

26. FE—Mr. Marshall Green, SEA—John B. Dexter, "Secret, Status Report on Cambodia," 16 October 1964, folder Cambodia (July—Dec. 1964), RG 59, General Records of the Department of State, Bureau of Far Eastern Affairs, Office of the Country Director for Burma and Cambodia, Records Relating to

Cambodia 1964–1967, 1964: AID 7, Program Operation to 1965: Political Affairs and Relations, box 1, NAII, 2.

27. FE—Mr. Marshall Green, SEA—John B. Dexter, "Secret, Status Report on Cambodia," 1.

28. FE—Mr. Bundy, FE/RA—Joseph A. Mendenhall, "United States Policy Toward Cambodia," 28 October 1964, folder POL—Political Affairs & Rel., United States—Cambodia, RG 59, General Records of the Department of State, Bureau of Far Eastern Affairs, Office of the Country Director for Burma and Cambodia, Records Relating to Cambodia 1964–1967, 1964: AID 7, Program Operation to 1965: Political Affairs and Relations, box 1, NAII, 1–2.

29. FE—Mr. Bundy, FE/RA—Joseph A. Mendenhall, "United States Policy Toward Cambodia," 1–2.

30. Alf E. Bergesen to Philip W. Bonsal, 31 December 1964, folder: Official Informal Correspondence, RG 59, General records of the Department of State, Bureau of Far Eastern Affairs, Office of the Country Director for Burma and Cambodia, Records Relating to Cambodia 1964–1967, 1964: AID 7, Program Operation to 1965: Political Affairs and Relations, box 1, NAII, 1–2.

31. Jack Taylor, "Contingency Planning for Cambodia," 17 December 1964, folder: DEF—Defense affairs, 1–1 Contingency Planning, RG 59, General Records of the Department of State, Bureau of Far Eastern Affairs, Office of the Country Director for Burma and Cambodia, Records Relating to Cambodia 1964–1967, 1964: AID 7, Program Operation to 1965: Political Affairs and Relations, box 1, NAII, 1–4.

32. Brian Toohey and William Pinwill, *Oyster: The Story of the Australian Secret Intelligence Service* (William Heinemann Australia: Port Melbourne, Victoria, Australia, 1989), 127.

33. T. D. Allman, untitled draft, July 1971, folder: Allman file, box 67, Papers of George McT. Kahin, Division of Rare and Manuscript Collections, Cornell University, 3.

34. E. W. Pfeiffer, "Remember Cambodia?" *Nation*, 27 November 1972, CIA Records, CREST, NAII, 52–54, https://www.cia.gov/readingroom/docs/CIA-RDP77-00432R000100020001-4.pdf; Turkoly-Joczik, "The Khmer Serei Movement," 54.

35. "Memorandum From James C. Thomson, Jr., of the National Security Council Staff to the President's Special Assistant for National Security Affairs (Bundy)," 16 August 1965, *Foreign Relations of the United States, 1964–1968*, vol. 27, *Mainland Southeast Asia; Regional Affairs* (Washington, DC: Government Printing Office, 2000), 350, https://history.state.gov/historicaldocuments/frus1964-68v27/d157.

36. George Ball to President Lyndon Johnson, "Memorandum for the President, Subject: Cambodia," 29 June 1966, folder: POL—Political Affairs & Rel., Pol 1 Cambodia/United States (April–June), RG 59, General Records of the Department of State, Bureau of Far Eastern Affairs, Office of the Country Director for Burma and Cambodia, Records Relating to Cambodia 1964–1967, 1966: POL 1, Cambodia/US (April–June) to 1967: POL 32.1–2, Prek Thnat (April–Dec), box 2, NAII, 1–3.

37. Memo for Mr. Bundy, "Two Weeks in Asia," 7 December 1965, folder: Cambodia—Miscellaneous 1951–75, box 67, Papers of George McT. Kahin, Division of Rare and Manuscript Collections, Cornell University.

38. "Telegram From the Department of State to the Embassy in Thailand," 29 December 1965, *Foreign Relations of the United States, 1964–1968*, vol. 27, *Mainland Southeast Asia; Regional Affairs* (Washington, DC: Government Printing Office, 2000), 377–78, https://history.state.gov/historicaldocuments/frus1964-68v27/d172.

39. "Memorandum From the Joint Chiefs of Staff to Secretary of Defense McNamara," 12 November 1965, *Foreign Relations of the United States, 1964–1968*, vol. 27, *Mainland Southeast Asia; Regional Affairs* (Washington, DC: Government Printing Office, 2000), 352–55, https://history.state.gov/historicaldocuments/frus1964-68v27/d159.

40. Turkoly-Joczik, "Khmer Serei Movement," 54.

41. "Cambodian Rebels Report Attacks on Military Posts," *New York Times*, 1 January 1966, 3.

42. "Cambodia Accuses Thailand of Attack on Frontier Post," *New York Times*, 2 January 1966, 72.

43. Robert Shaplen, "Letter From Cambodia," *New Yorker*, 13 January 1968, folder: Misc. Articles—Cambodia, Manuscripts File, Miscellaneous Press Releases re China, 1947, Africa—Vietnam, box #31, Papers of John F. Melby, Harry S. Truman Library, 80.

44. "Memorandum From James C. Thomson, Jr., to the President's Special Assistant for National Security Affairs (Bundy)," 5 January 1966, *Foreign Relations of the United States, 1964–1968*, vol. 27, *Mainland Southeast Asia; Regional Affairs* (Washington, DC: Government Printing Office, 2000), 382–83, https://history.state.gov/historicaldocuments/frus1964-68v27/d175.

45. "Letter From Acting Secretary of State Ball to Secretary of Defense McNamara," 17 January 1966, *Foreign Relations of the United States, 1964–1968*, vol. 27, *Mainland Southeast Asia; Regional Affairs* (Washington, DC: Government Printing Office, 2000), 383–84, https://history.state.gov/historicaldocuments/frus1964-68v27/d176.

46. "L'agression Contre Preah Vihear: Plus qu'un Crime, Une Faute," *Réalités Cambodgiennes*, no. 497, 8 April 1966, box 678, Charles Meyer Collection, NAC, 5.

47. Phnom Penh to Foreign Office, Canberra telegram No. 526: Thai/Cambodian Relations, 22 April 1966, folder 8, Cambodia—Miscellaneous 1951–1975, box 67, Papers of George McT. Kahin, Division of Rare and Manuscript Collections, Cornell University.

48. Leslie Fielding letter to Patricia Stanbridge, British Embassy, Phnom Penh, 6 June 1966, folder 8, Cambodia—Miscellaneous 1951–1975, box 67, Papers of George McT. Kahin, Division of Rare and Manuscript Collections, Cornell University.

49. "Memorandum From the Joint Chiefs of Staff to Secretary of Defense McNamara," 24 September 1966, *Foreign Relations of the United States, 1964–1968*, vol. 27, *Mainland Southeast Asia; Regional Affairs* (Washington, DC: Government Printing Office, 2000), 419–21, https://history.state.gov/historicaldocuments/frus1964-68v27/d192.

50. William Shawcross, *Sideshow: Kissinger, Nixon, and the Destruction of Cambodia* (New York: Cooper Square Press, 2002), 66.

51. "Memorandum From the President's Special Assistant (Rostow) to Secretary of State Rusk," 21 June 1966, *Foreign Relations of the United States, 1964–1968*, vol. 27, *Mainland Southeast Asia; Regional Affairs* (Washington, DC: Government Printing Office, 2000), 397–98, 400, https://history.state.gov/historicaldocuments/frus1964-68v27/d183.

52. "Memorandum From the President's Special Assistant (Rostow) to Secretary of State Rusk," 21 June 1966, 395.

53. George Ball to President Lyndon Johnson, "Memorandum for the President, Subject: Cambodia," 29 June 1966, folder: POL—Political Affairs & Rel., Pol 1 Cambodia/United States (April–June), RG 59, General Records of the Department of State, Bureau of Far Eastern Affairs, Office of the Country Director for Burma and Cambodia, Records Relating to Cambodia 1964–1967, 1966: POL 1, Cambodia/US (April–June) to 1967: POL 32.1–2, Prek Thnat (April–Dec), box 2, NAII, 1–3.

54. George Ball to President Lyndon Johnson, "Memorandum for the President, Subject: Cambodia," 1–3.

55. "We Strongly Denounce Thai U.S. Agents' Sabotage Activities Against Cambodia," *Vietnam Courier*, no. 64 (23 June 1966), folder 6, box 1, Douglas Pike Collection: Unit 15—Cambodia, The Vietnam Center and Archive, Texas Tech University, https://vva.vietnam.ttu.edu/images.php?img=/images/243/2430106036.pdf.

56. "Sihanouk Press Conference on Thai Relations," 12 September 1966, folder: Cambodia—O—Z General, box no. RM4, The Personal Papers of Bernard Fall, John F. Kennedy Library, 2.

57. "Sihanouk Press Conference on Thai Relations," 4–5.

58. Central Intelligence Agency, "Central Intelligence Bulletin," 15 September 1966, General CIA Records, CREST, NAII, 4, https://www.cia.gov/reading room/docs/CIA-RDP79T00975A009200120001-6.pdf.

59. Quoted in David Chandler, *The Tragedy of Cambodian History: Politics, War, and Revolution since 1945* (New Haven, CT: Yale University Press, 1991), 161.

60. William C. Westmoreland, *A Soldier Reports* (Garden City, NY: Doubleday & Company, 1976), 289; Simpson III, *Inside the Green Berets*, 130–31; Turkoly-Joczik, "Military Role of Asian Ethnic Minorities," 314–15.

61. Westmoreland, *A Soldier Reports*, 289–90.

62. Westmoreland, *Soldier Reports*, 290–92; Simpson III, *Inside the Green Berets*, 132; Turkoly-Joczik, "Military Role of Asian Ethnic Minorities," 316. Westmoreland's account comes from Gritz himself and thus should not be taken at face value. Gritz is probably most famous for his failed attempts to locate and rescue supposed POWs being held in Vietnam and Laos in the early 1980s in what amounted to nothing more than a publicity stunt. An inspiration for the character Rambo, Gritz's long history of promoting conspiracy theories and self-aggrandizement culminated in his failed run for the presidency in 1992. See Stan Kranoff, *Shadows on the Wall: The Adrenalin-Pumping, Heart-Yammering True Story of Project Rapid Fire* (Crows Nest NSW 2065,

Australia: Allen & Unwin, 2002) for the perspective of an Australian officer attached to the US Special Forces on this mission.

63. Joseph A. McChristian, *The Role of Military Intelligence 1965–1967* (Washington: Government Printing Office, 1974), 108–9.

64. Shelby L. Stanton, *Vietnam Order of Battle* (Washington, DC: U.S. News Books, 1991), 251–52.

65. Shawcross, *Sideshow*, 65.

66. "Memorandum From Marshall Wright of the National Security Council Staff to the President's Special Assistant (Rostow)," 12 December 1967, *Foreign Relations of the United States, 1964–1968*, vol. 27, *Mainland Southeast Asia; Regional Affairs* (Washington, DC: Government Printing Office, 2000), 482, https://history.state.gov/historicaldocuments/frus1964-68v27/d219.

67. Richard A. Fineberg, "Ex-Beret Links New Cambodian Prime Minister to Murder Trial," *Dispatch News Service International*, n.d, document number D40116 (Se2007), DCCAM, 1.

68. Fineberg, "Ex-Beret Links New Cambodian Prime Minister to Murder Trial," 1.

69. "U.S. Is Reported to Have Hired Sihanouk Foes for '67 Missions," *New York Times*, 28 January 1970, 1, 9.

70. Memorandum of Conversation, "Professor Kahin's Visit to Indonesia, Cambodia, and Thailand," 28 August 1967, folder: Chron 9 1967, Memcons, RG 59, General Records of the Department of State, Bureau of Far Eastern Affairs, Office of the Country Director for Burma and Cambodia, Records Relating to Cambodia 1964–1967, 1966: POL 1, Cambodia/US (April–June) to 1967: POL 32.1–2, Prek Thnat (April–Dec), box 2, NAII, 1–2.

71. Memorandum of Conversation, "Professor Kahin's Visit to Indonesia, Cambodia, and Thailand," 1–2.

72. George McT. Kahin, interview with Noel St. Clair Deschamps, 3 August 1967, folder 23, 1967 Interviews–Cambodia, box 67, Papers of George McT. Kahin, Division of Rare and Manuscript Collections, Cornell University.

73. George McT. Kahin, interview with J. F. Engers, 10 August 1967, folder 23, 1967 Interviews–Cambodia, box 67, Papers of George McT. Kahin, Division of Rare and Manuscript Collections, Cornell University.

74. George McT. Kahin, interview with Donald Lancaster, 4 August 1967, folder 23, 1967 Interviews–Cambodia, box 67, Papers of George McT. Kahin, Division of Rare and Manuscript Collections, Cornell University.

75. George McT. Kahin, interview with J. F. Engers, 10 August 1967, folder 23, 1967 Interviews–Cambodia, box 67, Papers of George McT. Kahin, Division of Rare and Manuscript Collections, Cornell University.

76. George McT. Kahin, interview with M. K. L. Bindra, 12 August 1967, folder 23, 1967 Interviews–Cambodia, box 67, Papers of George McT. Kahin, Division of Rare and Manuscript Collections, Cornell University.

77. Shawcross, *Sideshow*, 67.

78. Khmer Rouge Trial Monitor, "KRT Trial Monitor Issue No. 7—Hearing on Evidence Week 2 (13–15 December)," *Khmer Rouge Trial Monitor*, December 15, 2011, 3, https://krttrialmonitor.files.wordpress.com/2011/11/7-wk-2_

13-15dec_final-2.pdf; in 1977, Pol Pot spoke of Bay Domram as the location where the armed struggle was launched and was "later celebrated as the first engagement of the Cambodian revolutionary army." See Chandler, *Tragedy of Cambodian History*, 175.

79. Chandler, *Tragedy of Cambodian History*, 159.

80. Central Intelligence Agency, "Central Intelligence Bulletin," 17 May 1968, General CIA Records, CREST, NAII, 9, https://www.cia.gov/readin groom/docs/CIA-RDP79T00975A011200060001-0.pdf.

81. "Memorandum for the Record," 16 October 1968, *Foreign Relations of the United States, 1964–1968*, vol. 27, *Mainland Southeast Asia; Regional Affairs* (Washington, DC: Government Printing Office, 2000), 904–5, https://history.state.gov/historicaldocuments/frus1964-68v27/d406.

82. Ben Kiernan, *How Pol Pot Came to Power: A History of Communism in Kampuchea, 1930–1975* (London: Verso, 1986), 300.

83. Osborne, *Sihanouk*, 202.

84. Shawcross, *Sideshow*, 112–13.

85. Chandler, *Tragedy of Cambodian History*, 190.

86. Wilfred Deac, *Road to the Killing Fields: The Cambodian War of 1970–1975* (College Station: Texas A&M University Press, 1997), 61, 66.

87. Kenneth Conboy, *The Cambodian Wars: Clashing Armies and CIA Covert Operations* (Lawrence: University Press of Kansas, 2013), 16, 20.

88. Richard Nixon, *RN: The Memoirs of Richard Nixon* (New York: Grosset & Dunlap, 1978), 446–47.

89. Henry Kissinger, *White House Years* (Boston: Little, Brown and Company, 1979), 458–59.

90. Shawcross, *Sideshow*, 122.

91. William Bundy, *A Tangled Web: The Making of Foreign Policy in the Nixon Presidency* (New York: Hill and Wang, 1998), 149.

92. Roger Morris, *Uncertain Greatness: Henry Kissinger and American Foreign Policy* (New York: Harper & Row, 1977), 173.

93. S. R. Thornton letter to editor of *The Economist* (unpublished), 11 October 1979, folder: Thornton re Coup, box 67, Papers of George McT. Kahin, Division of Rare and Manuscript Collections, Cornell University. See also T. D. Allman, *Unmanifest Destiny: Mayhem and Illusion in American Foreign Policy—from the Monroe Doctrine to Reagan's War in El Salvador* (Garden City, NY: The Dial Press, 1984); George McT. Kahin, *Southeast Asia: A Testament* (New York: RoutledgeCurzon, 2003).

94. S. R. Thornton letter to editor of *The Economist* (unpublished), 11 October 1979.

95. Re: Sunshine Park, see letter from Thornton to Andrew Knight, editor of the *Economist* (unpublished), 19 November 1979, folder: Thornton re Coup, box 67, Papers of George McT. Kahin, Division of Rare and Manuscript Collections, Cornell University.

96. S. R. Thornton letter to editor of *The Economist* (unpublished), 11 October 1979.

97. S. R. Thornton letter to editor of *The Economist* (unpublished), 11 October 1979.

98. S. R. Thornton letter to editor of *The Economist* (unpublished), 11 October 1979.

99. S. R. Thornton letter to editor of *The Economist* (unpublished), 11 October 1979; Allman, *Unmanifest Destiny*, 337.

100. Donald Kirk, "Cambodian Premier Confident: Sees Defeat of Reds," *Chicago Tribune*, 18 July 1972, General CIA Records, CREST, NAII, https://www.cia.gov/readingroom/docs/CIA-RDP80-01601R000400200001-8.pdf.

101. "The Overthrow of Prince Norodom Sihanouk of Kampuchea," Ben Kiernan interview with a senior Minister in the Sihanouk (1969–1970) and Lon Nol (1970–1973) governments in Kampuchea, 3 June 1980, folder: Course of Coup, box 67, Papers of George McT. Kahin, Division of Rare and Manuscript Collections, Cornell University, 1; Ben Kiernan, "The Impact on Cambodia of the U.S. Intervention in Vietnam," in *The Vietnam War: Vietnamese and American Perspectives*, ed. Jayne S. Werner and Luu Doan Huynh (Armonk, NY: M. E. Sharpe, 1993), 219.

102. Notes on interview with Lt. Gen. Budiardjo [sic], 22 May 1971, folder 8, Cambodia—Miscellaneous 1951–1975, box 67, Papers of George McT. Kahin, Division of Rare and Manuscript Collections, Cornell University.

103. Mark W. Zacher and R. Stephen Milne, eds., *Conflict and Stability in Southeast Asia* (Garden City, NY: Anchor Books, 1974), 214–15.

104. Allman, *Unmanifest Destiny*, 337.

105. "Overthrow of Prince Norodom Sihanouk of Kampuchea," 1.

106. T. D. Allman, untitled draft, July 1971, folder Allman file, box 67, Papers of George McT. Kahin, Division of Rare and Manuscript Collections, Cornell University, 3–4.

107. Hersh, *The Price of Power*, 177.

108. Philip Taubman, "The Secret World of a Green Beret," *New York Times Magazine*, 4 July 1982, folder 8, Cambodia—Miscellaneous 1951–1975, box 67, Papers of George McT. Kahin, Division of Rare and Manuscript Collections, Cornell University.

109. Pfeiffer, "Remember Cambodia?" 52–54.

110. See Osborne, *Sihanouk*, 210; Turkoly-Koczik, "Cambodia's Khmer Serei Movement," 57; Justin Corfield, *Khmers Stand Up! A History of the Cambodian Government 1970–1975* (Clayton, Victoria, Australia: Centre of Southeast Asian Studies, 1994), 55–58; Shawcross, *Sideshow*, 119–20.

111. Gerald C. Hickey, *Window on a War: An Anthropologist in the Vietnam Conflict* (Lubbock: Texas Tech University Press, 2002), 274–75.

112. T. D. Allman, untitled draft, July 1971, 2, 4. According to Thành, CIA agents he dealt with "ha[d] three names a month . . . We never knew their real names."

113. Shawcross, *Sideshow*, 113.

114. Shawcross, *Sideshow*, 114–15.

115. Shawcross, *Sideshow*, 115.

116. Chandler, *Tragedy of Cambodian History*, 193.

117. "Overthrow of Prince Norodom Sihanouk of Kampuchea," 2.

118. Chandler, *Tragedy of Cambodian History*, 193.

119. "Interview with General Chana Samuda-vanija," 1981, David Chandler Cambodia Collection, Monash University, 21, http://arrow.monash.edu.au/hdl/1959.1/483755.

120. Chandler, *Tragedy of Cambodian History*, 193–94.

121. T. D. Allman, untitled draft, July 1971, 2, 4.

122. George McT Kahin, *Cambodia*, 1 April 1997, folder *Cambodia*—M.S., box 67, Papers of George McT. Kahin, Division of Rare and Manuscript Collections, Cornell University, 73.

123. James G. Lowenstein and Richard M. Moose, "Cambodia: May 1970, A Staff Report Prepared for the Use of The Committee on Foreign Relations, United States Senate," 7 June 1970, B: 670, ID: 5755, Records of Post-Colonial Governments of Cambodia, NAC, 1.

124. Banning Garrett, "The Road to Phnom Penh: Cambodia Takes up the Gun," *Ramparts Magazine*, August 1970, 34; see also Corfield, *Khmers Stand Up!*, 67. Corfield suggests that, while not organized by Lon Nol, the demonstrations were instead hijacked by him.

125. See H. D. S. Greenway, "Cambodia," *Atlantic*, July 1970, 32–38. Greenway surmises that the demonstrations were organized by the government in an attempt to push Sihanouk toward a tougher stance against he communists.

126. "Overthrow of Prince Norodom Sihanouk of Kampuchea," 2.

127. Chandler, *Tragedy of Cambodian History*, 195.

128. "Saigon Artillery Aided Cambodians: Help is Reported to Have been Sought in Clash to Drive Out Vietcong," *New York Times*, 18 March 1970, 1.

129. T. D. Allman, "How Sihanouk Lost His Crown," *Bangkok Post*, 30 September 1971, folder: Clips Laos and Cambodia, box 2, Papers of T. D. Allman, Harvard University, 7.

130. "Appeals Court Clears Way For Bombing Until Aug. 13," *Daytona Beach Morning Journal*, 28 July 1973, 2A.

131. Allman, untitled draft, July 1971, 5–6.

132. Allman, untitled draft, July 1971, 4.

133. Pfeiffer, "Remember Cambodia?" 52–54.

134. Hersh, *Price of Power*, 178; see also Kahin, *Cambodia*, 65.

135. Hersh, *Price of Power*, 181.

136. Allman, untitled draft, July 1971, 5.

137. Hickey, *Window on a War*, 274.

138. Turkoly-Joczik, "Khmer Serei Movement," 56.

139. "Overthrow of Prince Norodom Sihanouk of Kampuchea."

140. *Far Eastern Economic Review*, April 1970, 7.

141. H. R. Haldeman, *The Haldeman Diaries: Inside the Nixon White House* (New York: G. P. Putnam's Sons, 1994), 143.

6. Always an Outsider, 1970–1972

1. "Far Eastern Round Up," *Far Eastern Economic Review*, 2 April 1970, 4.

2. Boris Baczynskyj, "'This is the Voice of . . .,'" *Far Eastern Economic Review*, 21 August 1971, 25.

3. T. D. Allman, "Sealing Their Own Doom?," *Far Eastern Economic Review*, 2 April 1970, 6.

4. Allman, "Sealing Their Own Doom?" 6

5. "Far Eastern Round Up," 4.

6. James G. Lowenstein and Richard M. Moose, "Cambodia: May 1970, A Staff Report Prepared for the Use of the Committee on Foreign Relations, United States Senate," 7 June 1970, B: 670, ID: 5755, Records of Post-Colonial Governments of Cambodia, NAC, 2, 5–6.

7. "Pas de Contact Avec Son Ngoc Thanh," in "Gazette du Royaume," *Réalités Cambodgiennes*, no. 691, 4 April 1970, box 680, Charles Meyer Collection, NAC, 21.

8. Lowenstein and Moose, "Cambodia: May 1970," 11–12.

9. "Memorandum From the President's Assistant for National Security Affairs (Kissinger) to President Nixon," 9 April 1970, *Foreign Relations of the United States, 1969–1976*, vol. 6, *Vietnam, January 1969–July 1970* (Washington, DC: Government Printing Office, 2006), 802–3, https://history.state.gov/historicaldocuments/frus1969-76v06/d226.

10. "Memorandum From the Acting Chairman of the Joint Chiefs of Staff (Westmoreland) to Secretary of Defense Laird," 21 April 1970, *Foreign Relations of the United States, 1969–1976*, vol. 6, *Vietnam, January 1969–July 1970* (Washington, DC: Government Printing Office, 2006), 844n3, https://history.state.gov/historicaldocuments/frus1969-76v06/d244.

11. "Telegram from Staff Secretary of the National Security Council Staff Secretariat (Watts) to Winston Lord of the National Security Council Staff," 20 April 1970, *Foreign Relations of the United States, 1969–1976*, vol. 6, *Vietnam, January 1969–July 1970* (Washington, DC: Government Printing Office, 2006), 837, https://history.state.gov/historicaldocuments/frus1969-76v06/d240.

12. Lowenstein and Moose, "Cambodia: May 1970," 3.

13. "Westmoreland to Laird," 842–44.

14. "National Security Council Decision Memorandum 56," *Foreign Relations of the United States, 1969–1976*, vol. 6, *Vietnam, January 1969–July 1970* (Washington, DC: Government Printing Office, 2006), 851, https://history.state.gov/historicaldocuments/frus1969-76v06/d249.

15. T. J. S. George, "Sheep to the Slaughter," *Far Eastern Economic Review*, 14 May 1970, 6.

16. Lowenstein and Moose, "Cambodia: May 1970," 11.

17. American Embassy in Saigon to Secretary of State, Department of the Army, Staff Communications Division, "Thieu, Ky comments on Cambodia," 13 May 1970, folder: Cambodia—US Policy and Assistance 1970 (13), RG 319 Records of the Army Staff, Center for Military History, Historians Background Material Files Relating to the Vietnam War, 1961-1975, PSYOPS, 1970 to Cambodia-Ops Talking Paper, 1970, box 8, NAII, 1–2.

18. Ralph Blumenthal, "U.S. Reported Recruiting Cambodians in Vietnam," *New York Times*, 28 May 1970, General CIA Records, CREST, NAII, 5, https://www.cia.gov/readingroom/docs/CIA-RDP72-00337R000200230001-1.pdf.

19. T. J. S. George, "The Crusaders' Cross," *Far Eastern Economic Review*, 28 May 1970, 5.

20. Quoted in Banning Garrett, "The Road to Phnom Penh: Cambodia Takes up the Gun," *Ramparts*, August 1970, 34.

21. R. L. Turkoly-Joczik, "The Military Role of Asian Ethnic Minorities in the Second Indochina War, 1959–1975" (PhD diss., University of Wales, 1986), 346.

22. American Embassy in Phnom Penh to Secretary of State, Department of the Army, Staff Communications Division, 7 June 1970, folder: Cambodia–US Policy and Assistance 1970 (13), RG 319 Records of the Army Staff, Center for Military History, Historians Background Material Files Relating to the Vietnam War, 1961–1975, PSYOPS, 1970 to Cambodia-Ops Talking Paper, 1970, box 8, NAII, 1–2.

23. Ellsworth Bunker to Secretary of State, "SVN/Cambodian Relations," 9 June 1970, folder: Cambodia–US Policy and Assistance 1970 (13), RG 319 Records of the Army Staff, Center for Military History, Historians Background Material Files Relating to the Vietnam War, 1961–1975, PSYOPS, 1970 to Cambodia-Ops Talking Paper, 1970, box 8, NAII, 1–2.

24. Ellsworth Bunker to Secretary of State, "SVN/Cambodian Relations," 2.

25. Ellsworth Bunker to Secretary of State, "SVN/Cambodian Relations," 3.

26. American Embassy in Phnom Penh to Secretary of State, "ICRC/LICROSS Appeal for Refugee Relief and PL-480 Title II Assistance," 11 June 1970, folder: Cambodia–US Policy and Assistance 1970 (13), RG 319 Records of the Army Staff, Center for Military History, Historians Background Material Files Relating to the Vietnam War, 1961–1975, PSYOPS, 1970 to Cambodia-Ops Talking Paper, 1970, box 8, NAII.

27. "Far Eastern Round Up," *Far Eastern Economic Review*, 2 July 1970, 4; Harald Munthe-Kaas, "C'est Fini," *Far Eastern Economic Review*, 2 July 1970, 6.

28. T. D. Allman, "Cambodia: Into an Iceberg War," *Far Eastern Economic Review*, 23 July 1970, 16.

29. T. J. S. George, "A Long War to Come," *Far Eastern Economic Review*, 21 May 1970, 64.

30. Quoted in "Far Eastern Round Up," *Far Eastern Economic Review*, 28 May 1970, 4.

31. Munthe-Kass, "C'est Fini," 6.

32. Charles Meyer, "Behind Phnom Penh's Musical," *National Guardian*, 2 June 1971, General CIA Records, CREST, NAII, https://www.cia.gov/readingroom/docs/CIA-RDP80-01601R000800200001-4.pdf.

33. "743 Enemy Killed During Offensive by South Vietnam," *Lawrence Daily Journal-World*, 22 March 1972, 1.

34. T. D. Allman, "Cambodia: Dismantling the Monarchy," *Far Eastern Economic Review*, 5 September 1970, 8.

35. Allman, "Cambodia: Dismantling the Monarchy," 8.

36. "Son Ngoc Thanh à Saigon," in "Actualites," *Réalités Cambodgiennes*, no. 712, 4 September 1970, box 680, Charles Meyer Collection, NAC, 26.

37. Justin Corfield, *Khmers Stand Up! A History of the Cambodian Government 1970–1975* (Clayton, Victoria, Australia: Centre of Southeast Asian Studies, 1994), 104.

38. Corfield, *Khmers Stand Up!*, 110–11.

39. "Pnompenh [*sic*] Aides to Ask Lon Nol to Reconsider His Resignation," *New York Times*, 21 April 1971, 10.

40. "Pnompenh [*sic*] Aides to Ask Lon Nol," 10.

41. Corfield, *Khmers Stand Up!*, 111.

42. Henry Kamm, "Aide Says Lon Nol Must Be Premier: Asserts Cambodian Crisis Requires Him to Serve," *New York Times*, 27 April 1971, 9.

43. "Far Eastern Round Up," *Far Eastern Economic Review*, 1 May 1971, 4.

44. Kamm, "Aide Says Lon Nol Must Be Premier," 9.

45. Central Intelligence Agency, "Central Intelligence Bulletin," 30 April 1971, General CIA Records, CREST, NAII, 1, https://www.cia.gov/readin groom/docs/CIA-RDP79T00975A018900060001-6.pdf.

46. Central Intelligence Agency, "Central Intelligence Bulletin," 3 May 1971, General CIA Records, CREST, NAII, 1, https://www.cia.gov/readingroom/ docs/CIA-RDP79T00975A018900080002-3.pdf.

47. Corfield, *Khmers Stand Up!*, 112.

48. Central Intelligence Agency, "Central Intelligence Bulletin," 6 May 1971, General CIA Records, CREST, NAII, 1, https://www.cia.gov/readingroom/ docs/CIA-RDP79T00975A018900110002-9.pdf.

49. Corfield, *Khmers Stand Up!*, 112–13.

50. Central Intelligence Agency, "Weekly Summary," 21 May 1971, General CIA Records, CREST, NAII, 5–6, https://www.cia.gov/readingroom/docs/ CIA-RDP79-00927A008800020001-5.pdf.

51. Corfield, *Khmers Stand Up!*, 113–15.

52. "Le Maréchal Lon Nol Preside Une Important Réunion," *Réalités Cambodgiennes*, no. 757, 6 August 1971, box 680, Charles Meyer Collection, NAC, 5.

53. Central Intelligence Agency, "Central Intelligence Bulletin," 30 July 1971, General CIA Records, CREST, NAII, 1, https://www.cia.gov/reading room/docs/CIA-RDP79T00975A019600090001-5.pdf.

54. "Far Eastern Round Up," *Far Eastern Economic Review*, 2 October 1971, 4.

55. T. D. Allman, "Forever Khmer," *Far Eastern Economic Review*, 4 September 1971, 22–23.

56. "Far Eastern Round Up," *Far Eastern Economic Review*, 23 October 1971, 4.

57. "Far Eastern Round Up," *Far Eastern Economic Review*, 30 October 1971, 4.

58. Judith Coburn, "Cambodia: New Game—Old Wicket," *Far Eastern Economic Review*, 30 October 1971, 12.

59. Central Intelligence Agency, "Political Developments in Phnom Penh," 26 October 1971, General CIA Records, CREST, NAII, 6–7, https://www.cia. gov/readingroom/docs/CIA-RDP85T00875R001100100127-5.pdf; David Chandler, *The Tragedy of Cambodian History: Politics, War, and Revolution since 1945* (New Haven, CT: Yale University Press, 1991), 213–14.

60. Central Intelligence Agency, "Weekly Summary," 12 November 1971, General CIA Records, CREST, NAII, 9, https://www.cia.gov/readingroom/ docs/CIA-RDP79-00927A009200040001-8.pdf.

61. Joseph Fried, "Report U.S. Spy Units Active in Cambo," *New York Daily News*, 17 November 1971, General CIA Records, CREST, NAII, 43, https://www. cia.gov/readingroom/docs/CIA-RDP80-01601R000400200001-8.pdf.

62. Central Intelligence Agency, "Developments in Indochina," 26 November 1971, General CIA Records, CREST, NAII, 1, https://www.cia.gov/reading room/docs/CIA-RDP79M00098A000200150025-7.pdf.

63. Central Intelligence Agency, "Central Intelligence Bulletin," 8 December 1971, General CIA Records, CREST, NAII, 3, https://www.cia.gov/readin groom/docs/CIA-RDP79T00975A020600100002-0.pdf; Chandler, *Tragedy of Cambodian History*, 213–14.

64. Judith Coburn, "Cambodia: Bruised Egos and Coup Talk," *Far Eastern Economic Review*, 8 January 1972, 6–7.

65. Central Intelligence Agency, "Developments in Indochina," 1–2.

66. Far Eastern Round Up," *Far Eastern Economic Review*, 25 December 1971, 4.

67. Peter Osnos, "Cambodians Compete to Succeed Lon Nol," *Washington Post*, 19 December 1971, General CIA Records, CREST, NAII, 37, https://www.cia.gov/readingroom/docs/CIA-RDP80-01601R000400200001-8.pdf.

68. Central Intelligence Agency, "Taking Stock in Cambodia," 18 February 1972, General CIA Records, CREST, NAII, 9–10, https://www.cia.gov/read ingroom/docs/CIA-RDP79R00967A000400030005-0.pdf.

69. "Far Eastern Round Up," *Far Eastern Economic Review*, 18 March 1972, 4; "Lon Nol Takes Cambodia Posts," *The Palm Beach Post*, 14 March 1972, A2.

70. Fox Butterfield, "Lon Nol Names a Cambodian Premier," *New York Times*, 19 March 1972, 3.

71. "Far Eastern Round Up," *Far Eastern Economic Review*, 18 March 1972, 4.

72. Corfield, *Khmers Stand Up!*, 131; "Far Eastern Round Up," *Far Eastern Economic Review*, 18 March 1972, 4; Judith Coburn, "And Now a King in Khaki," *Far Eastern Economic Review*, 18 March 1972, 5–6.

73. Donald Kirk, "Cambodian Premier Confident: Sees Defeat of Reds," *Chicago Tribune*, 18 July 1972, General CIA Records, CREST, NAII, 10, https://www.cia.gov/readingroom/docs/CIA-RDP80-01601R000400200001-8.pdf; Central Intelligence Agency, "Weekly Vietnam Indicators: Week Ending 18 March 1972," General CIA Records, CREST, NAII, https://www.cia.gov/read ingroom/docs/CIA-RDP80T01719R000100100014-8.pdf; Corfield, *Khmers Stand Up!*, 132.

74. Fox Butterfield, "Lon Nol Names a Cambodian Premier," *New York Times*, 19 March 1972, 3.

75. Butterfield, "Lon Nol Names a Cambodian Premier," 3.

76. CIA, "The Presidential Daily Brief," 20 March 1972, https://www.cia.gov/readingroom/docs/DOC_0005993201.pdf, 3.

77. Central Intelligence Agency, "Weekly Summary," 24 March 1972, General CIA Records, CREST, NAII, 6. https://www.cia.gov/readingroom/docs/CIA-RDP79-00927A009500010001-8.pdf.

78. T. J. S. George, "Last Round for Lon Nol," *Far Eastern Economic Review*, 25 March 1972, 5.

79. Fox Butterfield, "Lon Nol Gets Full Control in Cambodia," *New York Times*, 23 March 1972.

80. Quoted in "Lon Nol Aide Accepts Post," *Washington Star*, 19 March 1972, General CIA Records, CREST, NAII, 29, https://www.cia.gov/readingroom/docs/CIA-RDP80-01601R000400200001-8.pdf.

81. Central Intelligence Agency, "Weekly Vietnam Indicators: Week Ending 18 March 1972."

82. "Enemy Troops Launch Attacks Near Capital," *St. Petersburg Times*, 22 March 1972, 1.

83. Central Intelligence Agency, "Central Intelligence Bulletin," 20 March 1972, General CIA Records, CREST, NAII, 4–5, https://www.cia.gov/readingroom/docs/CIA-RDP79T00975A021500010001-1.pdf.

84. Judith Coburn, "Guerilla in Government," *Far Eastern Economic Review*, 8 April 1972, 6–7.

85. Central Intelligence Agency, "Central Intelligence Bulletin," 21 March 1972,General CIA Records, CREST, NAII, 2, https://www.cia.gov/readingroom/docs/CIA-RDP79T00975A021500020001-0.pdf.

86. "Cambodia Worried by Enemy Offensive in Vietnam: Premier Sees Glimmering of World War," *Schenectady Gazette*, 13 April 1972, 40.

87. Central Intelligence Agency, "Central Intelligence Bulletin," 4 May 1972, General CIA Records, CREST, NAII, 1, https://www.cia.gov/readingroom/docs/CIA-RDP79T00975A021800060001-3.pdf.

88. Central Intelligence Agency, "Central Intelligence Bulletin," 4 May 1972.

89. "Cambodia Worried by Enemy Offensive in Vietnam," 40.

90. Central Intelligence Agency, "Central Intelligence Bulletin," 4 May 1972, 1.

91. "News Roundup," *Far Eastern Economic Review*, 20 May 1972, 3.

92. "News Roundup," *Far Eastern Economic Review*, 10 June 1972, 3; for more on fraudulent election, see Chandler, *Tragedy of Cambodian History*, 221–22.

93. *Republic* (Ann Arbor, MI), May and June 1972, 2.

94. "News Roundup," *Far Eastern Economic Review*, 24 June 1972, 5.

95. "News Roundup," *Far Eastern Economic Review*, 1 July 1972, 5; Boris Baczynskyj, "Lon Nol's Private War," *Far Eastern Economic Review*, 1 July 1972, 23.

96. Central Intelligence Agency, "Central Intelligence Bulletin," 13 June 1972, General CIA Records, CREST, NAII, 15, https://www.cia.gov/readingroom/docs/CIA-RDP79T00975A022100040001-1.pdf.

97. Boris Baczynskyj, "Withering Muscle," *Far Eastern Economic Review*, 15 July 1972, 15.

98. Baczynskyj, "Withering Muscle," 15.

99. "Cambodia Worried by Enemy Offensive in Vietnam," 40.

100. Central Intelligence Agency, "Central Intelligence Bulletin," 17 June 1972, General CIA Records, CREST, NAII, 6, https://www.cia.gov/readingroom/docs/CIA-RDP79T00975A022100080001-7.pdf.

101. Central Intelligence Agency, "Weekly Summary," 23 June 1972, General CIA Records, CREST, NAII, 9–10, https://www.cia.gov/readingroom/docs/CIA-RDP79-00927A009600050001-2.pdf.

102. Central Intelligence Agency, "Weekly Summary," 30 June 1972, General CIA Records, CREST, NAII, 5–6, https://www.cia.gov/readingroom/docs/CIA-RDP79-00927A009600060001-1.pdf.

103. Edith Lenart, "Lon Nol's Dilemma," *Far Eastern Economic Review*, 7 October 1972, 20.

104. Donald Kirk, "Cambodian Premier Confident."

105. Quoted in T. D. Allman, "Lesser Danger?" *Far Eastern Economic Review*, 18 September 1971, 18.

106. "Vietnam Positions See-Saw: Cambodian Leader Said Bomb Target," *Palm Beach Post*, 21 August 1972, A-2.

107. So'n Ngọc Thành, "Communiqué de Presse," *Le Républicain*, 30 August 1972, box 42, *"France Cambodge*, 25/12/1945–19/01/1946; *Républicain (Le)*, 30/08/1972–13/02/1975, Cambodian Publications and Periodicals, NAC, 1; "Visite Du Premier Ministre Khmer A Saigon," *Le Républicain*, 31 August 1972, box 42, *"France Cambodge*, 25/12/1945–19/01/1946; *Républicain (Le)*, 30/08/1972–13/02/1975, Cambodian Publications and Periodicals, NAC, 1; "La Visite de M. Son Ngoc Thanh à Saigon," *Le Républicain*, 1 September 1972, box 42, *"France Cambodge*, 25/12/1945–19/01/1946; *Républicain (Le)*, 30/08/1972–13/02/1975, Cambodian Publications and Periodicals, NAC, 2.

108. So'n Ngọc Thành, "Communiqué de Presse," *Le Républicain*, 30 August 1972, 1; "Visite Du Premier Ministre Khmer A Saigon," *Le Républicain*, 31 August 1972, 1; "Visite de M. Son Ngoc Thanh à Saigon," *Le Républicain*, 1 September 1972, 2; "Indochina Peace Near, Thieu Assures Cambodia," *Milwaukee Sentinel*, 1 September 1972, 2.

109. Lenart, "Lon Nol's Dilemma," 20.

110. Central Intelligence Agency, "Central Intelligence Bulletin," 5 September 1972, General CIA Records, CREST, NAII, 9, https://www.cia.gov/reading room/docs/CIA-RDP79T00975A022700040002-4.pdf.

111. "News Roundup," *Far Eastern Economic Review*, 21 October 1972, 5.

112. *Republic* (Ann Arbor, MI), December 1972, 2.

113. Central Intelligence Agency, "Central Intelligence Bulletin," 16 October 1972, General CIA Records, CREST, NAII, 2, https://www.cia.gov/reading room/docs/CIA-RDP79T00975A023000030001-2.pdf.

114. Boris Baczynskyi, "Socio-synicism," *Far Eastern Economic Review*, 28 October 1972, 24.

Conclusion

1. Thomas W. Lippman, "Bats, Bolts Bold Ill in Jittery Cambodia," *Washington Post*, 27 November 1972, General CIA Records, CREST, NAII, 49–50, https://www.cia.gov/readingroom/docs/CIA-RDP77-00432R000100020001-4.pdf.

2. Ellsworth Bunker, "Son Ngoc Thanh," 25 April 1973, document number 1973SAIGON07183, AAD, NAII, http://aad.archives.gov/aad/createpdf?rid=11959&dt=2472&dl=1345; "Cambodian Reds Urge Phnom Penh Rioting," *Evening Independent* (St. Petersburg, FL), 27 April 1973, 20-A.

3. William Rodgers, "April 30 Indochina Press Summary," document number 1973STATE080977, Central Foreign Policy Files, 1973–1976, RG59, AAD, NAII, accessed 11 January 2013, 1–2, https://aad.archives.gov/aad/create pdf?rid=1705&dt=2472&dl=1345

4. Emory Swank, "Recruitment of Khmer Krom," 11 August 1973, document number 1973PHNOM08333, Central Foreign Policy Files, 1973–1976,

RG59, AAD, NAII, 1-2, http://aad.archives.gov/aad/createpdf?rid=55293&dt=2472&dl=1345.

5. Graham Martin to Secretary of State, "Mr IV Sitrep for August 27, 1973, also summarizing week of August 20-26," 28 August 1973, document number 1973SAIGON15487, Central Foreign Policy Files, 1973–1976, RG59, AAD, NAII, https://aad.archives.gov/aad/createpdf?rid=25475&dt=2472&dl=1345 3.

6. William Rodgers, "August 13 EA Press Summary," document number 1973STATE160037, Central Foreign Policy Files, 1973–1976, RG59, AAD, NAII, https://aad.archives.gov/aad/createpdf?rid=13187&dt=2472&dl=1345, 1-2.

7. James Fenton, *All the Wrong Places: Adrift in the Politics of the Pacific Rim* (New York: The Atlantic Monthly Press, 1988), 39.

8. Rowland Evans and Robert Novak, "Ending Aid Won't Halt Bloodshed," *Free Lance-Star* (Fredericksburg, VA), 17 March 1975, 4.

9. Fenton, *All the Wrong Places*, 39.

10. Fenton, *All the Wrong Places*, 101-2.

11. Fenton, *All the Wrong Places*, 102-3.

12. Kenneth Rush, "Meeting of Khmer Libre Movement (Son Ngoc Thanh)," 1 October 1975, document number 1975PARIS25401, AAD, NAII, http://aad.archives.gov/aad/createpdf?rid=186080&dt=2476&dl=1345.

13. Charles Whitehouse, "Resistance to the New Cambodian Regime," 29 July 1975, document number 1975BANGKO15352, Central Foreign Policy Files, 1973–1976, RG59, AAD, NAII, http://aad.archives.gov/aad/createpdf?rid=152670&dt=2476&dl=1345.

14. Whitehouse, "Resistance to the New Cambodian Regime."

15. Whitehouse, "Resistance to the New Cambodian Regime."

16. Charles Whitehouse, "Sample Cases of Cat III Refugees Remaining in Thailand," 23 February 1976, document number 1976 BANGKO03981, Central Foreign Policy Files, 1973–1976, RG59, AAD, NAII, https://aad.archives.gov/aad/createpdf?rid=88268&dt=2082&dl=1345, 1, 3.

17. Robert L. Turkoly-Joczik, "Cambodia's Khmer Serei Movement," *Asian Affairs* 15, no. 1 (Spring, 1988): 58-59; William Shawcross, *The Quality of Mercy: Cambodia, Holocaust and Modern Conscience* (New York: Simon and Schuster, 1984), 224-28.

18. Vasinh Son, email to author, 6 January 2022.

Bibliography

Unpublished Primary Sources

United States

Division of Rare and Manuscript Collections, Cornell University
Library, Ithaca, NY

Papers of George McT. Kahin

Harry S. Truman Presidential Library, Independence, MO

Papers of John F. Melby
Papers of Harry S. Truman

Houghton Library, Harvard College Library, Cambridge, MA

Papers of T. D. Allman

John F. Kennedy Presidential Library and Museum, Boston, MA

Papers of Bernard Fall
Papers of Roger Hilsman
Papers of John F. Kennedy

National Archives II, College Park, MD

Record Group 59—General Records of the Department of State
Record Group 319—Records of the Army Staff
Record Group 472—Records of the US Forces in Southeast Asia,
1950–1975
CIA CREST Database

Northern Illinois University Library, DeKalb, IL

Kenton Clymer Collection

Vietnam Center and Sam Johnson Vietnam Archive, Texas Tech
University, Lubbock, TX

Douglas Pike Collection

Cambodia

Bophana Center, Phnom Penh

ECPAD (French Institution for Communication and Audiovisual Production)
Cinema and Cultural Diffusion Department of Cambodia

Center for Khmer Studies, Phnom Penh and Siem Reap
Documentation Center of Cambodia, Phnom Penh
National Archives of Cambodia, Phnom Penh

Records of the Résidence Supérieure du Cambodge (French Colonial Administration)
Records of Post-Colonial Governments of Cambodia
Cambodian Publications and Periodicals
Charles Meyer Collection
Relations Diplomatique

Australia

Monash University Library, Melbourne, Victoria, Australia

David Chandler Cambodia Collection, Son Ngoc Thanh Papers

National Archives of Australia, Canberra

Series A1838—Records of the External Affairs Office

Published Primary Sources

Bundy, William. *A Tangled Web: The Making of Foreign Policy in the Nixon Presidency*. New York: Hill and Wang, 1998.
Colby, William and Peter Forbath. *Honorable Men: My Life in the CIA*. New York: Simon and Schuster, 1978.
Documents Relating to British Involvement in the Indochina Conflict 1945–1965, cmnd. 2834 London: Her Majesty's Stationery Office, 1965.
Fenton, James. *All the Wrong Places: Adrift in the Politics of the Pacific Rim*. New York: The Atlantic Monthly Press, 1988.
Foreign Relations of the United States: Diplomatic Papers, 1940. Vol. 4, *The Far East*. Washington, DC: Government Publishing Office, 1955. https://history.state.gov/historicaldocuments/frus1940v04.
Foreign Relations of the United States: Diplomatic Papers, 1945. Vol. 6, *The Far East*. Washington, DC: Government Publishing Office, 1969. https://history.state.gov/historicaldocuments/frus1945v06.
Foreign Relations of the United States, 1946. Vol. 8, *The Far East*. Washington, DC: Government Publishing Office, 1971. https://history.state.gov/historicaldocuments/frus1946v08.

Foreign Relations of the United States, 1947. Vol. 6, *The Far East.* Washington, DC: Government Publishing Office, 1972. https://history.state.gov/historicaldocuments/frus1947v06.

Foreign Relations of the United States, 1950. Vol. 6, *The Far East.* Washington, DC: Government Printing Office, 1976. https://history.state.gov/historical documents/frus1950v06.

Foreign Relations of the United States, 1952–1954. Vol. 2, part 2, *National Security Affairs.* Washington, DC: Government Publishing Office, 1984. https:// history.state.gov/historicaldocuments/frus1952-54v02p2.

Foreign Relations of the United States, 1952–1954. Vol. 13, part 1, *Indochina.* Washington, DC: Government Publishing Office, 1982. https://history.state. gov/historicaldocuments/frus1952-54v13p1.

Foreign Relations of the United States, 1955–1957. Vol. 1, *Vietnam.* Washington, DC: Government Printing Office, 1985. https://history.state.gov/historicaldocuments/frus1955-57v01.

Foreign Relations of the United States, 1955–1957. Vol. 21, *East Asian Security; Cambodia; Laos.* Washington, DC: Government Printing Office, 1990. https:// history.state.gov/historicaldocuments/frus1955-57v21.

Foreign Relations of the United States, 1955–1957. Vol. 22, *Southeast Asia.* Washington, DC: Government Printing Office, 1989. https://history.state.gov/historicaldocuments/frus1955-57v22.

Foreign Relations of the United States, 1958–1960. Vols. 15/16, part 1, microfiche supplement, *Burma; Malaya-Singapore; East Asia Region; Cambodia.* Washington, DC: Government Printing Office, 1993.

Foreign Relations of the United States, 1958–1960. Vol. 16, *East Asia–Pacific Region; Cambodia; Laos.* Washington, DC: Government Printing Office, 1992. https://history.state.gov/historicaldocuments/frus1958-60v16.

Foreign Relations of the United States, 1961–1963. Vol. 23, *Southeast Asia.* Washington, DC: Government Printing Office, 1994. https://history.state.gov/historicaldocuments/frus1961-63v23.

Foreign Relations of the United States, 1964–1968. Vol. 27, *Mainland Southeast Asia; Regional Affairs.* Washington, DC: Government Printing Office, 2000. https://history.state.gov/historicaldocuments/frus1964-68v27.

Foreign Relations of the United States, 1969–1976. Vol. 6, *Vietnam, January 1969–July 1970.* Washington, DC: Government Printing Office, 2006. https:// history.state.gov/historicaldocuments/frus1969-76v06.

Haldeman, H. R. *The Haldeman Diaries: Inside the Nixon White House.* New York: G. P. Putnam's Sons, 1994.

Hickey, Gerald C. *Window on a War: An Anthropologist in the Vietnam Conflict.* Lubbock: Texas Tech University Press, 2002.

Hilsman, Roger. *To Move a Nation: The Politics of Foreign Policy in the Administration of John F. Kennedy.* Garden City, NY: Doubleday, 1967.

Kiernan, Ben and Chanthou Boua, eds. *Peasants and Politics in Kampuchea, 1942–1981.* New York: M. E. Sharpe, 1982.

Kissinger, Henry. *White House Years.* Boston: Little, Brown and Company, 1979.

Lansdale, Edward Geary. *In the Midst of Wars: An American's Mission to Southeast Asia.* New York: Fordham University Press, 1991.

Lewis, Norman. *A Dragon Apparent: Travels in Indo-China.* Oxford: The Book Society, 1951.

Morris, Roger. *Uncertain Greatness: Henry Kissinger and American Foreign Policy.* New York: Harper & Row, 1977.

Nixon, Richard. *RN: The Memoirs of Richard Nixon.* New York: Grosset & Dunlap, 1978.

Norodom Sihanouk. *My War with the CIA: The Memoirs of Prince Norodom Sihanouk.* New York: Pantheon, 1972.

Norodom Sihanouk. *Shadow Over Angkor.* Vol. 1, *Memoirs of His Majesty King Norodom Sihanouk of Cambodia,* edited by Julio A. Jeldres. Phnom Penh, Cambodia: Monument Books, 2005.

Papers Relating to the Foreign Relations of the United States, with the Annual Message of the President Transmitted to Congress December 5, 1905 (Washington, DC: Government Printing Office, 1906. https://history.state.gov/historicaldocuments/frus1905.

Westmoreland, William C. *A Soldier Reports.* Garden City, NY: Doubleday, 1976.

Published Secondary Sources

Allman, T. D. *Unmanifest Destiny: Mayhem and Illusion in American Foreign Policy—from the Monroe Doctrine to Reagan's War in El Salvador.* Garden City, NY: The Dial Press, 1984.

Anderson, David L. *Trapped by Success: The Eisenhower Administration and Vietnam, 1953–1961.* New York: Columbia University Press, 1991.

Armstrong, John P. *Sihanouk Speaks: Cambodia's Chief of State Explains His Controversial Policies.* New York: Walker and Company, 1964.

Becker, Elizabeth. *When the War Was Over: The Voices of Cambodia's Revolution and Its People.* New York: Simon and Schuster, 1986.

Chandler, David. *A History of Cambodia.* Boulder, CO: Westview Press, 2007.

Chandler, David. *The Tragedy of Cambodian History: Politics, War, and Revolution since 1945.* New Haven, CT: Yale University Press, 1991.

Chandler, David P. "The Kingdom of Kampuchea, March–October 1945: Japanese-Sponsored Independence in Cambodia in World War II." *Journal of Southeast Asian Studies* 17, no. 1 (March 1986): 83–93.

Chawla, Sudershan, Melvin Gurtov, and Alain-Gerard Marsot, eds. *Southeast Asia under the New Balance of Power.* New York: Praeger, 1975.

Clymer, Kenton. *Troubled Relations: The United States and Cambodia since 1870.* DeKalb: Northern Illinois University Press, 2007.

Clymer, Kenton. *The United States and Cambodia, 1870–1969: From Curiosity to Confrontation.* London: RoutledgeCurzon, 2004.

Clymer, Kenton. *The United States and Cambodia, 1969–2000: A Troubled Relationship.* London: RoutledgeCurzon, 2004.

Conboy, Kenneth. *The Cambodian Wars: Clashing Armies and CIA Covert Operations.* Lawrence: University Press of Kansas, 2013.

Corfield, Justin. *Khmers Stand Up! A History of the Cambodian Government 1970–1975.* Clayton, Victoria, Australia: Centre of Southeast Asian Studies, Monash University, 1994.

Currey, Cecil B. *Edward Lansdale: The Unquiet American*. Boston: Houghton Mifflin, 1988.

Deac, Wilfred. *Road to the Killing Fields: The Cambodian War of 1970–1975*. College Station: Texas A&M University Press, 1997.

Dommen, Arthur J. *The Indochinese Experience of the French and the Americans: Nationalism and Communism in Cambodia, Laos, and Vietnam*. Bloomington: Indiana University Press, 2001.

Duus, Peter, Ramon Myers, and Mark Peattie, eds. *The Japanese Wartime Empire, 1931–1945*. Princeton, NJ: Princeton University Press, 1996.

Edwards, Penny. *Cambodge: The Cultivation of a Nation, 1860–1945*. Honolulu: University of Hawaii Press, 2007.

Etcheson, Craig. "The Khmer Way of Exile: Lessons from Three Indochinese Wars." *Journal of Political Science* 18, no. 1 (November 1990): 94–123.

Etcheson, Craig. *The Rise and Demise of Democratic Kampuchea*. Boulder, CO: Westview, 1984.

Frederick, Cynthia. "Cambodia: 'Operation Total Victory No. 43.'" *Bulletin of Concerned Asian Scholars* 2, no. 3 (April–July 1970): 3–18.

Gardner, Lloyd C. *Approaching Vietnam: From World War II through Dienbienphu, 1941–1954*. New York: W. W. Norton, 1988.

Gibson, Richard M. and Wenhua Chen. *The Secret Army: Chiang Kai-shek and the Drug Warlords of the Golden Triangle*. Solaris, South Tower, Singapore: John Wiley & Sons (Asia), 2011.

Goodman, Allan E. *Government and the Countryside: Political Accommodation and South Vietnam's Communal Groups*. Santa Monica, CA: The RAND Corporation, 1968. https://www.rand.org/content/dam/rand/pubs/papers/2008/P3924.pdf.

Goto, Ken'ichi. *Tensions of Empire: Japan and Southeast Asia in the Colonial and Postcolonial World*. Athens: Ohio University Press, 2003.

Hammer, Ellen J. *The Struggle for Indochina, 1940–1955*. Stanford, CA: Stanford University Press, 1966.

Harris, Ian. *Cambodian Buddhism: History and Practice*. Honolulu: University of Hawaii Press, 2005.

Hersh, Seymour M. *The Price of Power: Kissinger in the White House*. New York: Summit Books, 1983.

Herz, Martin Florian. *A Short History of Cambodia: From the Days of Angkor to the Present*. New York: F. A. Praeger, 1958.

Hickey, Gerald C. *Accommodation and Coalition in South Vietnam*. Santa Monica, CA: The RAND Corporation, 1970. https://www.rand.org/content/dam/rand/pubs/papers/2008/P4213.pdf.

Issacs, Arnold R. *Without Honor: Defeat in Vietnam and Cambodia*. Baltimore: Johns Hopkins University Press, 1983.

Jacobsen, Trude. *Lost Goddesses: The Denial of Female Power in Cambodian History*. Copenhagen: NIAS Press, 2008.

Kahin, George McT. *Southeast Asia: A Testament*. New York: RoutledgeCurzon, 2003.

Kelley, Francis J. *The Green Berets in Vietnam, 1961–1971*. Washington, DC: Brassey's, Inc., 1991.

Kiernan, Ben. *How Pol Pot Came to Power: Colonialism, Nationalism, and Communism in Cambodia, 1930–1975.* New Haven, CT: Yale University Press, 2004.

Kiernan, Ben. *How Pol Pot Came to Power: A History of Communism in Kampuchea, 1930–1975.* London: Verso, 1986.

Kiernan, Ben. "The Impact on Cambodia of the U.S. Intervention in Vietnam." In *The Vietnam War: Vietnamese and American Perspectives,* edited by Jayne S. Werner and Luu Doan Huynh, 216–232. Armonk, NY: M. E. Sharpe, 1993.

Kiernan, Ben. "Origins of Khmer Communism." *Southeast Asian Affairs* (1981): 161–180.

Kiernan, Ben. *The Pol Pot Regime: Race, Power, and Genocide in Cambodia under the Khmer Rouge.* 3rd ed. New Haven, CT: Yale University Press, 2008.

Lacey, Michael J., ed. *The Truman Presidency.* New York: Woodrow Wilson International Center for Scholars, 1989.

LaFeber, Walter. *America, Russia, and the Cold War, 1945–2006.* New York: McGraw-Hill, 2008.

Leifer, Michael. *Cambodia: The Search for Security.* New York: Frederick A. Praeger, 1967.

Leifer, Michael. "The Cambodian Opposition." *Asian Survey* 2, no. 2 (April, 1962): 11–15.

Locard, Henri. "*Achar* Hem Chieu (1898–1943), the 'Umbrella Demonstration' of 20th July 1942 and the Vichy Regime." *Siksacakr,* no. 8–9 (2006–2007): 70–81.

McChristian, Joseph A. *The Role of Military Intelligence 1965–1967.* Washington, DC: Government Printing Office, 1974.

McClain, James L. *Japan: A Modern History.* New York: W. W. Norton, 2002.

McMahon, Robert J. "Toward A Post-Colonial Order: Truman Administration Policies Toward South and Southeast Asia." In *The Truman Presidency,* edited by Michael J. Lacey, 339–365. New York: Woodrow Wilson International Center for Scholars, 1989.

Nohlen, Dieter, Florian Grotz, and Christof Hartmann, eds. *Elections in Asia and the Pacific: A Data Handbook,* vol. 2, *Southeast Asia, East Asia, and the South Pacific.* Oxford: Oxford University Press, 2001.

Osborne, Milton. *Sihanouk: Prince of Light, Prince of Darkness.* Honolulu: University of Hawaii Press, 1994.

Peattie, Mark R. "*Nanshin*: The 'Southward Advance,' 1931–1941, as a Prelude to the Japanese Occupation of Southeast Asia." In *The Japanese Wartime Empire, 1931–1945,* edited by Peter Duus, Ramon Myers, and Mark Peattie, 189–242. Princeton, NJ: Princeton University Press, 1996.

Prados, John. *Lost Crusader: The Secret Wars of CIA Director William Colby.* New York: Oxford University Press, 2003.

Reddi, V.M. *A History of the Cambodian Independence Movement, 1863–1955.* Tirupati, India: Sri Venkateswara University Press, 1970.

Rust, William J. *Before the Quagmire: American Intervention in Laos, 1954–1961.* Lexington: University Press of Kentucky, 2012.

Rust, William J. *Eisenhower & Cambodia: Diplomacy, Covert Action, and the Origins of the Second Indochinese War.* Lexington: University Press of Kentucky, 2016.

Schrock, Joann L., William Stockton, Jr., Elaine M. Murphy, and Marilou Fromme. *Minority Groups in the Republic of Vietnam.* Washington DC: Department of the Army, 1966.

Shawcross, William. *Sideshow: Kissinger, Nixon, and the Destruction of Cambodia.* New York: Cooper Square Press, 2002.

Shawcross, William. *The Quality of Mercy: Cambodia, Holocaust and Modern Conscience.* New York: Simon and Schuster, 1984.

Short, Philip. *Pol Pot: Anatomy of a Nightmare.* New York: Henry Holt, 2005.

Simpson, Charles M., III. *Inside the Green Berets: The First Thirty Years—A History of the U.S. Army Special Forces.* Novato, CA: Presidio Press, 1983.

Smith, Ralph B. "The Japanese in Indochina and the Coup of March 1945." *Journal of Southeast Asian Studies* 9, no. 2 (September 1978): 268-301.

Stanton, Shelby L. *Vietnam Order of Battle.* Washington, DC: U.S. News Books, 1991.

Steinberg, David J. *Cambodia: Its People, Its Society, Its Culture.* New Haven, CT: Hraf Press, 1959.

Strate, Shane. "A Pile of Stones? Preah Vihear as a Thai Symbol of National Humiliation." *South East Asia Research* 21, no. 1 (March 2013): 41-68.

Tarling, Nicholas. *Britain and Sihanouk's Cambodia.* Singapore: National University of Singapore Press, 2014.

Ton That Thien. *Indian and South East Asia, 1947–1960: A Study of India's Policies towards the South East Asian Countries in the Period 1947–1960.* Geneve: Librairie Droz, 1963.

Toohey, Brian and William Pinwill. *Oyster: The Story of the Australian Secret Intelligence Service.* Port Melbourne, Victoria, Australia: William Heinemann Australia, 1989.

Tully, John. *France on the Mekong: A History of the Protectorate in Cambodia, 1863–1953.* Lanham, MD: University Press of America, 2002.

Tully, John. *A Short History of Cambodia: From Empire to Survival.* Crows Nest, NSW, Australia: Allen & Unwin, 2005.

Turkoly-Joczik, R. L. "The Military Role of Asian Ethnic Minorities in the Second Indochina War, 1959-1975." PhD diss., University of Wales, 1986.

Turkoly-Joczik, Robert L. "Cambodia's Khmer Serei Movement." *Asian Affairs* vol. 15, no. 1 (Spring, 1988): 48-62.

Vickery, Michael. *Cambodia, 1975–1982.* Boston: South End Press, 1984.

Waite, James. *The End of the First Indochina War: A Global History.* New York: Routledge, 2012.

Werner, Jayne S. and Luu Doan Huynh, eds. *The Vietnam War: Vietnamese and American Perspectives.* Armonk, NY: M. E. Sharpe, 1993.

Zacher, Mark W. and R. Stephen Milne, eds. *Conflict and Stability in Southeast Asia.* Garden City, NY: Anchor Books, 1974.

INDEX

CPSIA information can be obtained
at www.ICGtesting.com
Printed in the USA
LVHW112240040423
743528LV00005B/309